The general history of Africa: studies and documents   3

In this series:

1. *The peopling of ancient Egypt and the deciphering of Meroitic script*
2. *The African slave trade from the fifteenth to the nineteenth century*
3. *Historical relations across the Indian Ocean*

DR WALTER RODNEY

IN MEMORIAM

In June 1980, the Unesco Project on the General History of Africa lost an illustrious participating member: Dr Walter Rodney was killed in a bomb explosion in Georgetown, Guyana.

Walter Rodney's career was brief but dazzling. He was born in Georgetown in March 1942. His training as a historian was first at the University of the West Indies at Mona, Jamaica, where he graduated with a bachelor's degree. He received his doctorate in history from the University of London in 1966.

Dr Rodney's first major teaching appointment was at the University College, Dar es Salaam (now the University of Dar es Salaam). He returned to the University of the West Indies at Mona in 1968 but in October of the same year Rodney was declared *persona non grata* in Jamaica. He went back to Dar es Salaam and resumed his teaching position there. After a few more years he decided to return home to his native Guyana.

On arrival in Guyana, Rodney was officially prevented from assuming a teaching role at the university. He was forced to live for a while on ad hoc lecture fees and royalties. He subsequently decided to become more of a political activist. On 16 June 1980, he was killed in circumstances which were indeed political.

Internationally Walter Rodney is perhaps best known for his 'best-seller' *How Europe Underdeveloped Africa*. But among professional historians he is particularly admired for his work on the Upper Guinea coast and the West Atlantic slave trade.

It is clear that Dr Rodney brought to the study of African history the skills of political economy at their most versatile. His range in scale was from the localized specificity of an aspect of Angolan history to the global perspectives of the history of capitalism. His range across time was from the origins of the trans atlantic slave trade to the significance of the Arusha Declaration in contemporary Tanzania.

To the Unesco General History of Africa, Dr Rodney contributed chapters to two volumes, and was being considered as an author for yet another volume. The Director-General of Unesco had also invited him to serve on the International Scientific Committee of the project. Dr Rodney had accepted to serve in that capacity, but before he could attend his first formal session as a committee member he was killed.

In evaluating Walter Rodney one characteristic stands out in sharp relief. He was a scholar who recognized no distinction between academic concerns and service to society, between science and social commitment. His career spanned at least four continents—Africa, Europe, North America and his native South America. He was concerned about people as well as archives, about the workplace as well as the classroom. He found time to be attentive to the practical issues of the day. He found time to be both a historian and a sensitive social reformer.

Dr Rodney was particularly gifted in inspiring students. Perhaps no Africanist historian of his generation demonstrated a greater capacity for such inspirational relationships with students. From Dar es Salaam to Kingston, from the campuses of the Northern Hemisphere to the streets of Georgetown, Dr Walter Rodney was a symbol of both compassion and vision to the young.

The world of scholarship has lost a creative intellect and African history has lost a brilliant interpreter of its own meaning.

Historical relations across the Indian Ocean

Report and papers of the meeting of experts
organized by Unesco at Port Louis, Mauritius,
from 15 to 19 July 1974

Published in 1980 by the United Nations
Educational, Scientific and Cultural Organization
7 Place de Fontenoy, 75700 Paris
Printed by NICI, Ghent

ISBN 92-3-101740-3
French edition: 92-3-201740-7

© Unesco 1980
Printed in Belgium

Preface

Published in the series 'The General History of Africa: Studies and Documents', the present volume contains the working documents and the Report of the Meeting of Experts on the Historical Contacts between East Africa and Madagascar on the One Hand, and South-East Asia on the Other, Across the Indian Ocean, which was organized by Unesco at Port Louis, Mauritius, from 15 to 19 July 1974, in response to a proposal made by the International Scientific Committee for the Drafting of a General History of Africa.

The discussions were on all aspects of the relations that have developed from the earliest times between the countries on either side of the Indian Ocean, which was described by one participant as 'the largest cultural continuum in the world during the first millennium and a half A.D.'.

The effects of these exchanges on the settlement and development of the Indian Ocean islands near Africa, and particularly on the peopling of Madagascar, which remains in many respects an enigma, were also examined.

The authors are responsible for the choice and the presentation of the facts contained in this book, and for the opinions expressed therein, which are not necessarily those of Unesco and do not engage the responsibility of the Organization.

The designations employed and the presentation of material throughout the publication do not imply the expression of any opinion whatsoever on the part of Unesco concerning the legal status of any country or territory or of its authorities, or concerning the delimitations of any country or territory.

Contents

Introduction   9

Part I: Historical, cultural and commercial contacts across the Indian Ocean

East Africa and the Orient: ports and trade before the arrival of the Portuguese, *Neville Chittick*   13
Historical relations between the Horn of Africa and the Persian Gulf and the Indian Ocean islands through Islam, *Musa H. I. Galaal*   23
Indian cultural and commercial influences in the Indian Ocean from Africa and Madagascar to South-East Asia, *D. G. Keswani*   31
Historical contacts of Africa and Madagascar with South and South-East Asia: the role of the Indian Ocean, *Michel Mollat*   45
The Chinese and the countries across the Indian Ocean, *Wang Gungwu*   61

Part II: The settlement of Madagascar and neighbouring islands

Various theses concerning the settlement of Madagascar, *Jacques Rabemananjara*   71
The settlement of Madagascar: two approaches, *Charles Ravoajanahary*   83
Cultural influences and the contribution of Africa to the settlement of Madagascar, *Pierre Vérin*   95
The role of trade in the settlement of Mauritius, *Auguste Toussaint*   117
The part played by agriculture in the settlement of Réunion, *Hubert Gerbeau*   125

Part III: Indian Ocean studies

A proposal for Indian Ocean studies, *J. de V. Allen*   137
Historical studies on the Indian Ocean, *Auguste Toussaint*   153

Part IV: Meeting of experts
    Report on the discussions   165
    Recommendations   185

    List of participants   189
    Bibliography   191

Introduction

The subject of the meeting of experts held at Port Louis reflected the principle underlying the project for the *General History of Africa,* namely that Africa is considered as a whole, including the neighbouring islands that have formed and maintained historical links with it and have all too often been regarded in works published hitherto as being quite unconnected with each other. It has now been scientifically established that Africa has kept up economic, commercial and cultural relations not only with Madagascar and the islands of the Indian Ocean, but also across that ocean with South-East Asia and the countries of the Persian Gulf. It is therefore planned to devote part of Volume III of the *General History of Africa* to the study of trade across the Indian Ocean, and the role of Africans in India and South-East Asia and their contacts with Arabia. In the same volume a chapter will trace the successive stages in the settlement of Madagascar, and the island's relations with South-East Asia, the Indian Ocean and Africa. Likewise, in Volume IV, one chapter will deal with Madagascar, particularly in relation to Islam, and another with Africa and the Indian Ocean.

The inaugural session of the meeting was presided over by H.E. Mr Louis Régis Chaperon, Minister of Education and Cultural Affairs of Mauritius, who in his welcoming address expressed the hope that the work of the experts would lead to a better understanding of the intercultural exchanges in the Indian Ocean. In reply, the representative of the Director-General of Unesco described the background of the meeting, which had been convened to study the relations of Africa and Madagascar with Asia in all their aspects: history of ideas and civilizations, societies and institutions. Special attention was to be paid to the original features of the island societies—in particular of Madagascar and Mauritius—as viewed also from the inside, for the *General History of Africa* should be thought of as a history of civilizations and institutions as lived, received and felt by the peoples concerned.

Accordingly, the twofold purpose of the meeting was, first, to take stock of the present state of knowledge and, secondly, to co-ordinate several existing programmes and, possibly, to put forward proposals for a new pluricontinental and intercultural programme among the various research specialists and institutions concerned.

The meeting appointed the following officers: Professor B. A. Ogot (Kenya), chairman; Professors Y. A. Talib (Singapore) and G. Rantoandro (Madagascar), vice-chairman; Professor J. Devisse (France), rapporteur.

In order to enable the experts to go directly to the heart of the matter, Unesco had asked them to prepare papers which would serve as a basis for the discussions. These papers are reproduced in the first two parts of this book.

The studies in the first part deal with the historical contacts between countries bordering on the Indian Ocean. Neville Chittick discusses the situation of the African ports on the Indian Ocean and the trade they carried on before the arrival of the Portuguese. Musa H. I. Galaal emphasizes the role played by Islam in establishing historical links between the Horn of Africa, the Persian Gulf and the Indian Ocean. D. G. Keswani analyses the Indian cultural and commercial influences in the Indian Ocean, while M. Mollat examines the relations between Africa and Madagascar on the one hand, and South and South-East Asia on the other. Finally, Professor Wang Gungwu traces Chinese sea expeditions across the Indian Ocean.

The contributions in the second part concern the influences that exchanges across the Indian Ocean have had on their settlement of Madagascar and the neighbouring islands. Jacques Rabemananjara sets forth the various theses concerning the peopling of Madagascar, and C. Ravoajanahary tackles the problem from both a global and a regional approach. Pierre Vérin stresses the importance of African cultural contributions and the African contribution to the peopling of Madagascar. The studies by Auguste Toussaint and Hubert Gerbeau deal with the history and development of Mauritius and Réunion respectively.

The third part contains two papers on Indian Ocean studies submitted during the meeting by J. de V. Allen and Auguste Toussaint.

The report of the Meeting of Experts is given in the fourth part of the work.

As the reader will note, all the papers presented at the meeting in Port Louis end with suggestions on research work that should be undertaken or intensified concerning the topics under discussion. The experts were specifically invited to make such proposals, since the International Scientific Committee for the Drafting of a General History of Africa felt that it was urgently necessary to draw the attention of research workers to the importance of the historical role played by the Indian Ocean, with a view to the establishment of a programme of Africa/South-East Asia studies. By opening up new avenues of research, such a programme would promote interdisciplinary work and collaboration between specialists on Africa and Asia.

Part I
Historical, cultural and commercial contacts across the Indian Ocean

East Africa and the Orient: ports and trade before the arrival of the Portuguese

Neville Chittick

If we take a reasonable load for a man to transport on foot as 25 kg, it may be said that the same energy expended is sufficient to move roughly 250 kg on wheels on a road, 2,500 kg on rails, and 25,000 kg on water. These figures bring home forcefully the economic advantage of sea communications, once men are capable of constructing vessels adequate to transport cargo with a degree of safety and reliability. Given such sea-going vessels, the oceans and seas unite, rather than divide, the peoples of the world. It is as profitable to think in terms of oceans as in terms of continents when we consider cultural spheres of influence.

The huge basin of the Indian Ocean is outstandingly suitable for such sea communications. The climatic regime of alternating monsoons is particularly suited to regular and reliable sailing voyages, as is the comparative lack of storms over most of the area. This has resulted in its constituting what is arguably the largest cultural continuum in the world during the first millennium and a half A.D. In the western part of the basin, at least, the coasts had a greater community of culture with each other and with the islands than they had with the land masses of which they form the littorals. And besides the intermingling of cultural elements, there was much mixing of peoples, as is dramatically presented in Mauritius.

The contrast between the culture of the coast and that of the interior is particularly marked in the case of the African littoral. Land communication between Africa south of the Sahara and the rest of the world was almost non-existent, save in the case of the regions just south of the Sudan belt. The ports accessible to ocean-going vessels were thus effectively the only route for the transport of goods, and also the transmission of cultural influences, leaving aside the effect of the large-scale movements of peoples which we know took place in the interior of the continent. Nevertheless, the people of the coast of East Africa were oriented to such an extent towards the ocean that their social and cultural interaction with the peoples of the interior before the nineteenth century was very slight. There was little penetration of the hinterland, save in the Zambezi region; goods needed for export were brought to the coast, rather than sought out in the interior.

Before considering in more detail the pattern of ports and trade, it is well to consider the character of the ports themselves. Under the influence of the modern model, we tend to think of the ideal port as a largely enclosed expanse of deep water, suitable for the construction of quays alongside which ships may be moored. This is a type evolved in north-western Europe, originally because of the heavy swells found there and the nature of the beaches. It was developed subsequently to accommodate the very large vessels built in recent times and is now, of course, found throughout the world. In much of the Indian Ocean region, on the other hand, the circumstances were different. The winds are comparatively moderate, steady and predictable, save for the cyclones in the south, outside the region with which we are primarily concerned. The beaches, at least in the west, usually have an almost flat foreshore below a steep sandy beach. Boats can therefore conveniently be beached at high tide on the foreshore, unloaded on to men's shoulders and carried up the beach after the tide recedes. Vessels are consequently built in a fashion to make such beaching possible. Quays and lighters are in general unnecessary. Only where there is inadequate shelter is it necessary for ships to anchor and unload cargoes into small boats. Such adequate shelter is, however, available in numerous localities along very long stretches of coast. The shelter may be provided by either a coral fringing reef or by an offshore island, or by an inlet or creek, or even by a headland, used on either side according to the duration of the monsoon (a combination of such elements may also be found).

A further requirement is fresh water. Even taking this into account, there are a great many places suitable for adoption as ports around the Indian Ocean. The corollary to this is that the geographical reasons (in the widest sense) for a substantial port having come into being in a given place are insufficient for it necessarily to continue to exist, or to continue to be of significance. Ports have come and gone throughout the last 2,000 years; there seems to be a curious, but presumably fortuitous flourishing of such ports with a cycle of 200 or 300 years.

Navigation in the Indian Ocean was pioneered by the Arabs, and they were the dominant element throughout history, as, so far as sailing ships in the western part of the basin are concerned, they were until the present. As early as around 2000 B.C., as we know from Sumerian records, timber was being imported from India to Megan (probably Oman), and a reference to head shipwrights of Megan indicates that ships were being built there in Sumerian times (Tibbetts). It is permissible to assume that these ships were owned and crewed by Arab traders of Oman. It is probable that both the Persians and Greeks gained their knowledge of navigation from the Arabs; the Persians did not undertake long-distance voyages until the fifth century B.C. and the Greeks not until Hellenistic times. Before then voyages were coast-wise or at best by dead reckoning; at night, ships were usually beached.

The ports of Oman and the Persian Gulf were, except for short periods, the most important for the eastern trade, though at times most of the trade passed through the ports of southern Arabia, especially Aden, and in the time of the *Periplus* of the Erythraean Sea in the first centuries A.D. Mocha was the most important. When the trade with the eastern coast of Africa south of the equator became important, after Islamic towns came into being, from the ninth century A.D. onwards, all the goods seem to have been transshipped in the Gulf ports (see al-Mas'udi). The merchandise intended for the Far East was for the most part probably transshipped again in the western seaboard of India, chiefly in the region of Gujarat.

The first ports to be developed on the East African coast, as we know from the *Periplus* and Ptolemy, were on what is now the Somali coast, and at Rhapta, the most likely site for which is in the delta of the Rufiji river (8° S.). This position corresponds roughly to the limit to which ships may sail on the north-eastern monsoon, and be certain of returning on the south-western later in the year. Below this approximate latitude the number of days on which the monsoon may be relied upon to blow with adequate force at the end of the season and at the beginning of the next, respectively, are too few to be sure of being able to make the round trip within the year.

The first Islamic settlements were on the coast of Somalia, northern Kenya (one site was Manda, an island adjacent to the coast) and on the islands of Pemba and Zanzibar. Manda, the only site as yet excavated (and now quite deserted, although fulfilling all the conditions for a port), shows evidence of having been a colony (or factory, in the eighteenth-century sense) of immigrants; these and the other settlements are probably to be associated with the traditions of immigration from the Persian Gulf ('Shiraz' and al-Hasa, near Bahrain).

By the twelfth century the main port had come to be Mogadishu, which indeed remained of the first rank subsequently. Trade developed to substantial proportions during this time with the lands far to the south, primarily with the Sofala region following the discovery that gold was to be obtained from there, but probably also with the Comoros and Madagascar. Then there arose the need for an entrepot well south of the equator, given, as explained above, the difficulty of voyaging to those southern parts and back within one year. (Navigation far to the south where the town of Sofala was to come into being was virtually impossible because of the difficulty of returning against the Mozambique current.) Thus, Mafia, and soon after Kilwa, because the main ports south of the equator, equal to Mogadishu in importance. The members of the dynasty associated with the name of Shiraz, who had settled there were themselves offshoots of a family or families of the northern coast who were in part descended from immigrants of Gulf origin, but by the period concerned had mixed with African stock and were in a sense Swahilized. Similar, but much smaller city or village states, where rulers also claimed Shiraz origin, established themselves at the same time or soon after in the Comoros, at other places on the mainland coast between Kilwa and Mogadishu, and (probably later), on the west coast of Madagascar. The ports on the eastern side of that island, though theoretically Muslim, seem more likely to derive ultimately from a further step of immigration from the Comoros.

Soon Kilwa gained control of the whole trade originally established by Mogadishu, and dominated and governed a number of ports in this Sofala region. Throughout this period, and through that of Portuguese domination, the influence of the ports on the interior was minimal except in the Zambezi region. Even on the coast, control by the towns extended only a small distance from their limits, and much of the population of the littoral was still pagan when the Portuguese appeared on the scene.

According to tradition the cause (or the occasion) of the original migrations was religious persecution, and in other cases family disputes. The latter seem somewhat improbable; and persecuted religious dissidents in the Gulf area could have found refuge with coreligionists in other parts of the region. Probably the reason for the migration of most of these people was the pursuit of trade, coupled perhaps with a desire to live in a less arid and usually cooler climate. (An exception is the emigration of the Banu Majid to Mogadishu.) Certainly the movement to the southern region was prompted by the pursuit of trade.

The goods sought for export to the countries of the Middle and Far East were the natural products of Africa. Of these, there is no doubt that throughout history ivory has been the most important; this is as true (as we know from the *Periplus*) of Ethiopia and its port Adulis as it is of the southern-most regions. For a rather restricted period—probably only in the fourteenth and fifteenth centuries but perhaps rather earlier—gold was the most important commodity for the trade of Kilwa. Interesting also in this period is the trade in vessels of chlorite schist (soapstone), brought to Kilwa, probably mostly for re-export, from the Vohémar region in north-eastern Madagascar. One suspects also that in the Arab literature (our main source of information) the more evocative and precious goods may have been given a place of excessive pre-eminence, at the expense of more mundane merchandise, particularly because most of this literature was of the *adab* type, accounts written to divert as well as instruct the reader. Timber (mangrove poles) was probably always an important export of the equatorial African coast, and is mentioned (as *saj*) as early as Al-Istakhri. A mention of rice imported from Kilwa has recently been discovered in fifteenth-century customs records at Aden; as the production of rice in the Kilwa area can never (because of the soil and topography) have been great, one suspects that it may have been imported to Kilwa from Madagascar. A further commodity that was probably of importance was iron, the only manufactured product mentioned by our sources. Its importance is supported by the finding of plentiful remains of iron smelting at Manda, and some indications at Kilwa. We are told by one source that East African iron was exported to India for the manufacture of the famous swords made there. Indeed, iron smelted by the simplest, most primitive methods makes the best steel. Making iron by the blooming process, where in the furnace the iron coagulates as it were into a spongy mass, and has to be subsequently hammered to produce workable metal, results in the greatest possible amount of carbon being incorporated. Duly forged, this is the finest tempered product.

The question of the trade in slaves on the East African coast is puzzling. No mention of such trade is made in the *Periplus* in regard to the region south of the equator, and there is only one mention known to me in the works of the Arab authors. It would seem, therefore, that slaves were not a significant item of commerce on this part of the littoral. On the other hand, the fact that the slaves in Iraq, largely of African origin, were able to stage the massive and largely successful Zanj revolt shows that there must have been such trade with Africa on a considerable scale. While, however, the term Zanj is applied to a particular stretch of the East African coast, mostly south of the equator, it is also applied to the whole of the East African region. It seems propable therefore, that most of the slaves exported from Eastern Africa were shipped from the Horn. Given the evidence, now being reinforced by archaeological finds in the recent excavations at Axum of trade between the Axumite Kingdom and the middle Nile valley, it may well be that many of those slaves descended from the people of that region.

We may mention here the importance throughout history of frankincense from the Horn of Africa, as well, of course, as aromatic gums from southern Arabia and Socotra. The reference in the *Periplus* to the export of cinnamon from the Horn is puzzling. Cinnamon would seem to be a substance only produced in South-East Asia, and there appears here to be evidence of trade from that region to the Horn. However, this reference may be an ill-informed reflection of the fact that cinnamon from Asia was probably transshipped in southern Arabia.

A word as to the imports to East Africa. They were for the most part objects of a more or less luxury nature—Chinese porcelain, Islamic glazed wares, glass, cloth (cotton from India, and probably silk from China) and copper objects. With regard to copper, however, it is very possible that some of the metal itself was also imported, perhaps from the Central African copper belt, to be made into articles of daily use, and particularly for the coinage struck in Kilwa, Zanzibar, and Mogadishu. A last important item was beads—carmelians and agates from Bombay, but more importantly glass beads. The latter, probably for the most part also of Indian origin, were used both by the women of the coast, and for trade with the interior. For this trade imported cloth may also have been used. A large amount of cloth was, however, made on the coast (as evidenced by the plentiful spindle whorls at Kilwa). This appears (from the first reports of the Portuguese) to have been of inferior quality, and it seems likely that it was used mostly for trade, the imported material of higher quality being retained for use by the wealthy inhabitants of the coastal towns.

A word, lastly, on the modes of sea transport to and from the African coast. This trade would seem to have been in the hands mainly of the Arabs of the Gulf and of South Arabia, and at certain periods, probably to a lesser extent, of the Persians and possibly Indians. Though sizeable vessels of the *mtepe* (sewn) type were used by the inhabitants of the coast, there is no evidence that their ships were used to carry the merchandise over the ocean (as opposed to the coastwise trade, and probably that to the coasts of Mozambique and Madagascar). As observed, the trade was mostly directed towards the Persian Gulf and Omar, as indicated by al-Masudi. Goods destined for points farther east were transshipped here, and those destined for China and the Far East probably again in ports on the coast of western India.

Subjects for future research

I would put the production of new editions of the passages in the Arabic sources concerning East Africa and the Indian Ocean region as of high priority, together with the publishing of any known manuscript texts offering useful information in this field. (Such texts include Arabic navigational treatises, two of which are reviewed and interpreted by H. Grosset-Grange in an article in *Azania*, IX (1974).) The new editions should include translations and notes on the interpretation. The last should be extremely important, and to this end the editions should be produced by Arabists well acquainted with the areas with which the texts deal, or by Arabists in collaboration with persons who have such knowledge. A recent scheme under the aegis of Unesco is concerned with the publication of texts concerning Africa under the title of *Fontes Historiae Africanae*[1] and edited by Dr J. O. Hunwick. The intention is to concentrate initially on the texts con-

---

1. Published under the auspices of the International Council of Philosophy and Humanistic Studies, Paris.

cerning West Africa, but the Arab documents concerning East Africa should have at least equal priority.

Further research is also urgently necessary in the archaeological sphere. Much information can be gained at little expense by surface survey, in the way of identifying sites of ports of importance, gauging from surface findings, mainly of imported and datable glazed pottery, the periods during which these ports were occupied, and the regions with which they were trading. From the sites identified through such archaeological reconnaissances particular settlements can be selected for careful, stratigraphic excavation. Recent work on the East African coast in Madagascar and at Banbhore near Karachi has demonstrated that valuable historical deductions can be made from such excavation at maritime settlements.

Certain areas may be indicated as deserving detailed survey work. In Africa, I think that priority should be given to the coast round the Horn, from Mogadishu round into the Red Sea to at least as far north as Aidhab, on the border of Sudan and Egypt. This coast is almost unknown archaeologically. The most important sites for excavation would include Adulis, the port of Axum (hitherto only summarily investigated), and Hafun (Opone of the *Periplus*), near the tip of the Horn. Farther south, work is needed in the Comoros, and on the northern coast of Mozambique. In Asia, Ceylon and the Maldive islands (the latter a likely staging port on voyages from the Far East) might be given the greatest priority. But hardly any of the coast of southern Arabia and Oman has been examined; methodical archaeological survey work should be undertaken. The same is true of the southern coast of Iran and the western coast of India. Excavations have taken place at three or four sites in the Gulf, notably at Siraf, but given the commercial importance of the area in the past, much more needs to be done.

It is of great importance to establish more securely the date of the *Periplus of the Erythraean Sea,* our only substantial source of information concerning the East African coast in the first half of the first millennium A.D., and the most important source of information concerning the products and commerce of the Indian Ocean region in general. Views as to the date of this document, which appears to have been written by a Greek merchant (perhaps an agent of the Roman government) living in Alexandria, vary between the latter part of the first century A.D. and the early third century. One of the crucial clues to the date is the reference to a king in western India, and the state of affairs there at the time. It would seem that the received chronology of the kings of this area, and of the coins they minted, rests on rather unsatisfactory evidence. It is thus important that there should be a new examination of this evidence, without preconception. This should be associated with excavations directed, at least in part, to finding stratigraphic evidence of the dates of the kings and coins of the region.

Much of the archaeological field work can be done at comparatively little expense. Only the archaeologists are lacking in this region. It is much to be hoped that more professional archaeologists may be trained in the countries concerned (some have none at all among their nationals), and that, in the meanwhile, more professionals from other regions may be attracted to these fascinating studies.

Bibliographical notes

It may be permissible here to call attention to *East Africa and the Orient*, edited by H. N. Chittick and R. I. Rotberg, New York, Africana Press, 1975. This volume is a collection of papers presented at a conference held in Nairobi in 1967. Of particular concern to the present paper are the chapters by J. S. Trimingham, 'The Arab Geographers and the East African Coast', and by Paul Wheatley, 'Analecta Sino-Africana Recensa'. Gervase Mathew, 'The Dating and Significance of the Erythraean Sea' examines the problem concerned and offers a tentative solution to the dating problem.

The writings of Ferrand remain after half a century of great importance; only a selection of these valuable works is given below.

The works of J. S. Kirkman and various publications by the present writer give some account of early ports of the East African coast, and those of P. Vérin of Madagascar; the latter's *Histoire Ancienne* (the first volume of a larger work) is a landmark.

The work of Tibbetts and Grosset-Grange open up new vistas on the information to be gained from the Arabic 'pilots': besides the navigational aspect, there is much information about the ports therein.

A collection of papers given at a conference in Oxford, *Islam and the Trade of Asia* (edited by Richards), is very pertinent to our subject. There are also useful papers in *Sociétés et Compagnies de Commerce en Orient et dans l'Océan Indien*, edited by M. Mollat, Paris, SEVPEN, 1971.

The Interim Reports on the recent excavations at Siraf, by D. Whitehouse and published in *Iran*, give the first hard evidence of dating on stratigraphic grounds of the various trade goods in that region. The excavations by the Pakistan Department of Antiquities at Banbhore, the probable site of the great port of Daibul, those of the University of Arhus in the important Islamic levels at Qala' Bahrain, are so far only referred to in brief articles of a popular nature.

Bibliography

BIVAR, A. D. H. Trade between China and the Near East in the Sasanian and early Muslim Periods. In: W. Watson (ed.), *Pottery and Metalwork in T'ang China*, London, 1970.

CAHEN, C. Le Commerce Musulman dans l'Océan Indien au Moyen Age. *Sociétés et Compagnies de Commerce en Orient et dans l'Océan Indien*, p. 180-93. Paris, SEVPEN, 1970.

CERULLI, E. *Somalia, Scritti Editi ed Inediti*. Vol. I: Storia della Somalia, l'Islam in Somalia, Libro degli Zenji. Rome, 1957.

CHITTICK, H. N. East African Trade with the Orient (1967). In: D. S. Richards (ed.), *Islam and the Trade of Asia*, Oxford, Cassirer, 1970.

——. *Kilwa: an Islamic Trading City on the East African Coast*. Vol. I, The Monuments and Excavations; Vol. II: The Finds. Nairobi, BIEA, 1974.

DATOO, B. Rhapta: the Location and Importance of East Africa's First Port, *Azania*, V, 1970, p. 65–75.

DECARY, R. *L'Etablissement de Sainte-Marie de Madagascar sous la Restauration et le Rôle de Sylvain Roux*, Paris, Soc. Edit. Géo. Mar. et Col., 1937.

DI MEGLIO, R. R. Arab Trade with Indonesia and the Malay Peninsula from the 8th to the 16th Century. In: D. S. Richards (ed.), *Islam and the Trade of Asia*, Oxford, Cassirer, 1970.

DONQUE, G. Le Contexte Océanique des Anciennes Migrations: Vents et Courants dans l'Océan Indien. *Taloha*, I, 1965, p. 43–69.

DUYVENDAK, J. J. *China's Discovery of Africa*. London, Probstain, 1948.

FAUBLEE, J.; FAUBLEE, M. Madagascar vu par les Auteurs Arabes avant le XIe Siècle, *Communication au Congrès d'Histoire Maritime de Lourenço Marques*. Paris, SEVPEN, 1964, and *Studia*, 1963, No. 11.

FERRAND, G. *Relation des Voyages et Textes Géographiques Arabes, Persans et Turks Relatifs à l'Extreme-Orient du VIIIe au XVIIIe Siècles*. Paris, Leroux.

——. Le K'ouen Louen et les Anciennes Navigations Interocéaniques dans les Mers du Sud. *Journal Asiatique*, 1919, p. 443–92.

FILESI, T. *Le Relazioni della Cina con l'Africa nel Medioevo*, Milan, Dott. A. Giuffre, 1962. In English as *China and Africa in the Middle Ages*, trans. D. L. Morison, London, Cass, 1970

GOITEIN, S. Letters and Documents on the Indian Trade in Medieval Times. *Islamic Culture*, 1963.

GROSSET-GRANGE, H. I. Les Procédés Arabes de Navigation en Océan Indien au Moment des Grandes Découvertes. *Sociétés et Compagnies de Commerce en Orient et dans l'Océan Indien*, p. 227–46. Paris, SEVPEN, 1970.

——. La Côte Africaine dans les Routiers Nautiques Arabes au Moment des Grandes Découvertes. *Azania*, Vol. IX.

GROTTANELLI, V. *Pescatori dell'Oceano Indiano*, Rome, 1955.

——. The Peopling of the Horn of Africa. In: H. N. Chittick and R. I. Rotberg (eds.), *East Africa and the Orient*, New York, Africana Press, 1975, p. 44–75, and *Africa* (Rome).

GUILLAIN, C. *Documents sur l'Histoire, la Géographie et le Commerce de la Partie Occidentale de Madagascar*. Paris, Imprimerie Royale, 1845.

HASAN, H. *A History of Persian Navigation*, London, 1928.

HOURANI, F. I. *Arab Seafaring in the Indian Ocean*. Princeton, N.J., Princeton University Press, 1951.

KIRKMAN, J. S. The Coast of Kenya as a Factor in the Trade and Culture of the Indian Ocean. *Sociétés et Compagnies de Commerce en Orient et dans l'Océan Indien*, p. 247–53, Paris, SEVPEN, 1970.

KUBBEL, L. E.; MATVEYEV, V. V. (eds.). *Drevniye i sredyevekoviye istochniki po Etnografii i istorii Narodor Afriki Yozhnyeye Sachari*. Arabskiye Istochniki, Vol. I, VII-X Vekov. Vol. II, X-XII Vekov. Moscow, Leningrad, 1960-65. (Arabic sources on Africa.)

MAUNY, R. Le Periple de la Mer Erythrée et le Problème du Commerce Romain en Afrique au Sud du Limes. *Journal de la Société des Africanistes*, 1968, p. 38–41.

MEILINK-ROELOFSZ, M. Trade and Islam in the Malayo-Indonesian Archipelago prior to the Arrival of the Europeans. In: D. S. Richards (ed.), *Islam and the Trade of Asia*, Oxford, Cassirer, 1970.

MILLOT, J. *Considérations sur le Commerce dans l'Océan Indien au Moyen Age et au Pré-Moyen Age à Propos des Perles du Zanaha*, Mém. I.R.S.M. Série C. Vol. II, No. 2, 1952, p. 153–65.

PICARD, R.; KERNEIS, J. P.; BRUNEAU, Y. *Les Campagnes des Indes, Route de la Porcelaine*. Paris, Arthaud, 1966.

RICHARDS, D. S. (ed.). *Islam and the Trade of Asia*, Oxford, Cassirer, 1970.

RODINSON, M. Le Marchand Musulman. In: D. S. Richards (ed.), *Islam and the Trade of Asia*, Oxford, Cassirer, 1970.
ROGERS, M. China and Islam. In: D. S. Richards (ed.), *Islam and the Trade of Asia*, Oxford, Cassirer, 1970.
SCHOFF, W. H. *The Periplus of the Erythraean Sea*, London, 1912.
STEIN, A. *Archaeological Reconnaissances in North Western India and South Eastern Asia*, London, 1937.
TIBBETTS, G. R. Early Muslim traders in South East Asia. *J. Malaysian Branch of R. Asiatic Soc.*, XXX/1, 1957, p. 1–45.
——. *Arab Navigation in the Indian Ocean before the Coming of the Portuguese*. London, Luzac, 1957.
VÉRIN, P. Histoire Ancienne du Nord-Ouest de Madagascar, *Taloha*, Vol. 5. Université de Madagascar, 1972.
WINDSTEDT (ed.). *The Christian Topography of Cosmas Indicopleustes*. London.

Historical relations between the Horn of Africa and the Persian Gulf and the Indian Ocean islands through Islam

Musa H. I. Galaal

I should like to point out that in starting to put the result of my survey into writing I found a number of points that could not be incorporated into the report.

First, the Somali culture reflects an ample amount of information about the countries and people of the Persian Gulf, but there is no reference to the existence of islands in the Gulf.

Secondly, some of the islands in the Indian Ocean, owing perhaps to their having more favourable geographical locations and commercial importance, have been known to the people of the Horn of Africa for generations, while others in the same ocean, in spite of being much larger, are never mentioned in the Somali oral tradition. Madagascar, which is by far the largest and the most important island in the Indian Ocean, is unfortunately an example, although it is well documented in books.

Thirdly, Somali seafarers of both ancient as well as more modern times seem to have had an understandable way of defining the islands within the reach of their navigation, for each group of islands or a whole archipelago was referred to under the name of one of the islands, usually the most important one from the Somali point of view.

Finally, I should like to point out that until 1972 the Somali language had no system of writing. Until then, all the thoughts and actions of the people were recorded in the oral literature. Luckily, the Somali oral poetry has an infinite number of genres, in which one can record any information or thought. In fact the chief source I employed in this résumé was the oral tradition. Where written records were found the source is in the bibliography at the end of this paper. The list of names of Somali researchers in the field is also given.

Historical relations through Islam

Religion is one of the strongest forces through which historical, commercial, political and cultural relations can be established between countries and peoples. This is a point of general fact that becomes more important when we know that the countries and peoples concerned are in addition geographically close to one another. But when this is not so and the mode of life of the two peoples concerned is widely different, our special interest is aroused and we realize the need for further research in the field.

During a preliminary investigation on the origin of the idea of written Somali in the Horn of Africa, I was led to trace the activities of a famous native saint, called Sheikh Barkhadle, who is known to have been the most active sheikh in the dissemination of Islam in the interior of the Horn of Africa. He is believed to have lived some time between 700 and 900 years ago. Barkhadle was a name given to him by the people as a result of his pious conduct and the saintly power he is said to have possessed. *Barkhad* is the Somali translation of the Arabic term *baraka,* meaning 'virtues', and the ending *le* means 'the owner'. The religious name of the saint was Sheikh Yusuf el Kawneyn.

Apart from propagating Islam in the interior, he was first to succeed in teaching the Somalis how to read and write the Arabic vowel-point system. He did this by devising a vernacular way of reading the difficult Arabic vowel point system, when the Arabic system *Aanisbaa aa, ii kisraa ii, uu thummaa uu* became difficult. The new Somali version he devised was *Alif la kor dhebey, Alif la hoos dhebey, Alif la godey.* From that period, Somalis understood both the Arabic Harakat (a, i, u) and their own basic vowel system as well.

The innovation here is that this saint seems to be the same whom the people of the Maldive Islands near India called Saint Abu Barakath Al-Barbari and who disseminated Islam there, as he did in the Horn of Africa. It is not known, however, in which of the two places he lived first, and what inspired him to change his area of activity.[1] Sheikh Barkhadle's tomb is in a ruined city, called Dhogor, near Hargeisa in the north of the Somali Democratic Republic, which is also known after his local name 'Sheikh Barkhadle'.

Seafaring in the Horn of Africa

Seafaring is an old profession in the Horn of Africa. Until the advent of colonialism in this region at the beginning of the century, hundreds of dhows were registered in the various ports of the Horn. An ample amount

---

1. See page 539 of the *World Muslim Gazetteer* of 1964, and page 4 of my notes on the history of written Somali, available at the library of the Academy of Somali Culture, Mogadishu, Somalia.

of oral poetry on sailing, monsoons and marine experience existing in Somalia is indicative of this history; the following are selected examples:

Bad nin tegey yaab, waxuu ku warramana ma yaqaan. (A man who has been to sea has had a bewildering experience which will be difficult for him to explain.)

Musureen dhacyey madaxu i xanuun. (The occurrence of hurricane gales causes me severe headaches.)

Sidii doonni dhooftay duufaan, cidlaan hadba diirad saaraa. (Like a sailing-ship pulled by a storm, I set my compass towards a place empty of people.)

Doonni buuxdaba bad lagaga teg. (Even a full dhow is sometimes abandoned.)

Ilaahow xaayadda iyo maayadda noo hagaaji. (Oh Allah, may you calm down the winds and the currents for us in our journey.)

Caliyow dabuubtaada gabay, Daayinkaa wadaye,
Dabaylaa, xagaagii bafliyo, daafigaa sidaye.
(Oh Cali, the everlasting one has driven on the words of your poems. The rustling winds of summer and the warm breeze have carried them.)

Naa haddaan doonyii shammaal celin, amaan carabtii shil kale helin, shay noolba naga filo. (Oh my dear girl, unless the shammaal south-west monsoon hinders the sailing-ships, or some other misfortune retards the Arab merchants, expect every new make of clothes from us.)

Contacts between the Horn of Africa and adjacent islands

In the study of history, contacts between continents or subcontinents are regarded as more important than between countries or between islands. We talk about Christopher Colombus discovering America, belittling the significance of his landing at some of the Caribbean islands. Similarly, we complement Vasco da Gama for sailing to India, ignoring the historical significance of the already well-established commercial relationship between the East African coast and South-West Asia.

Oral literature, which is my chief source of information in this article, agrees with the above principle. Although it contains a number of allusions to ancient relationships between the Horn of Africa and the islands of the adjacent seas, there are far more references to old relationships with the countries and people of the mainlands. Many Somali words are indicative of this.

A beautiful woman's scarf is called a *hindia*, in recognition of its country of origin. The following terms are also part of the Somali vocabulary today: *bangaali* (rice from Bengal), *bombey* (a pointed fork dipped in sacks of rice to test the quality of the rice), *karaarshi* (rice from Karachi), *jaawi* (a good-quality incense from Java with which women perfume their bodies after a bath), *mureysi* (sugar from Mauritius, Mureys in Somali meaning Mauritius), *sinjibaari* (coloured cotton cloth from Zanzibar), *mesketi* (a lungi from Masqat), *xabashi* (a lightly woven Abyssinian cotton cloth), *bulgy* (strong cotton cloth made in Belgium, worn by women), *maraykaan* (American coarse cotton cloth).

The following two short extracts from marine songs show how difficult and intricate commerce in the East African and the Indian emporiums was about two hundred years ago: *Nin Sawaaxil tegey sahal ugama yami.* (A man who goes to East Africa cannot return on appointment.) *Hindiana nin tegey hammi waa qabaa.* (And a trader back from India has had a perplexing experience.)

In the adjacent seas and ocean of the Horn of Africa the current is either *shami* or *hindi,* according to the direction of its flow. A common belief in the Horn is that place names like Muqdisha and Gendershe are Persian in origin and originally meant: Maq'ad Shaah, and Gender Shaah, respectively. *Istambuuli* is a kind of perfume from Istanbul. The following lines are from a song by a woman who found it difficult to abstain from licking continuously a bag of sugar her husband had brought her from Mureys (Mauritius): *Mureysi qariir macaanaa Alla ha qabtee, sii dhig baan idhaahaa iyana waygu soo dhegtaa.* (Oh you temptingly sweet sugar of Mauritius, every time I say to myself, stop licking it, it says, 'Never, go on licking me'.) The Somali term *bogor* used in the official sense means 'king', 'sultan' or 'ruler'. It is believed to be Indonesian and still means 'palace' in that country.

Love in the ancient Land of Punt (a legend)

One of the immortal love stories of the Land of Punt is the tragic legend of Zeïla. In the Middle Ages, when Zeïla was a fabulously wealthy centre of trade, it is said that a boy fell in love with the beautiful girl who lived next door. The boy was tall, lean, strong and black.[1]

Normally, the girls were kept away from the boys. They were strictly forbidden to go out very often, and when they did they were chaperoned and veiled. In Zeïla, however, this boy saw the girl he loved quite regularly, though from a discreet distance, at the wall of Tokhoshi village, some five miles from the centre of the city.

---

1. A black boy is more favoured by mothers in Somaliland than a fair one. Note the maternal prayer of a woman asking: 'Almighty God, if Thou would not give me a black boy, wouldn't Thou give me at least a fair one?'

Here the youngsters came to fetch water, fruits and vegetables. Since they could not talk to each other in public, each sang while going about his own business:

> I love you
> And you love me;
> Let our sick hearts complement one another,
> Let them build us a home.

As the son of a wealthy merchant, the boy was usually sent abroad as his father's special envoy. This sometimes took him to Persia, India and Egypt. His father generally stayed at home in Zeïla, often playing 'Shax' with the girl's father, who owned a cotton mill in town. Seeing how deeply in love his son was (and noticing that it was reciprocal), the boy's father approached the girl's father, in typical Somali fashion, to negotiate the marriage of their two children. The girl's father hinted at a connection with another gentleman whom he considered quite appropriate. The boy's father insisted, offering more bride wealth and more attractive prospects for the would-be bride. This lured the other and agreement was reached.

The *Gabati* was paid in the usual traditional ceremony, and it was agreed that the wedding would take place in six months' time. Meanwhile the boy was sent to India on business by his father. He was instructed not to be late for the wedding. He agreed and parted.

As is known, seafaring in the ancient world was often hazardous, with frequently tragic results. The system of weather forecasting existing at that time was not as reliable as it is today. Ancient sailing-ships were crude, hard-to-manage junks which could not resist severely adverse conditions at sea, and the system of SOS in practice was poor. For these reasons, people in the Land of Punt often recorded their wills before they went to sea.

The year of our story happened to be a very bad one at sea. Heavy storms and earthquakes destroyed many ships and drove many more far off course. The famous ship of Zeïla the boy took to India was unfortunately among those that got lost in the high seas. It was caught by one of those bad storms, which threw it, as the saying went, 'behind the world', and all attempts to redirect it to Zeïla were in vain.

Time was running out and the boy, utterly distressed, lost hope of getting back by the marriage deadline. Every day he hoped for the return of fair winds, but the winds only got worse and the boy felt that he would not be back for two years. At times it seemed that the evil was over; but soon fresh gales, surpassing all that they had seen previously, would strike them from a different direction, causing the ship to become completely uncontrollable. Both captain and crew, knowing the distress of the boy, tried their utmost to direct the ship towards Zeïla, but always in vain. The six months passed, while every day pieces of sunken ships and corpses were seen drifting in the ocean. At times the crew saw some sailors, clutching pieces of their shattered ships, but they were unable to save them.

Two years indeed passed. The sea was calm at last. Now that the storm was over, how far was Zeïla? It might take yet another year to reach it. The boy could neither eat nor sleep. He sat day and night in a corner of the deck facing what he thought to be the direction of Zeïla, talking to himself, sometimes singing pathetically. He grew gaunt.

Meanwhile in Zeïla arrangements were being made according to plan for the wedding. A new stone house was built for the couple by the boy's father in time and in accordance with the custom. The usual open area for dancers was prepared within the house, just below the bedroom of the couple. From this room, a window was opened overlooking the floor so that the couple could watch the dancers and ceremonies. Everything was ready by the appointed date.

However, a feeling of anxiety grew when the ship carrying the bridegroom failed to return. Day after day conflicting reports arrived in Zeïla that the ship had sunk, was safe, damaged or due to arrive shortly.

Gradually it became clear that all these reports were unfounded, for in fact no one knew what had happened to the ship, as no other ship had arrived from India during the boy's absence.

A year passed and there was no news. Almost all the families of the crew members read the burial prayers (*Axan*) for their missing relatives. But the girl was still hopeful, as was the boy's father.

Now that the boy was generally considered lost, the man who had been considered as a prospective husband for the girl when her first engagement was being arranged, renewed his overtures. He saw the girl's father as well as the girl herself, offering more in bride wealth than the father of the missing boy. This news was very disturbing to the girl as well as to the still hopeful parents of the boy. They all prayed to Allah separately and secretly, on different parts of the seashore at night, for the safe return of the boy.

In one of her secret reveries, the girl sang these few lines while gazing at the distant sea:

>   The merchant ships that sailed
>   Have returned from Syria and Zanzibar
>   Where are those from Bombay?
>   Are they damaged or destroyed?

As she sang, her voice was carried by the wind far out to sea, out to the ears of the boy, who was as usual sitting on the deck of the ship. One can imagine his joy as he heard the musical sound echoed by the heavens. He jumped up and played about the deck happily, repeating the girl's melody.

Early the following morning he was out on the deck again, straining his ears to catch the faintest humming of the wind. He sang the following lines which he had composed during the night in the hope that she might hear them:

> I, too, wanted to be back in time
> But the cruel winds of winter
> Have barred my way.

On the beach of Zeïla, the girl stretched her hands towards the emptiness in a desperate gesture to catch the voice of her lover in the air. The heavens responded and she heard him sing. Learning the words by heart, the girl came happily home, singing the words over and over again. She told her close relatives about the miracle. A few believed her; most thought she was becoming crazy. In any case, she was resolutely convinced, from that day onward, that her betrothed was alive and that sooner or later he would be back home. Her father, however, regarded the story as a fabrication designed to avoid marriage to the other man.

While most people in Zeïla were gossiping about the girl's fantastic stories, she came with a fresh verse which she claimed she had heard in the same manner as before. In it, the boy was appealing to a lonely seabird on the mast of the ship:

> Holy bird, favourite of the saints,
> Let me soar high in the sky on your wings,
> And take me over the waves,
> To her for whom my heart craves.

Tiring of what he considered her childishness, the girl's father took a big stick and gave his daughter a sound thrashing. Furthermore, he declared that her wedding to the second lover was to take place immediately. No appeal from her would make him change his mind. As a result, an elaborate wedding ceremony was prepared. Within a short time a new house was built and all arrangements were made. The bride was escorted by the women to her new home, accompanied by the usual drums and flutes and impressive chorus songs. Later on, at night, the bridegroom was escorted there amidst spectacular dances. The inauguration was thus complete.

As the seven days of continuous entertainment were beginning, just before the conjugal bed of the newlyweds was furnished in the great hall prepared for this purpose, and as the whole town (except the parents of the missing boy) were having a good time, the missing ship arrived and anchored close to the beach. No sooner had it dropped anchor than the boy swam ashore and rushed into the town.

Asking the first old woman he met what the noisy festival was about, he discovered that it was the wedding of his betrothed to a stranger. 'Impossible', he declared, and ran to the house where the celebrations were taking place.

Upon entering, the boy saw an elaborate wedding feast in progress. Above the huge dancing crowd he saw his betrothed in the arms of the man she had been forced to marry. Looking at her face he saw that she had never consented. He rushed to join the dance. Directly below the conjugal bed, he sang to the rhythm of the drums and feet and the clapping of the hands:

> Beautiful eyes,
> Lavishing eyes,
> Oh! Cruel fortune.

Hearing his beautiful voice and then seeing his face, the girl jumped down from the window, leaving the undesired lover alone. She danced and sang:

> I waited too long,
> I could wait no more,
> Oh! Cruel fortune.

At the exchange of these lines they fell into each others arms. Having done so, they both died.

Bibliography

ANDRZEJEWSKI, B. W. The Art of the Miniature in Somali Poetry. *African Language Review*, 1967.
ANDRZEJEWSKI, B. W.; GALAAL, M. *Somali Poetic Combat*. East Lansing, Mich., Michigan State University, 1963.
BURTON, R. *First Footsteps in East Africa*, London, 1966.
CHITTICK, N. (ed.). *Azania*, Vol. IV, 1969.
GRIENFIELD, R. *Ethiopia*, 1965.
GROTTANELI, V. L. Somali Wood Engravings. *African Arts*, No. 16046, African Studies Center, University of California at Los Angeles.
World Muslim Gazetteer, 1964.

The following Somali historians are engaged on research into historical relations and movements across the Indian Ocean: Ali Abdirehman Hersi, Yassin Isman Kanadid, Sulsiman Mahamed Aslan, Sheikh Jama Omer Ese and Musa Galaal Ali, all of the Academy of Somali Studies; and Sased Ahmed Worsama, of the Somali National Museum.

Indian cultural and commercial influences in the Indian Ocean from Africa and Madagascar to South-East Asia

D. G. Keswani

From the prehistoric civilization of the Indus Valley, brought to light by excavations at Harappa and Moenjodaro, to the present time is a span in all probability of from five to six thousand years. During this period the peoples of India, an amalgam of various races, the dominant being the Ayans, who entered the subcontinent during the second millennium B.C., and the original inhabitants, the Dravidians, evolved an indigenous culture and civilization that has radiated far and wide. While the intellectual domination of India, particularly in East Asia, has been notable in extent, strength and duration, scant justice has hitherto been done to it by the world of scholarship and learning.

India has had a long and intimate relationship with the outside world, stretching back beyond the beginning of the Christian era. The Indus monuments reveal an influence from ancient Mesopotamia, which was the consequence of a continuous seaborne commerce from the mouths of the Tigris and Euphrates to the western coasts of India as well as of a contemporaneous overland trade of some kind. Later there were its flourishing commercial contacts with South-East Asia, the Graeco-Roman world, the Near East, overland with Persia and Central Asia, and by sea with the East African coast, the Persian Gulf and the Arab ports; and in their wake followed culture and civilization.

To begin with these voyages were slow, generally peaceful and attracted little attention at home. This is proved by the fact that no authentic historical evidences, apart from those derived from tradition as recorded in literature of various kinds, have survived. Be that as it may, when the definite chronological history begins for India, we find the permeation and infiltration of its superior culture beyond its borders already manifest.

India's South-East Asian trade

There is little doubt that Indian contact with the western ports of South-East Asia commenced centuries before the beginning of the Christian era. Indian literature has faithfully preserved the traditions of the early days of the perilous voyages to unknown lands beyond the seas. The Buddhist *Jataka* stories, the *Kathasaritsagar, Ramayana* and other similar collections frequently mention traders' voyages to Suvarnabhumi or Suvarnadvipa (Land of Gold or the Island of Gold) by which terms the lands or islands to the east of India were referred to. According to Ptolemy, by the second century A.D. there was a great intensification of Indian trade with South-East Asia as a consequence of a growing demand in the Roman empire for Asian luxuries and the thrust of its shipping from Egypt to South India and Ceylon. The principal port of departure for Suvarnabhumi was Guduru, undoubtedly the modern Kodura at the mouth of the Godaveri. This agrees well with the fact that it is really the art and culture of the Deccan of which traces are most apparent in the earlier art of Cambodia, Champa and Java. Some of the other ports that participated in the early trade were Muziris (Cranganore), Poduca (Pondicherry), Sopatma (Markanam), Tamralipti (Tamluk) and Barygaza (Broach). It was mainly from them and through the settlements of Indians at new trading posts in the Malayan peninsula or the archipelago, which bore Indian names, that Indian commerce, and with it its culture, penetrated peacefully but extensively, deeply and permanently in South-East Asia.

The term 'Hinduized' or 'Indianized' kingdoms has been suggested by some scholars to explain the florescence of Indian culture in the newly constituted kingdoms in these parts, ruled by kings with Indian names ending in the patronymic *Varman,* familiar with Manu's legal treatise and *varna,* expressing their new exuberance through the Sanskrit language, steeped in the mythology of the *Mahabharata* and *Ramayana* epics, fervently accepting the compound theology of Mahayanist Buddhism and Hinduism symbolized in the trinity of Brahma, Vishnu and Siva, and erecting splendid temples in the Indian style to express this devotion.

According to a legend recorded in *Mahavamsa* Ceylon is the first place where Indian civilization was introduced when a Prince Vijaya Simha (Lion) apparently started from the region of Broach about 500 B.C. with 700 followers. His entry there illustrates all the phenomena of infiltration, colonization and propaganda. Intercourse with the north was maintained, for in the reign of Asoka we find the King of Ceylon making overtures and receiving Asoka's son Mahindra and later his daughter Sanghamitta as apostles of Buddhism (247-207 B.C.). The earliest remains of Ceylonese art, stupas (or *dagabas* as they are called in Ceylon) at Anuradhapura, reflect the various traditions of the mainland from which they were derived. A number of fresco paintings that have survived in Ceylon are in a style closely related to that of Ajanta.

From the earliest times, Indian immigrants and Indian ideas found their way both by land and sea into Burma as well. From the fifth century onwards, Prome and Thaton were certainly important centres of Buddhist and Hindu culture. The architectural forms, though varied, reflect a contact with the Gupta and Pala periods of Indian history. Classical Burmese sculpture is best represented by the eighty-one reliefs of the Ananda Pagoda depicting the legend of the Buddha.

By the beginning of the Christian era, colonies of Indian merchants had appeared in the busier and more developed coastal settlements of South-East Asia. These colonies increased in number and size, and often included Brahmans and Buddhist monks among the settlers. Through the fertilizing impact of Hindu thought and culture, the indigenous culture achieved a rare synthesis and vigour. Chinese chronicles tell of the foundation of the Kingdom of Funan, the modern Kampuchea (Sanskrit Kamboj) in the first century by a Brahman from India named Kaundinya. It seems probable that the Hinduized dynasty of Champa was founded between A.D. 150 and 200, but there is no evidence to show whether a Malay race already settled in Champa was conquered and Hinduized or whether the Chams were already Hinduized when they arrived, possibly from Java. Immigration from South India to Java (Sanskrit Yava) or Yava-dvipa of *Ramayana* continued over an extended period, the earliest arrivals having been merchants who settled in the western end of the island. By at least the fifth century A.D., a Hindu or Hinduized State had been established in Java, though the possibility of earlier Hinduization is not ruled out. Probably in the eighth century, Bali came under the rule of the Javanese Kingdom of the Sailendras, which according to a legend gained the hegemony of most of Indonesia, Malaya, Sumatra and for a while Cambodia.

It is significant that the earliest material evidence of Indian contact with South-East Asia takes the form of Buddha images of the School of Amaravati, which have been found in Thailand, Cambodia, Annam, Sumatra, Java and the Celebes. No account of the Malay Peninsula and archipelago would be complete without reference to the splendid monuments in which their art found expression. A magnificent synthesis of the Malayo-Polynesian and Hindu-Buddhist styles was achieved in Champa and Cambodia, which in Angkor Wat has produced one of the noblest sculptural arts in the history of the human race. In Java, the Gupta, Pallava and Chola styles, and later the Pela from Bengal have fused with the native impulses of the Javanese genius. The eloquent reliefs, motifs and patterns of Borobudur, a veritable catechism in stone, clearly derived from Javanese life, represent a panorama of *Samsara,* the endless cycle of birth and death. Not to be overlooked are the stone inscriptions of Cambodia and Javanese adaptations of Indian epics, which attest to the flourishing state of the Sanskrit language and of Indian poetry and theology, which is surprising when we consider how far away from India they were composed. In Bali, one feels always the keen force of the brilliant tropical Polynesian element that was never quite submerged by the Indian impact.

Java, which witnessed the culmination of a native cultural renaissance in the tenth century, became a tremendous force in the Indian seas. Its merchant fleets touched Africa and China and went as far as Easter Island. This is proved by the fact that languages connected with Malay are spoken in Taiwan, New Zealand, Easter Island and Madagascar. In Madagascar, the ruling minority race of Hovas, light brown in colour with distinctly Mongoloid features, which has been identified as of Malay-Polynesian and Melanesian stock which emigrated there, is one startling example of the heights to which Javanese enterprise had reached under Indian impetus. It has even been suggested that Hinduized Malays carried some faint traces of Indian religion to Madagascar (*T'oung Pao,* 1906). There are of course other theories about several earlier Indonesian migrations across the Indian Ocean.

With the tide of Muslim invasion in the Indonesian Archipelago from the end of the thirteenth century, the arts of Hinduism and Mahayanism decayed and disappeared, as they did in India, under the puritanical iconoclasm of Islam.

In whatever way the expansion of Indian influence took place, there can be no doubt of its association with a great extension of Indian trade, not only in South-East Asia for gold and spices, but also with China for the silks so eagerly sought after by their Roman customers.

India's western trade

The overland commerce of India with western Asia dated from remote times and was conducted by several routes across Persia, Mesopotamia and Asia Minor. The Chinese silk trade followed the same route. The sea-borne trade of the peninsula with Europe through Egypt does not seem to have been considerable before the time of Claudius, when the course of the monsoons is said to have been known to the Roman merchants. Until Graeco-Egyptian mariners took this up, trade between Egypt and India had been largely in the hands of the Arab seamen who clung to the coasts of Arabia, Persia and India. But the new direct access to Egypt, coupled with greatly increased demands of Rome for Indian wares, had an enormous impact on South Indian ports.

We owe to one of the Greek sailors living in Egypt an informative handbook, *The Periplus of the Erythraean Sea,* in which he has recorded a minute account of his experiences of a voyage he undertook to India in the first century A.D. He found the Indian Malabar and Coromandel coasts studded with harbours from which Indian merchant vessels sailed to Persia, Arabia, Africa and Red Sea ports with their merchandise of pearls, precious stones, ebony, teak, sandalwood, spices and fine cotton cloth called muslin and re-export of China silk, all of which were in great demand. Ships were also customarily fitted out between the East African coast as far down as Madagascar and Barygaza (Broach) in India, bringing to these market towns the products of their respective places—rice, wheat, sugar, ghee, sesame oil, cinnamon, copal, cotton cloth and girdles from India and ivory, tortoise shell and rhinoceros horns from East Africa, much prized in Rome. Thus grew up the settlements of Indian traders in Socotra, Alexandria and in an island off the coast of Africa (Madagascar?).

The whole period of the Julio-Claudian and Flavian emperors was a golden age for Graeco-Roman commerce with Arabia and India. The magnitude of the Asian trade in this early period is clearly indicated by Pliny, a well-informed adviser of Vespasian (A.D. 69-79), who reckoned that no less than 50 million sesterces were annually drained from the Roman empire by India. This statement is corroborated by the discovery of a large number of Roman coins in India—a testimony to the extensive trade activity of the Indians. This trade almost ceased in the fourth century but revived to some extent in the fifth and sixth centuries.

Commercial relationship of such magnitude inevitably led to cultural contacts. The monumental discoveries at Harappa and Moenjodaro leave no doubt about a cultural intercourse between India and the western countries. When the Persian empire succeeded the Assyrians and Babylonians, in addition to brisk trade both by land and sea there was undoubtedly an intimate cultural contact. When Alexander the Great overthrew the Persian empire and extended the border of the Greek empire right up to the Punjab, the east and west became much more intimately acquainted with each other than ever before. The Hellenistic influence on Indian art, which is most plainly manifested in the Gandhara sculptures, and the influence of Buddhist ideas on Christian doctrine flowed through the channels opened by Alexander.

With the Greek sovereigns of Asia and Africa who inherited the vast dominions of Alexander, Indian kings were on terms of closest intimacy. The strongest testimony to the dissemination of Buddhist ideas and the 'conquest of religion' claimed by Asoka is to be found in his celebrated edict (256 B.C.), in which he proclaimed the spread of *Dharma* as far as the dominions of Antiochus 'and beyond where dwell the four kings named Ptolemy, Antigonus, Magar and Alexander', identified as rulers of Egypt, Syria, Crete and Macedonia. While we have no knowledge that these missions reached their destination, the fact is indicative of his friendly relations with the Seleucids. From the age of Augustus, Indian embassies to the Roman Empire became almost a regular feature.

In Central Asia, the cultural conquest almost completely overshadowed the trade relations of India. The influence of Buddhism was profound and penetrating and it travelled far and wide into China, Japan and Korea.

Arab-Indian trade

India's glorious maritime supremacy was not long sustained. With the slackening of the outward thrust as a result of the Hun and Muslim incursions and India's preoccupation with resisting external pressures, the Farther India movement soon became choked, dried up and decayed. With the conquest of Egypt and Persia by the Arabs in the seventh century, both the sea and land routes came under their control. This Arab navigation was entirely independent of the earlier Graeco-Arabian trade. Henceforth the Arabs held a complete monopoly in the overseas trade between the East and the West, and India resigned herself to accepting seafarers as middlemen for carrying her wares. The conquest of Sind soon after 710 gave Arabs the use of the valuable ports of Al-Daybul and Al-Mansurah and brought them a stage nearer to the Far East and China. The sea route from the Persian Gulf to Canton was the longest in regular use by the Arabs. They amassed enormous profits by carrying articles such as Indian textiles and piece-goods, Persian and Arabian horses, gold and ivory from East Africa as well as spices from Indonesia, Ceylon and Malabar and Chinese silks across the Indian Ocean and China seas. But by the fourteenth century the Arab advance seems to have exhausted itself, for when Ibn-Batuta visited China he noticed that the voyages from Calicut and other Malabar ports to China were made only in Chinese junks.

Indian cultural influence seems to have been sporadic and diffuse in this period. The Neoplatonists of Alexandria and the Sufis of Arabia seem to have listened to the voice of Hindu mysticism but rather as individuals than as leaders of popular movements. Arabs acquired from India some knowledge of Indian philosophy, medicine, mathematics, astronomy and folklore and carried it not only to their own land but also to Europe.

Western commercial enterprises in India

It has been observed how spices and silks, which were the characteristic exports of the Orient, could reach the European markets for several centuries only through a hostile intermediary, the Arabs. Indeed some of the ancient cities and ports all along the Indian Ocean seaboard rose to affluence and power only because either they were directly participating in the eastern trade or thus occupied strategic positions on the trade routes along which the produce of the East was transported. Such a profitable trade naturally excited the cupidity of the European powers and in its quest came the Portuguese, the Dutch, the British, the French, the Danes and other hopefuls.

In this context, Vasco da Gama's epic voyage of discovery of the all-sea route to India via the Cape of Good Hope was a feat of great significance inasmuch as it broke the monopoly of Arab trade and channelled the stream of eastern trade towards European seaboards. It is one of the ironies of history that a great Arab seaman, Ahmad ibn-Majid, helped to bring about the undoing of Arab navigation when he agreed to pilot to India Vasco da Gama, who had worked his way to Malindi, one of the wealthy Arab trading settlements on the east coast of Africa. Before long Portugal acquired strategic control of the Indian Ocean and engrossed almost the entire Asiatic trade.

The beginning of the seventeenth century saw the Dutch and the British almost simultaneously taking measures to contest the claim of Portugal to the monopoly of Oriental commerce. While the Dutch entrenched themselves in the remoter waters of the Indonesian archipelago in Java, Sumatra and the Moluccas, the British East India Company switched its area of operation to the western coast of India. Very soon these companies, instead of confining themselves to purely commercial activities, made territorial ownership a legitimate part of their business. The French were the last to enter the race.

Europe indeed had few exports to match the unique gems, aromatics, cotton fabrics and spices it sought from Asia. There was a heavy adverse balance of trade, which had to be settled in gold and silver. The echo of Pliny's complaint about the drain of bullion from Rome was resounding across the corridors of time some sixteen centuries later. But the industrial revolution gave Great Britain an unprecedented ability to produce those very goods in which India had so long held superiority. Thus from its age-old predominance in Asian markets, the Indian cotton industry was reduced to supplying coarse products for domestic consumption. The drain was reversed irrevocably, wrecking the Indian economy.

Politically subjugated, economically emasculated and intellectually apathetic, India withdrew within herself and ceased to exert any influence outside.

India's trade with East Africa

It is more than probable that a good deal of the African trade, such as it was, which found its way to Tyre and Syria was carried on by Indian merchants who had their houses of agency at African ports. That there was a flourishing commerce between India, Arabia and East Africa from the earliest times has been testified to by Greek and Roman writers. The *Periplus* mentions several East African places that traded with India. The ruling power at these ports was generally in the hands of foreigners of Arab or Persian extraction, and all trade was monopolized by Indians or Arabs with Indian connections, and having their homes or chief places of business sometimes on the Egyptian, Arabian or Persian coast, but more often in India, at Tatta in Sind, Mandavie in Cutch, the ports of Kathiawar or the Gulf of Cambay, Surat, Calicut and other ports on the Malabar coast.

The earliest travellers, both those who came from the north of Africa and those who came with the Portuguese, found Indian traders at every port along the East African coast, and the trade carried on much in the same fashion as in olden days by vessels of the same build and character as the dhows, availing themselves of the regular trade-winds to sail to and fro between the ports, on the same coasts of Africa, India, Arabia and Persia, and carrying articles of much the same character, and what is more all this trade was in the hands of men whose homes were in India or closely connected with India.

This vast Indian trade seems to have been sorely crippled by Arab piracy and the advent of Europeans in the Indian Ocean. First the Portuguese and then the British dealt lethal blows to the Indian trade, since the Indian Ocean had become unsafe to all but large and well-armed vessels. Nevertheless a few ships still managed to elude the adversary and bring ivory and other African produce in exchange for Indian blue cotton cloth, metals and beads in demand in Africa.

Sir Bartle Frere, who had been deputed by Great Britain to the Sultans of Zanzibar and Muscat to settle the question of the suppression of the East African slave trade, in a memorandum, had this to say in 1873 on the extent of the Indian trade: 'Of all classes connected with the trade of East Africa, there is none more influential than the natives of India generally known as "Banians" ', a term applied to all Indians be they Bhattias, Lohana Wanias, Khojas, Momens or Bohras. Continuing on the same theme, Sir Bartle says:

Everywhere, wherever there is any foreign trade, it passes through the hands of some Indian trader. No produce can be collected for the European, American or Indian market but through him; no imports can be distributed to the natives of the country but through his agency. At every port the shops which collect or distribute articles or commerce are kept almost exclusively by Indians. Throughout our whole circuit from Zanzibar round by Mozambique and Madagascar and up to Cape Guardafui, we did not, except at Johanna, meet half a dozen exceptions to the rule that every shopkeeper was *an Indian*.

He knew of 'nothing like it in the history of Commerce, and it is difficult to convey to those at a distance an adequate idea of the extent and completeness of the monopoly'.

'Banians' generally kept to the ports, trade with the far interior being exclusively in the hands of Arabs and Swahilis.

Temporarily smothered by the European onslaught, the Indian trade revived by the beginning of the nineteenth century. Along some six thousand miles of sea coast in Africa and its islands and nearly the same extent in Asia, from Delagoa Bay to Karachi, the Indian trader was if not the monopolist, the most influential, permanent and all-pervading element of the commercial community. That such a trade could have grown up so little noticed by the commercial world elsewhere was due to the fact that Indians engaged in it all belonged to the commercial classes, not high up in the Indian hierarchy. As such they exerted hardly any cultural influence in the countries they traded with.

African diaspora

Slavery is an age-old institution, but the real change in its character, as well as in its expansion, came as a result of the change from a subsistence to a market economy. The study here will be restricted to the sixteenth century onwards, when the Christian nations of Europe introduced the system into Africa, which was till then literally a blank in geography to them, to bolster up the sagging growth of their colonial plantation economy. The British became the most important importers on the west coast of Africa, for which their charter provided the 'sole, entire and only trade' in Negroes to feed their West Indies colonies, although the French, the Dutch and others also participated in the commerce, to supply their own colonies or the larger and richer Spanish possessions. On the other hand, the Portuguese, the first to introduce slavery and the slave-trade, reserved the monopoly of the South Atlantic slave-route to Brazil. Indeed the traffic in slaves was the sole means of survival for the shaky structure of the Portuguese East African colony of Mozambique.

The eastern flank of Africa, with its convenient island rendezvous, was ideally suited for the scandalous slave-trade. The coves and creeks south of Cape Delgado fed the barracoons of Ibo, the Querimba islands, Quiliman and Sofala, and supported the depots and markets of Mozambique, the Comoro Islands, Madagascar, Bourbon and Mauritius. Thence, most of the human cargoes were transferred to the stifling holds of French, American, Portuguese or Spanish brigs or barques bound for the South Atlantic voyage and the markets of Rio de Janeiro, Pernambuco and Santos. The highest stakes lay in the New World. Soon North Americans came out undisguised under their own flag. The shuttle service along the East African coast and to the islands was almost entirely in the hands of the Arabs. To escape surveillance of the British during the slavery suppression campaign, even the French- and Portuguese-owned dhows normally sailed under the borrowed Arab flag, and faked papers to avoid detection.

The most important slave market in the north was located in Zanzibar. In general, the slave-hunting area included the country lying between the equator and Delagoa Bay and extended as far inland as Lake Tanganyika and the Mountains of the Moon; but most of the captives came from the region of Lake Nyasa and west of Lake Victoria. This teeming hinterland was like a quarry for the Arab slavers to exploit. The coasting dhow, the principal vehicle of transport, travelled as far as the Red Sea transit bases of Jeddah and Mocha for shipments to Mediterranean Turkey and the coastal Arab States, to Masqat and Sur for supplying slaves to South-East Arabia, Persia, Sind and even parts of British West India; and Bushire, which fed the markets of Basra and Baghdad, which supplied south-eastern Turkey as well.

The overland slave caravans from East Africa terminated at the shores of the Mediterranean, the Red Sea, the Persian Gulf and the Indian Ocean. Some of the slaves brought there were sold for local employment, but most were sent further, usually in small crafts, to insatiable Turkey and Egypt, Arabia, Persia, Tunisia, Morocco and other countries.

It is impossible to be precise about the number of slaves exported from the east coast. On an average, in a year some 20,000 reached Zanzibar, of which about 15,000 were exported to the Red Sea, Arabia, the Persian Gulf and the borders of India. From the southern coastal zone, centring around Mozambique, which fed the transports en route to Madagascar, Bourbon and thence to Latin America, the average yearly export does not seem to have been far below that of the northern one. The figure of 50 million has been suggested for the overall African diaspora.

The assault against slavery on an international scale started immediately after the end of the Napoleonic Wars in 1814. The Congress of Vienna had succeeded in obtaining from the great powers not only a general condemnation but an agreement in principle to seek co-operative means for its abolition. But the trade continued clandestinely throughout the nineteenth century and even later.

African slaves in India

There was a great influx of Abyssinians and other East Africans into western India around the middle of the fifteenth century. Though most of these *habshis* came as slaves, by dint of their faithfulness, courage and energy they rose to positions of high trust. Later known as 'Sidis of Janjira', they rose to great power in Ahmadnagar. The import of African slaves continued briskly during the Portuguese period. But by the time of the British conquest of Sind in 1842, the annual import of African slaves into India, including Baluchistan, was probably no more than 200-800. Official documents of the Bombay Government show that African slaves were imported in Arab vessels and sent to the native States of Cutch, Kathiawar, Sind and into the Portuguese ports of Goa, Daman and Diu. *Coffrees,* as the slaves were called in Calcutta, seemed to have been in great demand. The Bombay Government became perturbed by the reports in 1841 that Masqat vessels were bringing negro slaves from Africa and taking back Hindu women for sale in Zanzibar (Bombay Archives, 1840-1843). The National Archives of India (New Delhi) records indicate the several stages of the progress of the measures taken by the British for the suppression of slavery in the Indian Ocean and Persian Gulf, culminating in the treaties concluded with the Sultans of Masqat and Zanzibar and the assurances obtained from the Maritime Arab Chiefs in 1873.

Indian diaspora

With the abolition of slavery in the British colonies in 1834 and in the French colonies in 1849, a new slave-trade sprang up under a new alias—Indian immigration under the indentured system. The British Guyana Commission of 1871 had this to say:

The indenture system differs from slavery principally in this respect—that of his proper civil rights, those which are left to the slave, if any, are the exception while in the case of indentured labourer the exceptions are those of which he is deprived. Hence it is the freedom of the slave and the bondage of the indentured labourer against which all the unforeseen incidents and accidents of law must tell.

The colonial plantations, starved of Negro slaves, created the dire need for large supplies of cheap labour. At this psychological moment in history, it was the penuric conditions in India, which gave an impetus to the tide of Indian emigration, for the most part unlettered. Indeed it presents a pathetic but none the less striking contrast to the earlier Indian emigration, where the emigrants were the ambassadors of a great civilization and culture or traders in rare commodities.

At the scale at which the emigration of indentured labour took place from India in the latter half of the nineteenth century, it was only natural that a series of Indian ghettos should burgeon in the colonies concerned. Massive in size were those at Mauritius, Reunion, Madagascar and Fiji in the South Indian and Pacific Oceans; Malaya, Burma and Ceylon in South-East and South Asia; Kenya, Tanganyika, Uganda, Zanzibar and Natal in Africa; Trinidad and Jamaica in the Caribbean basin, and British Guyana and Surinam in South America.

Though Indian labour has played a conspicuous role in the development of colonial economies, yet in many countries, like their African counterparts, they have been denied even the elementary rights of citizenship, apart from the racial discrimination of which they are victims. Under circumstances such as these sprouted Gandhi's new philosophy of dissent or *satyagraha,* which was tried with apparent success in South Africa in 1906.

Research possibilities

The following lines of research are suggested:
The maritime and emigration propensities of the Indonesians from the earliest times.
The indigenous art and culture of the Polynesians in early times.
The 'Greater India' movement—political, commercial, religious and cultural.
India and Africa: (a) the Mangalore settlers in Madagascar and Mozambique and the identity of the Wadebulis, (b) East African trade with India, and (c) the Indian merchant shipping which traded with East Africa.
The Malay-Polynesian settlers (Hovas) of Madagascar. When and how did they appear? Also, an ethnological study of Malagasy.
The Arab ascendancy in the Indian Ocean.
The Muslims in Africa.
The early history of the islands off the coast of East Africa.

Among the interested Indian research groups are the Centre for West Asian and African Studies, School of International Studies, Jawaharlal Nehru University, New Delhi; the Centre for South, South-East and Central Asian Studies, at the same university; the Department of African Studies, University of Delhi, Delhi; and Area Studies, Department of Civics and Politics, University of Bombay.

The following scholars are concerned:

Dr Anirudha Gupta, Head, Centre of West Asian and African Studies, School of International Studies, Jawaharlal Nehru University, Delhi-30. Compiler of *Source Material on Indo-African Relations from the Early British Rule in India to the Present Day.*

Dr C. S. Chattopadhyaya, Department of African Studies, University of Delhi, Delhi.

Indian cultural and commercial influences in the Indian Ocean from Africa and Madagascar to South-East Asia

Author of *Indians Abroad—Asia and Africa*, New Delhi, Orient Longman, 1971. Materials on Africa in the National Archives of India.

Dr S. P. Chawdhury, Lecturer, Desh Bandhu College, Kalkaji, New Delhi. Interested in Indian emigration to East Africa.

Dr Ann Peascatello, 8 William Street, Paw Catuck Coun, Los Angeles, Calif. Interested in Brazil and Africa and in trade with Goa.

Dr S. L. Tesnak, Institute of Oriental Studies, USSR Academy of Sciences, Moscow. Interested in relations between China and Asian and African Countries, 1920–1969.

Dr D. Devahonti, Delhi University, Delhi. Interested in Indian cultural influence in Borneo.

Commander K. Sridharan, Indian Navy. Author of *A Maritime History of India*, Delhi, Publications Division, 1965.

Historical contacts of Africa and Madagascar with South and South-East Asia: the role of the Indian Ocean

Michel Mollat

Certain circumstances seem to stand in the way of Africa's belonging to the natural community of the Indian Ocean countries. The massiveness of the continent, the fact that some sectors of the seaboard are difficult of access, the narrowness of the coastal zone, the impediment constituted by mountain or desert areas, seem at first sight to oppose the penetration of influences from the sea and to deter the African populations, basically landsmen in general, from seeking outside contacts. Nevertheless, the persistence of contacts between the African continent and Madagascar, on the one hand, and the countries of South and South-East Asia, on the other, on the most diverse planes, are borne out by all forms of historical inquiry. The search for examples, and *a fortiori* their analysis and synthetic interpretation, are far from complete. But the efforts of individual research workers, research centres and frequent congresses yield sufficient documentary material and partial results to justify an attempt to sum up the situation. As I had occasion to contribute to the *Journal of World History* (Vol. XIII, No. 2) an essay on this subject in 1971, reference will be made to it. Since then, expert reports on Malay culture submitted by Denys Lombard and Siméon Rajaona at the meetings held in Kuala Lumpur in 1972[1] and Bangkok in 1973[2] have helped to shed light on the question. Further elements can also be drawn from partial surveys recently published in Africa and Madagascar. I shall therefore endeavour to consider the facts, of course in relation to the history of Africa with which we are concerned here, but not from the standpoint of any particular region. Viewing the subject from the aspect of the sea routes linking Africa with its partners may offer a broad horizon.

---

1. International Meeting of Experts for the Launching of the Malay Culture Project, organized by Unesco, Kuala Lumpur, 21–28 January 1972.
2. Meeting of the Council for the Study of Malay Culture, organized by the Thailand National Commission for Unesco with Unesco assistance, Bangkok, 5–9 February 1973.

The natural environment

At a very early stage, nature seems to have prepared for the lands bordering on the Indian Ocean the conditions for their relations with Africa. In this connection history needs the co-operation of disciplines very different from itself.
   Geology teaches us that Madagascar became separated, as an island, after the end of the primary era, in the course of alternate phases of breaking away from the African continent and being reattached to it during the secondary and tertiary eras. When the shelf of the great island tipped westwards, penetrable valleys were opened, while the easterly direction, on the contrary, offered a less hospitable aspect. The mountain tops that remained above water made of the Comoro Islands a series of ports of call between Madagascar and Africa, where conditions for navigation were highly variable. For its part, the bathymetric chart, which the oceanographers are trying to make more accurate, already shows clearly, despite the depths separating Africa from Madagascar, a contrast with the great troughs situated to the east of the latter. Here, only the relays of the Mascarene and Chagos Islands, too distant one from the other, emerge. This situation has had several consequences: geographical affinities, the conditions under which people and things move about—in a word, all that constitutes the natural environment modified by man.
   Among the geographical factors affecting relations in the Indian Ocean, it will suffice to recall that the regularity of the contrasts in atmospheric pressures between the continents and the sea, combined with the seasonal rhythm of the monsoons and the trade-winds, gives rise to a regular alternation of the movement of sailing ships between Africa, Madagascar and their Asian partners, and vice versa. These wind conditions prevail to the east of Madagascar and the Mascarenes as they do in the northern part of the ocean, and this raises the question of the possibility of direct navigation between Madagascar and the East Indies in ancient times with precarious craft. Then again, can it be supposed that there were communications between South Africa and Australasia before the cold west winds, the roaring forties, were used by eighteenth-century sailing vessels?
   The natural sciences reveal that the vegetation first consisted of untransportable common elements, whose presence today, in Madagascar and Africa, for example, testifies to the old continental links. Marine currents, winds and birds subsequently contributed to the modification of the flora, even before the intervention of man and independently of his action. The latter was of course decisive and, on this point, botany supplements the information supplied by history. Madagascar, even more than Africa, affords in its flora a typical example of the meeting place of different types of

vegetation. It was not so much the presence of the Mozambique Channel which prevented the penetration of plant species from outside as the vast stretches of ocean to the east, even before the island was inhabited. However, human intervention has had considerable effects. Madagascar has probably preserved a greater wealth of endemic flora than have many other regions in the world; but the equilibrium of the vegetation is fragile, and some plants, faced by competition from imported tropical species, are doomed by this assault either to die out, or to undergo transformation or differentiation. The least deteriorated formations observable at present were the ones that served as a basis for the vegetation map of the island made by Humbert and Cours in 1965. Botanists estimate that 27 per cent of the Malagasy flora affinities and 7 per cent has Indonesian affinities. It is significant that the plants showing an Indonesian influence are some of the forest and steppe formations and, above all, crop plants such as rice; as is well known, the cultivation of rice was developed in the island by the Malayan immigrants.

A study of the fauna also provides valuable information in regard to contacts between one region and another. Is there need to mention, beside the survival of lemurs in Madagascar and the originality of the fauna of Europa Island, the fact that the zebu, so characteristic of Madagascar, is believed to have come from Africa? Zoologists note that the existence of the pygmy hippopotamus on either side of the Mozambique Channel is due to the fact that Madagascar was once joined to the African mainland. Ethnography would also have something to say concerning the widespread significance of the taboo preserving crocodiles. Lastly, returning to Africa, there are many findings which history can take over as a result of the efforts made by students of natural history. Two very different cases may be quoted as examples. One is that of the clove, which used to be imported from Indonesia and with which, reversely, Zanzibar now supplies that region. The other is that of the African giraffe, which as we know was offered in the Middle Ages as a present to the sovereigns of Bengal and China, where it created a sensation. More prosaically, but backed by the deductions of ethnologists and sociologists, botany and zoology bring us to the history of nutrition. Man draws his subsistence from his environment and from the supplements procured through contacts with the outside world. Here, there is still much to be expected. This last remark leads to the problems deriving from the relations between peoples on one side and the other of the Indian Ocean.

Indonesian migrations across the ocean

The most notable ethnic contacts—and those that have given rise to the most controversy because they date from a very long time ago and there is no direct documentary evidence—result from the Indonesian migrations. In Madagascar the fact is anthropologically evident; but the extent, the locality and the date of these migrations, the route they followed and their consequences, have to be determined. In the absence of written and dated documents, the historian must have recourse to other disciplines to test his working hypotheses and partial conclusions. Anthropological examination is aimed at determining and classifying the somatic characteristics of individuals. J. Poirier devised a kind of standardized anthropological profile for male subjects of the same age, for the purpose of detecting Melanoid or Melanesian features in them. Other methods compatible with this one are the haematological studies conducted by M. C. Chamla (1958) and Pingache (1970) and the serological tests carried out in East Africa by Hiernaux (1968). The findings are still recent and fragmentary, the chief impediment, especially in Madagascar, being the mixed character of races and ethnic groups. At all events, they seem to converge towards a solution midway between the theories favouring Asia, in accordance with the views of A. Grandidier and J. Poirier, and those defended by R. K. Kent following in the footsteps of G. Ferrand.

Anthropology alone cannot suffice to decide between these theories. At present research workers are better equipped in regard to linguistics, ethnology and sociology. No one now disputes the fact that Malagasy belongs to the Malayo-Polynesian linguistic group. O. Dahl's work (1951), which we agree with D. Lombard in describing as masterly, concludes in favour of a close relationship between Malagasy and the Maanjan spoken in Borneo. It was noted by S. Rajaona that 80 per cent of the roots in Malagasy were of Indonesian origin. Might not the Asian language containing the largest number of common terms with Malagasy be regarded as the parent stock? The problem is not simple, for the Malagasy language contains African intrusions at two levels, noted by Dahl and J. Dez: an extremely old Bantu base corresponding to a stock-raising society, and more recent additions, relating mainly to navigation, borrowed from Swahili. All things considered, the fact that a language of Indonesian origin has become a vehicular language poses a problem with many unknowns and almost impossible to solve that of the size of the ethnic groups involved, their intellectual level, the route followed by the migrants, and the locality where they settled.

At present little more can be done than to propound the problem of numbers. Elements for a reply to the question of cultural levels are to be found in the results of comparative ethnographic surveys. In addition to the language, Madagascar presents notable traditional elements of the culture from across the ocean, which D. Lombard describes by the new and ingenious term 'Nusantaran'. These are the resemblances in kinship systems, the collective organization of the village (the *foko*), the sense of community between the living and the ancestors, an ethic of courtesy regarded as a strategy for interpersonal relations, certain religious myths, a series of customs that have acquired the force of law and, lastly, certain practices in connection with dwellings (quadrangular huts, figures of birds on the eaves, villages set on hills and surrounded by ditches), with techniques (irrigated ricefields, coconut grater, pirogue with balancing pole) and with the arts (musical instruments: flute and perhaps xylophone). In fact the situation is very complex, for in Madagascar cultural features of Indonesian origin are mingled with or exist alongside African traditions and Arab elements, while on the African coast the same mixture is to be found with the proportions reversed. Thus, archaeology can also help in the search for origins. The localization of the sites excavated in Imérine (A. Mille counted 16,000 in 1972) and their stratigraphy should make it possible to assign dates. So far, the findings yielded by archaeology, anthropology and linguistics seem to indicate two main waves: one, known as the Proto-Malagasy, around the fourth to fifth centuries, in the north of the island; the other, known as the Neo-Indonesian, which settled on the high inland plateaux (eleventh to fourteenth centuries).

As for the route followed, the simplest would be the direct line of about 6,000 km from the East Indies to the east coast of Madagascar. This is theoretically possible but, in the absence of islands to stop at on the way, it is impracticable, despite the seaworthiness of the pirogue with a balancing pole and freedom from cyclones during the Austral winter. A second, semi-direct, route was possible, with a stop at Ceylon. Fishermen from the Laccadive Islands drifted as far as Madagascar in 1930 without encountering any island. However, if this route had been used, the Mascarenes would have remained uninhabited until the arrival of the Dutch in Mauritius and the French in Réunion. A further possibility is the roundabout way by Africa; a number of arguments militate in favour of this and several historians consider it likely. No routes are better reconnoitred than that from the coasts of India to East Africa and thence to Madagascar. The crossing is easy from Cape Delgado to Great Comoro, because in clear weather Kartola Volcano is visible from Cape Delgado. Then, going on from one island to another presents practically no problem. The area between Madagascar and the African coast where the pirogue with a balancing pole circulates seems to correspond to the Indonesian zone of influence. However, up to now few evidences of this influence have been revealed by ethnography, and the deeper strata of the sites excavated have produced nothing in this connection.

Later settlements acted differently, overlaying the existing elements in one place, pushing them back in another, even on the island. But, on this side of the ocean, archaeology has not said its last word.

Indians and Islam on the African coast: the Swahili culture

Less the subject of controversy than are the Indonesian voyages, the contacts of Africa and Madagascar with South and South-East Asia are better testified to, from ancient times, by written documents and by archaeology. The only point of historical interest in the adventure of Hippalos is that it bears witness to the use of the monsoon before the Christian era. It also means that, while the African coast was reached by Indonesian craft opposite Madagascar, it was from the north, in the Red Sea and around the Horn of Africa, that it was aroused to maritime life.

Written sources are a guide for the locating of archaeological sites. Without going back as far as Phoenician times and Nechao's voyage—on which, however, any further light would be welcome—Cosmas of Alexandria's *Topographia Christiana* and the *Periplus* (or coastal guide) of the Eritrean Sea are too universally accepted to be disregarded. Arab sources are the most plentiful. In many cases the geographers have copied one another, but it is still advisable to consult Mas'udi, Ibn Hauqal, Idrisi, Abu Sa'id, Yaqut, Abulfeda and that inexhaustible story-teller, Ibn Batuta, without forgetting, on the other side of Arabia, the *Livre des Merveilles de l'Inde*.[1] Ethiopian literature is not absent: in the *Kebra nagaset*, one element of the 'Glory of the Kings', to which it is devoted, is found in the Indian trade. Even far-away China, according to a ninth-century chronicle and to information given by the high-placed official Chau Ju'Kua, was not unaware of the whereabouts of Popali, that is, Africa, or the possibilities of trade with it. This information had perhaps not been forgotten by those who launched the ephemeral but powerful Chinese naval expeditions to East Africa in the fifteenth century. Western sources are more plentiful from the fourteenth century onwards. Marco Polo said about Africa what his Arab informers had conveyed to him at Ormuz; but shortly afterwards missionaries such as Guillaume Adam and Etienne Raymond at Socotra, or Odoric de Pordenone in India, observed maritime activity in the Indian Ocean. After that, we must wait for the time of the voyages of discovery—that of João de Barros—to find, in addition to numerous accounts of travel, archival

---

1. *Mémorial Jean Sauvaget*, Vol. A, p. 159–312, Beirut, 1954.

Historical contacts of Africa and Madagascar with South and South-East Asia: the role of the Indian Ocean

documents, containing a wealth of quantitative information, which made their appearance in the sixteenth century.

On such bases, archaeologists have recognized certain port sites in Africa and Madagascar and, owning to the monuments brought to light and the material found in the course of excavations, they have sometimes confirmed and supplemented what was known concerning the nature and the trends of exchanges, the individuals and peoples who were the agents or the subjects of these relations and the types of culture that shaped their existence.

The results achieved are already notable, though much remains to be excavated on the coasts of Eritrea and the Horn of Africa, from the site of Adulis, the lung of the ancient kingdom of Axum, and that of Zeïla as far as the Mogadishu region, where exploration seems promising. The zone in which the old port of Rhapta was situated is now being marked out. From Lamu through Gedi to the south of Kilwa the commercial ports have been located and in some cases brought to light. The first excavations made on the Comoro Islands are also promising. The efforts that revealed Vohémar in the north east of Madagascar have been renewed, with more reliable methods, on sites at various points along the west coast, and the map of archaeological sites on the two coasts appears well filled.

The configuration of the western Indian Ocean and the system of circulation of the monsoons determined Africa's contacts with the outside world as much as did economic and human circumstances. In the north, relations between Ethiopia and India developed very early in a latitudinal direction; it was here that Indians began to settle in Africa. A hoard of some hundred Indian gold coins dating back to the third century, found at Dabra Dammo, provides evidence of these relations, traces of which can be seen in other features of Ethiopian civilization: the use of spices (pepper and cinnamon), the introduction of sugar-cane, of the art of cotton weaving, influences in art and architecture revealed at Axum, dissemination of literary themes (for instance, the story of Barlaam and Josaphat, which also reached Europe in the Middle Ages). In the opposite direction, from the beginning of the thirteenth century Ethiopian slaves—'Habshis' or 'Siddis'—were highly appreciated from Gujerat to Ceylon. They were used as soldiers and on the boats. There were many of them in the hinterland of Cambay, and their descendants are still to be found in a few groups of African origin that are among the most underprivileged in the country. From the sixteenth century, exchanges were in the hands of the Banian merchants established at Massawa, who made the port's fortune and their own right up to our own time.

A second axis, which was to give rise to far-reaching consequences, linked up, as it were, with the first one and developed to begin with in a southerly direction, from the Arabo-Iranian zone, the Horn of Africa and

Socotra, where ships were accustomed to pass. The complementary nature of the sailing of the Rea Sea and Persian Gulf merchants down the coasts of Africa, in relation to their trade with India, is undisputed. The statements of the geographers and chroniclers are confirmed by documents in the *genizah* near Cairo and what is known of the Kharimis. In fact, were they not following an example previously set by the Indians? The latter, not confining themselves to the Ethiopian market, appear to have penetrated as far as Kilwa, where they were still dominant at the end of the thirteenth century. Coins found in that city bear out the theory that the Dabol coins served as models for African workshops; and, according to one tradition, it was from Dabol that the 'Wadebuli' came to Africa in boats 'made from palm leaves'. Besides the economic incentive that drew the Arabs and the Persians in the same direction as the Indians, there were also religious and social reasons: Africa was a haven for Sunnite and Karmathian dissidents from Syria, Iraq and Arabia.

The state of knowledge concerning Muslim settlements was the subject of a communication submitted by H. Neville Chittick in 1972 to the Congress on Population Movements in the Indian Ocean, which was held at Réunion by the International Commission for Maritime History and the International Historical Association of the Indian Ocean, and also of a contribution by P. Vérin to No. 5 of *Taloha,* published by the University of Madagascar. A few particularly important facts will be borne in mind. The immigrants arrived at different points offering natural protection, situated close to estuaries and trails used by bearers, and showed a preference for the islands. The place names quoted by ancient authors cannot always be verified, but some have yielded to archaeological investigation—for example, Gedi near Malindi (the old Mulanda), Qanbalu, found in the islands of Pemba, Manda, and above all Kilia. The stratigraphy of the excavations makes it possible to check the chronology followed by ancient authors, more recent chronicles such as that of Kilwa, and systematically collected oral traditions. Unfortunately for the interpretation of the material found, this seldom includes coins, which would fix a *terminus a quo* for the stratigraphic layer where it was discovered. Ceramics are very plentiful and here, as elsewhere, they lend themselves to comparison with known types. For instance, they provide proof of importations from Siraf and China.

Texts and excavations point towards an evolution along the following lines. From the beginning of the Abbasside period the African slave trade was extensive enough to explain the famous revolt of the Zenj slaves in lower Iraq at the end of the ninth century. The first Muslims, traders or refugees from the persecuted sects, to settle in East Africa probably came from Shiraz at the time of the port of Siraf's prosperity. The legend of Hussein ibn Ali and his sons, who came in the tenth century with seven ships, has a historical basis not refuted by archaeology: even in the north-east of Madagascar, Islamic pottery similar to that of Siraf in the ninth century and that of Unguja Ukun in Zanzibar has been found at the Irondo site, along with a gold dinar dating from the time of Harun Al-Rashid (798).

While, from the outset, Islam reached as far as the Comoro Islands and Madagascar, which is recognized to be identical with the Wakwak of the old texts, the sites seem gradually to have spread southwards. Owing to the unequal progress of archaeological investigation in the various countries, no definitive conclusions can be reached. Mogadishu seems to have played a vital part and in the thirteenth century reached an importance to which its mosques still bear witness, but the secret of which remains buried in the ground. In former times Manda had from four to five thousand inhabitants. Mas'udi himself noted *de visu* as far as Pemba a trade in Chinese and Persian ceramics, which were exchanged for iron, ivory and slaves. The Shirazians laid the foundations of the prosperity of Kilwa, which was first a stopping-place on the way from Mogadishu to the southern regions, Madagascar and—above all—the gold country, Sofala, before it became a direct link with Arabia under the Mahaly dynasty in the fourteenth century. Aden and the Bahrain area were other centres of expansion in Africa. When Kilwa declined, even before the advent of the Portuguese, under the effects of the independence of Sofala, a series of Muslim towns prospered in the tenth century all along the African coast, mainly at Lamu, at Pate and especially at Mombasa. It is sometimes difficult to assign dates; but means of checking the deductions made from stratigraphy are provided by numerous inscriptions. The little towns whose ruins archaeologists are beginning to clear in the Comoro Islands and on the west and north-east coasts of Madagascar, though lesser in size and importance than the 'dead cities' of East Africa, are none the less representative of an original type of Swahili Muslim civilization.

The Swahili culture is a maritime culture: the way of life, social organization, mentality and language all derive from the contacts with the sea of those whose culture it was. In this, the immigrants who came from Asia across the ocean and their descendants offer a contrast with the indigenous Africans, farmers and graziers—although this contrast must have become diminished by the mutual influences that have necessarily been exerted over the centuries. Travellers, including Batuta and Mas'udi, and later on Portuguese visitors, remarked on the autonomy of each of the towns, organized as separate, and in some cases rival, sultanates, similar in some respects to the Mediterranean city States. These cities were rivals or allies because they had similar interests, almost solely commercial, and because their trade and their trade routes were the same. Life there followed a common course, governed by the monsoons, and the instruments of their activity were likewise practically identical: sailing-ships of medium or low tonnage, whose ribs were joined by means of coconut fibre, the rigging consisting of one, two or even three masts and a triangular mainsail carried by a long yard. This kind of vessel still exists in various forms but basically the same. Navigation founded on empirical observation of the sky and atmospheric conditions, as in the experiment conducted recently by Commandant Grosset-Grange, has remained up to our time a common technique. Lastly, as in all maritime areas traversed by the same peoples, an idiom combining contributions from various languages serves as a means of communication for men sharing the same life and facing the same dangers. Swahili, mixed with Bantu in Africa and with Malay in Madagascar, is nevertheless essentially related to the language of the predominant groups, Arabic. Language is a vehicle for ideas, and the Muslim faith held in common constitutes a very strong bond between those already associated by the ocean: the Africans among themselves and with their Asian partners. Ways of thinking are matched by customs and practices. Here again, the sea exerts its influence. A native of Tangiers such as Ibn Batuta, in the fourteenth century, did not feel at all strange in Mogadishu or Kilwa, where he was received by seafarers and traders. However, he noted customs peculiar to these places, differences in language, contrasts in development, even contradictions between the rulers and the ruled in a colonial-type social State. Some research has opened a way for the study of local aspects of the African and Malagasy maritime societies, for instance, in respect of Lamu and, in Madagascar, the Vezo, Betsimiramaka and Sakalava. There are many particular aspects to be studied: besides the coastwise trade and the transoceanic trade, all forms of fishing; and, under the Muslim faith and practices, the survival of magic and ancestor cults. Nor have the Malagasy *Sorabe* revealed all their contents.

Continuity and change

The Swahili culture, which had almost reached its full flowering before the arrival of the Portuguese, was not profoundly changed by the coming of Europeans. The regional currents of exchange continued despite the efforts of the Portuguese to take them over. The first objective of the European traders was to seize upon the most profitable products (especially spices) from India or the East Indies, and they took an interest in East Africa up to the nineteenth century in that, situated as it was on the 'route to India', it commanded the access to and trading on that route. One of the first effects was that south-east Africa, from the Cape to Sofala, was integrated in the general circuits. The Portuguese tried to draw the traffic from the northern sector, even from the Red Sea, in this direction. This explains the role of

Mombasa, head of the direct line to Western India; but the diversion thus attempted and partially achieved was largely superficial. Africa, in exchange for its skins, ivory and rubber, continued to receive Indian cotton goods, Malayan spices and Persian and Chinese ceramics, which are always found in the upper layers of the excavations. The fleets used to sail round Madagascar and, up to the seventeenth century, the Mascarene Islands, mainly in order to take on fresh provisions, that is, water and fruit to combat scurvy. No doubt the Monomotapa's gold was evacuated by the Portuguese under the noses of the Arab traders, but it met with keen competition from the Ethiopian and south-east Asian gold. Although no numerical evaluation can be made, it is not improbable that J. C. van Leur was right in estimating that the regional trade and the European trade in the Indian Ocean were equal in volume and in value. So true is this that the Europeans did not hesitate to avoid the coasts of Africa and save time on the journey to India or the Far East by using first the outer route, that is, the route to India passing east of Madagascar and, later, the roaring forties, which carried them towards Australia.

While the sea traffic was unable for centuries to change the course of tradition in Africa, the continent was seriously affected by the manpower problem, which took two successive forms. The slave trade in the hands of the Arabs lasted a millennium, from the ninth to the nineteenth century, uninterrupted by the slave trade in the hands of the Europeans in the seventeenth and eighteenth centuries, which barely rivalled it. Recent studies and the work of the 1972 Congress in Réunion have shed some light on the volume of the slave trade and the manner in which it was carried on. Without going into details, we would observe once again that Madagascar offers complex and significant features. In the eighteenth century there was a sort of division of tasks and equalizing current between the Muslim traders and the European merchants—the Muslims bringing their human cargo from the African continent and the Europeans supplying the Mascarene Islands with manpower.

It was in a different way that the migrations affected contacts between Africa and Asia in the nineteenth and the beginning of the twentieth centuries. To offset the shortage of manpower due to the abolition of the slave trade, the sugar-cane planters peopled the Mascarene Islands with Indian immigrants. Similarly, the development of southern Africa and the centre of eastern Africa in the nineteenth century provided Indian merchants and workmen with opportunities for speculation and employment.

Population movements and the intermingling which has resulted from them have therefore exerted on Africa an influence at least as great as that exerted by investment of capital, the introduction of techniques and the arrival of Christian missionaries, specialists and intellectuals.

The influence of outside contacts is as stimulating for societies as it is for individuals. That East Africa was opened up before West Africa no longer needs to be demonstrated. The antiquity, extent and intensity of its relations, the existence of urban life from very early times, provide perhaps the clearest proofs. The good fortune to which these are due certainly resides in the possession of a very long coastline facing an ocean predestined to fruitful exchanges. The mediterranean seas—for the Indian Ocean is such— have always been centres of civilization. Awareness of this circumstance provides not only matter for a chapter, or even a volume, of African history; rather it sheds light on the whole course of that history. However, all is not yet perfectly clear; some areas of shadow still remain to be dealt with by research.

Directions and centres for research

To begin with, let us endorse two principles stated by S. Rajaona in his report of 1973— enumeration, comparison. The collection of material is far from being completed in certain spheres. No analysis, and still less synthesis, is possible without measurement of the data; and measuring means comparing.

Sources and working tools

Prospecting of sources presupposes inventorying of the archives available. The *Guide to the Sources of African History*, under the direction of Unesco, has made a breakthrough. But we must reach the level of detailed thematic directories; and the work in progress at the National Archives of India, of which we have been given some idea by D. G. Keswani, may be quoted as an example.

Pending arrival of a corpus of epigraphs, the trail has been blazed by the publication of a provisional list of Arabic inscriptions from the eastern African coast (G. S. P. Freeman-Grenville and B. G. Martin, 'A Preliminary Handlist of the Arabic Inscriptions of the Eastern African Coast', (with bibliography), in the *Journal of the Royal Asiatic Society*, 1973 (2), p. 98–122). For the purpose of comparison, the inscriptions found in Indonesia, for which a publication plan has been prepared, should be used.

An urgent task is the speeding up of archaeological excavation. The results achieved in Africa are stimulating but they are confined to fairly narrowly circumscribed points. Much is expected from the excavations being carried out by the French *Centre National de la Recherche Scientifique*, particularly on the sites at Adulis and Matara in Ethiopia. In respect of the Somali coast, H. Neville Chittick has published a precise account of the sites to be cleared ('An Archaeological Reconnaissance of the Southern Somali Coast', in *Azania*, IV, 1969, p. 115–61). Under the impetus of the British Institute in East Africa, Nairobi, many places have been explored in Kenya and Tanzania, but others have yet to be excavated. Zanzibar has scarcely been touched on, except at Unguja Ukuu and Kizimkazi Dimbani. Further south, Angoche has been studied, but elsewhere nothing has as yet been done. On the initiative of the University of Madagascar, work has begun on the Great Comoro, and a map has been drawn up of the sites in Madagascar. This work has already proved so re-

*Historical contacts of Africa
and Madagascar with South
and South-East Asia:
the role of the Indian Ocean*

warding (P. Vérin) that there is every reason for continuing it on the eastern coast. Moreover even the excavations in the interior of Africa (at Tete and Zimbabwe) and of Madagascar (the high Imèrima plateau) are essential to the study of outside contacts. Some interesting projects are being prepared at Lamu (J. de V. Allen). To enable the archaeologists to make comparisons, excavations must be carried out in the countries which were in contact with Africa—first, in Yemen, Hadramut, Oman, so frequently and so constantly linked with the East African ports; we know of little more than the yellow pottery of Kawd-an-Saila. As for the ports of southern Iran, the results of the excavations carried out at Siraf by D. Whitehouse can be quoted, but that is all. Yet so many secrets lie hidden in the sites of Qays and Ormuz. In India much excavation is going on, and Africanists can glean information from the publications of the Archaeological Survey of India and from the productions of the *Ecole Française d'Extrême Orient*. What has been found at Dahol, Cananor and elsewhere is of great interest. In Indonesia, the archaeological service maintained by the Dinas Purbakala has not confined its activities to the restoration of Borobudur, but is contributing material to the history of Malayan influences west of the Indian Ocean. Some of this material, found in Bali and on the north coast of Java, dates back to the neolithic period; it also includes Chinese ceramics comparable to those in African museums. All these resources, which will increase in the near future, must be used.

A basic working tool is the atlas. Some atlases exist, as for example, the *Atlas de Madagascar*. What is needed, in respect both of Africa and of the countries maintaining relations with it, is many maps prepared from the historical standpoint: archaeological, linguistic, ethnographical maps; maps showing religions, trade routes, food resources, mineral resources, handicrafts, distribution of settlements, maps of towns; and of course maps showing the distribution of fauna and flora.

Lastly, texts. Collections of the kind produced by Grandidier and Ferrand can no longer suffice. What is required is systematic and critical collections of annotated documents, critical editions of accounts of voyages, log-books and route-books of Arabic and Malayan texts compared with each other. The task of collecting the Sorabe in Madagascar and oral traditions everywhere must be completed without delay. A great deal of material is available for linguistic analysis, provided that use is made of it with the most modern means such as computers. Then, besides the critical editions, semantic studies and multilingual dictionaries should be published.

As the current trend in historical research all over the world is towards the inventorying of sources and the constitution of working tools, the history of Africa can only benefit thereby.

Research topics

The whole history of the Indian Ocean must be viewed afresh from the east, Denys Lombard wrote in connection with Indonesia. In the case of Africa, should it not be viewed afresh from the west as well? To be quite accurate, it would be advisable to approach the subject from the centre, so as to consider all aspects. In the collection and comparison of material it is well to co-operate with both sides of the ocean. We shall now group round a few topics the problems already mentioned.

The first topic, which governs all the others, is that of sea communications—ocean routes, ships, navigation. A great deal remains to be done. However, assuming the problem to be solved, or rather pending its solution, we shall proceed to the second topic: the routes followed by people and cultures, which brings us back to such questions as the Indonesian migrations, the Muslim expansion, the slave trade, the spread of technical, intellectual and religious influences and particularly the influence of languages (Malay, Arabic, French, English) and religions (Islam, Christianity). The third topic would be economic exchanges.

An interdisciplinary approach and work over a long period are the prerequisites for a breakthrough, the need for which seem to inspire the projects and programmes that have sprung up on all sides as signs of scientific vitality, on the three seabords of the Indian Ocean. Although Africa is already fairly well equipped, it cannot do without international co-operation, and, in addition to the aid it receives from old-established and well-equipped centres in Europe and the United States, it could usefully enlist that of young institutions, which would have the advantage of operating in the world they are studying. The complementary character of archaeological centres was mentioned earlier; to this should be added the possibilities of exchange and co-operation between universities in Africa, Madagascar and Asia. International associations, by increasing their contacts, are coming more and more to understand the advantage of concentrating the work of their congresses on common topics—for example, 'Sociétés et Compagnies de Commerce en Méditerranée et dans l'Océan Indien' (Beirut, 1966), 'Symposium on the Indian Ocean and Adjacent Seas: Their Origin, Science and Resources' (Cochin, 1971), 'Mouvements de Population dans l'Océan Indian' (Réunion, 1972). The Combining of efforts has become so customary that the historians of Asia and South-East Asia have united in a single association since the congress held at Kuala Lumpur in 1968.

Lastly, sympathetic note will be taken of the opportunities for co-operation which the young *Institut d'Etude et de Recherches sur les Aspects Malgaches de la Culture Malaise* may find in Indonesia, with the LIPI research-workers, in respect of maritime history, human sciences, medicine, economics, and with the University of Indonesia (Jakarta) and the Universitas Gadjah Mada (Yogyakarta), in respect of economic and social questions, with particular reference to rural aspects; likewise in Malaysia, as a result of the stimulating emulation prevailing in linguistics and in the history proper of Malayan civilization and Islam, in the universities of Kuala Lumpur and Singapore.

In short, we shall not conclude on a negative note. On the contrary, what is required is to co-ordinate efforts and to make a choice among topics. To which projects should priority be given? No doubt to those that can contribute most effectively to the task of defining and manifesting the originality of African history.

Select bibliography

As a bibliography was attached to the article I contributed to the *Journal of World History* (Vol. XIII, No. 2, 1971, p. 291–316) under the title 'Les Relations de l'Afrique de l'Est avec l'Asie: Essai de Position de Quelques Problèmes Historiques', I shall confine myself here to supplementing it and bringing it up to date with the mention of the following works:

Archipel. Etudes Interdisciplinaires sur le Monde Insulindien, Paris (8 vols. since 1971.)
ASHTOR, E. The Karimi Merchants. *Journal of the Royal Asiatic Society*, 1956.
Atlas de Madagascar, Tananarive, 1969.
AUBIN, J. Quelques Remarques sur l'Etude de l'Océan Indien au XVIe Siècle. *Agrupamento de Estudos de Cartografia Antigua*, Vol. LXXV, Coimbra, 1972, 13 p.
BATTISTINI, P.; RICHARD-VINDRARD, G. *Biogeography and Ecology in Madagascar*. The Hague, 1972.
BHATTACHARYA, D. K. Indians of African Origin. *Journal of African History*, Vol. X, 1970, p. 579–82.
Bibliographie de l'Histoire des Grandes Routes Maritimes, Vol.III, Espagne, Grèce, Vol. IV, Royaume Uni, *Boletim Internacional de Bibliografia Luso-Brasileira*, XIII (3), 1972, p. 373–498, and XIV (1) 1973, p. 5–162, XV Océan Indien, 1976, Calouste Gulbenkian Foundation, for the International Commission for Maritime History.

BOUCHON, G. *La Communauté Musulmane de Cananor et ses Premiers Conflits avec le Portugal (1500-1528)*, thesis, Ecole Pratique des Hautes Etudes, IVe section, Paris, Sorbonne 1973 (typed), 2 vol. 509 p. (In the series Mare Luso Indicum, Vol. III.)

CARSWELL, J. Archaeology and the Study of late Islamic History. In: D. S. Eichards (ed.), *Islam and the Trade of Asia*. (Concerning Siraf excavations.)

CHATTERJII, S. K. *India and Ethiopia from the Seventh Century, B.C.*, Calcutta, 1967.

CHITTICK, H. Neville, Recent Archaeological Work in East Africa. In: *Actes du Premier Congrès International d'Archéologie Africaine*. Etudes et Documents Tchadiens, Mém. No. 1, Fort Lamy (1966) 1969.

———. East African Trade with the Orient. In: D. S. Richards (ed.), *Islam and the Trade of Asia*. (See below).

DAHL, O. Malgache et Maanjan. Une Comparaison Linguistique. In: *Avhandlinger utgitt av. Egede Instittuttet*, No. 3, Oslo, 1951 (Linguistics in the Service of the History of Migrations.)

DATOO, B. A. Rhapta. The Location and Importance of East Africa's First Port. *Azania*, Vol. V, 1970, p. 27–39.

DONQUE, G. Le Contexte Océanique des Anciennes Migrations, Vents et Courants dans l'Océan Indien. In: *Taloha* I, 1965, p. 43–69.

DORESSE, J. *Histoire Sommaire de la Corne Orientale de l'Afrique*, Paris, 1971.

FAUBLÉE, J. Les Manuscrits Arabico-Malgaches du Sud-Est. Leur Importance Historique. *Revue Française d'Histoire d'Outre-Mer*, Vol. LVII, 1970, p. 266–87.

———. Pirogues et Navigation chez les Vezo du Sud-Ouest de Madagascar. *Anthropologie*, Vol. LIV, 1954, p. 432–54.

FILLIOZAT, J. Les Echanges de l'Inde et de l'Empire Romain aux Premiers Siècles de l'Ere Chrétienne. *Revue Historique*, 1949, revised and supplemented in *Les Relations Extérieures de l'Inde*, Pondichéry, 1956, 60 p.

FINNEY, B. New Perspectives on Polynesian Voyages. *Polynesian Culture History* (Honolulu), 1967 (on the technical link between Polynesian and Indonesian voyages.)

GOPAL, Lallanji, *The Economic Life of Northern India A.D. 700-1200*, Delhi, Motilal Banarsidass, 1965.

GOITEIN, S. Letters and Documents on the Indian Trade in Mediaeval Times. *Islamic Culture*, Hyderabad, Vol. XXXVII, 1963, p. 188–205.

GREGORY, R. *India and East Africa. A History of Race Relations within the British Empire (1890-1939)*. Oxford, 1972.

GROTANELLI, V. L. *Pescatori del Oceano Indiano*. Rome, 1955.

———. Asiatic Influences on Somali Culture. *Ethnos*, Stockholm, Vol. IV, 1947, p. 153–81.

HAZAREE/SINGH, K. *Histoire des Indiens de l'Ile Maurice*. Paris, 1973, 223 p.

HORNELL, J. Indonesian Influence on East African Culture. *Journal of the Royal Anthropological Institute* (London), Vol. LXIV, 1934, p. 305–33.

JACKSON-HAIGHT, M. V. *European Powers and South-East Africa. A Study of International Relations on the South Eastern Coast of Africa 1796-1856*. London, 1967 (important for the history of the slave trade).

JONES, A. M. The Influence of Indonesia: the Musicological Evidence Reconsidered. *Azania*, Vol. IV, 1969, p. 131–91.

KENT R. K. *Early Kingdoms in Madagascar 1500-1700*. New York, 1970 (bibliography).

KOBISHCHANOV, Y. M. The Sea Voyages of Ancient Ethiopians in the Indian Ocean. In: *Proceedings 3rd International Conference of Ethiopian Studies*, Addis Ababa (1966), 1969, p. 19–25.

———. On the Problem of Sea Voyages of Ancient Africans in the Indian Ocean. *Journal of African History*, Vol. VI, 1965, p. 137–41.

KOECHLIN, J. Flora and Vegetation in Madagascar. See above, P. Battistini. *Biogeography*, p. 145-90.
KOUBBEL; TATVEIV. *Sources Anciennes et Médiévales pour l'Ethnographie et l'Histoire des Peuples de l'Afrique du Sud du Sahara*, 1. Sources arabes des VIIe-Xe s., Moscow, 1960; 2. Sources arabes des Xe-XIIe s., Moscow, 1965.
LEWIS A. Maritime Skills in the Indian Ocean 1368-1500. *Journal of the Economic and Social History of the Orient* (Leyden), Vol. XVI, 1973, p. 238-65.
LOMBARD, D. Les Indonésiens Font le Point sur l'Histoire de leur Pays. In: *Bulletin de l'Ecole Française d'Extrême Orient*, Vol. LVIII, 1971, p. 281-98. (Report of the second seminar on national history, Yogyakarta, 1970. Contains *inter alia* a progress report on the archaeological excavations.)
Mare Luso Indicum. Collection Ecole Pratique des Hautes Etudes. IVe section (under the direction of J. Aubin), 2 vols. issued in 1971 and 1973. (Important for the Kerala trade and the role of Ormuz and Cambay.)
NEWITT, M. D. D. The Early History of the Sultanate of Angoche. *Journal of African History*, Vol. XIII, 1972, p. 397-406.
PANKHURST, R. *The History of Ethiopia's Relations with India prior to the Nineteenth Century*. Roneo text presented at the fourth Conference of Ethiopian Studies, Rome, 1972, 121 p. (771 notes).
The Swahili-speaking Peoples of Zanzibar and the East African coast (Arab, Shirazi and Swahili). First ed., 1961; second ed., 1967. London, xvii + 146 p.
RICHARDS, D. S. *Islam and the Trade of Asia: a Colloquium*. Oxford, 1970, 267 p.
SANGEELEE, M. A Brief History of the Tamilans of Mauritius. In: *Proceedings of the First International Conference, Seminar of Tamil Studies*, Kuala Lumpur, 1966, p. 242-51.
SASTRI NILAN-KANDRA, K. A. *A History of South Africa*. Madras, 1956.
SCANLON, G. Egypt and China. In: D. S. Richards (ed.) *Islam and the Trade of Asia*. See above. (Concerning copies of Chinese ceramics in East Africa.)
SPRINS, A. H. S., *Sailing from Lamu. A Study of Maritime Culture in Islamic East Africa* Assen, 1965, 320 p.
STEIN, B. Coromandel Trade in Mediaeval India. In: J. Parker (ed.), *Merchants and Scholars*, Minneapolis, 1965.
TOUSSAINT, A. *Histoire des Iles Mascareignes*. Paris, Berger-Levrault, 1972.
TREGONNING, K. G. *A History of Modern Malaya*. The Hague, 1961.
VENKATARAMANAYYA, A. *The Early Muslim Expansion in South India*. Madras, 1942.
VÉRIN, P. *et al.* Civilisation du Sud Ouest ... de Madagascar. In: *Taloha* (Tananarive) 4, 1971. Roneo. 230 p. Histoire Ancienne du Nord Ouest de Madagascar. In: *Taloha*, 5, 1972, 175 p. (Extensive bibliography.)
WHEATLEY, P. *The Golden Khersonese, Studies in the Historical Geography of the Malay Peninsula Before A.D. 1500*, Kuala Lumpur, 1961.
WHITEHOUSE, D. Siraf, a Mediaeval Port on the Persian Gulf. *World Archaeology* (London), Vol. II, 1970, p. 141-58.
WIJETUNGA, W. M. K. South India Corporate Commercial Organization in South and South-East Asia. *Proceedings of the First 'International Conference, Seminar of Tamil Studies*, Kuala Lumpur, 1966, p. 494-508.
YAZDANI, G. *The Early History of Ceylon*, Colombo, 1960. *The Early History of Deccan*. Oxford, 1960.

The Chinese and the countries across the Indian Ocean

Wang Gungwu

Chinese sources suggest that the Chinese were aware of the great ocean we now call the Indian Ocean just before the beginning of the Christian era, at the latest by the first century A.D. The first Chinese to cross that ocean to India probably did so soon after that, and certainly by the third century. After that, there were more and more visits of Chinese Buddhist monks on pilgrimage to India, and, by the seventh century, it can be assumed that large numbers of Chinese traders and sailors of the southern Chinese coast were fully aware of the trading and even political conditions on the northern littoral of the Indian Ocean. But throughout this period it would appear that such Chinese as went across the Indian Ocean did so in Indian, Persian or Arab ships (Ferrand 1913-14, 1919). There is some speculation about Chinese shipping going beyond the Straits of Malacca by this time, but none of the evidence is conclusive on this point (Chang Hsing-lang, Needham, Filesi).

Although Chinese shipping may not have been used, ships of the Indian Ocean were communicating with China through the sea-lanes of South-East Asia soon after the beginning of the Christian era. That these ships were carrying on an active and prosperous trade throughout the first millennium is incontrovertible. Thus the research so far shows that the contacts between the Indian Ocean countries and China were first established and then maintained through the evolution of maritime techniques among the peoples of the Indian Ocean. This does not mean that Chinese shipping had not been developed to the point where it could do the journey across that ocean. There is evidence to suggest that, by the T'ang dynasty (618-906), Chinese ships were capable of doing long ocean voyages (Needham, Lo, 1955). It would seem that other cultural and institutional factors delayed the use of Chinese shipping beyond those areas that were of direct interest to China until after the tenth century. This suggests that there is no causal relationship between improvements in Chinese maritime techniques and Chinese trading across the Indian Ocean in Chinese ships. Although the techniques were already there, or could easily be adapted from the techniques developed by Indian Ocean sailors, reasons other than technological skills delayed China's decision to send its own ships across the Indian Ocean.

Nevertheless, it is important to note the fact that Indians and Arabs brought the Indian Ocean to China's attention. Because of this, it appears that the Chinese were not directly aware of a different continent on the western side of the Indian Ocean until they first saw European maps in the seventeenth century (for a possible exception, see Fuchs and Needham). Thus the perception of the Indian Ocean, even up to the time when Chinese ships themselves crossed it, was dominated by the glories of India and the Muslim world. The fragmentary Chinese reports of the peoples across that ocean suggest that they had a picture of Africa and Africans as seen through Arab eyes and that they saw such people as subjects of the Muslim rulers and extensions of the Arab world (Chao Ju-kua, Hirth and Rockhill, Wang Ta-yuan, Rockhill). At the same time, the Chinese found the trading goods from India and the Arab world sufficiently attractive and profitable to encourage that trade for several centuries. What we know now suggests that the Chinese increased their direct interest in the Indian Ocean countries only when Arab trade and Arab shipping to the Chinese coast had declined, during the thirteenth and fourteenth centuries (Hirth and Rockhill, Rockhill).

By the time the Chinese were directly interested in sending their own ships across the Indian Ocean, their ships were superior to the others sailing across that ocean at that time. I refer to the dramatic decision of the Ming Emperor Yung-lo to send a number of naval expeditions led by the eunuch admiral Cheng Ho to India and the Arab world. The way the expeditions dominated the seas at the time confirms the picture we have of rapid developments in Chinese shipping during the Southern Sung dynasty, especially during the thirteenth century (Liu, 1945; Lo, 1955). These developments were further supported by the world-conquering ambitions of the Mongols, and by the end of the thirteenth century the Chinese navy was clearly capable of crossing the Indian Ocean if it wanted to (Wang Ta-yuan, Chang Hsing-lang).

Chinese records on the development of maritime techniques are fragmentary until the fifteenth century. From then onwards, largely inspired by the grand designs of Emperor Yung-lo, the exploits of the great 'treasure ships' (*pao-ch'uan*) were fully recorded, and more details of how these large ships were constructed and manned became available (Man Huan, Fei Hsin, Huang Sheng-tseng, Kung Chen, Li Chao-hsiang, Mao Yuan-i). These records are not always accurate, and much of the reconstruction done by recent scholars has been based on interpretations of the surviving fifteenth- and sixteenth-century records collated with more accurate descriptions of eighteenth- and nineteenth-century coastal shipping and ships that sailed between China and South-East Asia (Pao Tsun-p'eng, Needham). The casualness of these early records about Chinese shipping confirms that the

Chinese did not place much score on the evolution of maritime techniques. This I think is due to two main reasons. First, the Chinese did not believe in travelling far across oceans unless absolutely necessary. They believed that politics was more important in determining the distance Chinese ships should and could travel than advances in maritime techniques. This reflects Chinese attitudes towards science and technology as contrasted with Chinese sensitivities concerning political and economic interests. Secondly, the maritime techniques needed to cross the Indian Ocean were already well known to the Chinese through their familiarity with Arab and Indian shipping, which had reached China so many centuries earlier. That they were not unduly impressed and did not turn them to their own use immediately confirms that the delay in Chinese shipping sailing across the Indian Ocean was not due to deficiencies in technology.

The dramatic events of the great naval expeditions of Cheng Ho in the first thirty years of the fifteenth century confirms this picture. These great naval forces experienced no difficulty whatsoever in reaching the Persian Gulf and the east coast of Africa (Cheng Ho-sheng; Hsiang Ta I and II; Liu, 1943). All the records suggest that the expeditions were carried out most effectively, and certainly there is no hint anywhere that there was any difficulty concerning techniques. Nor is there any suggestion of heavy shipping losses during the course of these long voyages (Pelliot; Duyvendak, 1933 and 1939; Mills). Most conclusively, the fact that the expeditions were ordered in 1403 and were quickly sent out in 1405, and that the last expedition on its return in 1433 was ordered never to be sent out again, makes it quite clear that the question of maritime techniques was not in any way the determining factor for the Chinese.

What was spectacular and also historic about these voyages across the Indian Ocean was the fact that the Chinese showed no great surprise or special curiosity about them. The well-known story about the giraffe brought to China reminds us that some strange creatures from Africa dazzled the Chinese (Duyvendak, 1949; Cheng Ho-sheng), but the total impression is one of having carried out a necessary task for an ambitious emperor without much glory or acclaim. On the contrary, as far as the Chinese ruling classes were concerned, these expeditions were unnecessary and wasteful, and at the first opportunity they arranged to have them ended. The popular impact of the voyages was more long-lasting; until the end of the Ming dynasty there was still much discussion about these spectacular voyages, and one major novel (the *San-pao T'ai-chien Hsi-yang Chi*) came out of the many tales about the great expeditions. All the same, their main effect was to confirm Chinese prejudices that voyages to distant lands were of no great benefit to China and that they could be discontinued without any serious consequences to Chinese politics or the Chinese economy.

Despite the fact that these voyages lasted only a short while and were not followed by other independent voyages, the results were very significant for our knowledge of the Indian Ocean situation during the first half of the fifteenth century. It was a period when Arab records were very slim and it was more than half a century before the Portuguese began to compile their great works. The Chinese records now fill a large gap in our knowledge of the Indian Ocean area.

Two points need to be emphasized that arise from these voyages. First, the many centuries of trade involving goods from China, which are clearly shown by the archaeological finds along long stretches of the east coast of Africa, show that Chinese maritime techniques and Chinese awareness of the continent of Africa played no part in the growth and expansion of a China trade on the western coasts of the Indian Ocean. Secondly, the evolution of maritime techniques in China was not a major factor in the extension of Chinese voyages to distant lands. We cannot say that the great voyages of the fifteenth century had to wait for the right set of maritime techniques, nor can we say that the Chinese were spurred on to rapid improvements in maritime techniques because they wanted to send great expeditions across the Indian Ocean. The lack of a causal relationship between the two here confirms the relatively insignificant role played by maritime techniques in the decisions made by the Chinese ruling élites about voyages of exploration and discovery or for that matter about voyages of distant and profitable trade.

Future lines of research

It is not easy now to suggest the best future lines of research. The surviving Chinese records have been fairly thoroughly combed. Records before the fifteenth century are too fragmentary for any substantial new information to emerge even with careful reinterpretation. Records after the fifteenth century (for example, Chang Hsieh, Wei Yuan) may still be subjected to careful collation and comparison to sift out insertions of new information from time to time, especially in the sixteenth and seventeenth centuries (Chang Wei-hua, T'ien Ju-k'ang). Such sifting may produce additional insights concerning changes in Chinese maritime techniques as well as changes in the nature of Chinese contacts with peoples and cultures on the Western side of the Indian Ocean. But it appears to me that the rewards will not be great, while such tasks that remain to be done will be extremely laborious. The most recent study in China on the relations between China and Africa (Chang T'ieh-sheng, 1965, 1973) draws so much upon the research of European scholars since the end of the nineteenth century, and in particular on the archaeological finds of the east coast of Africa during the last two or three decades, that it would appear that scholars in China with the best access to the remaining Chinese records find the literary materials too slim to make any further startling discoveries.

The most fruitful line remains in the field of archaeology. It would seem to me that ceramic and coin finds could probably be greatly augmented by more archaeological work in East Africa and that a more systematic collection and study of these finds might bring out new patterns in our understanding. But much would also depend upon whether these finds could be more closely related to the exact nature of Arab trade and the shipping and maritime techniques used at the height of the trade. There remains an important gap in establishing the time span of that China trade and the factors on which it depended. For one thing, whether any Chinese shipping was lost near enough to the shores of the Persian Gulf, the Red Sea and Eastern Africa for a discovery of their hulks remains an intriguing question. The recent growth of close relations between China and some of the countries on the eastern coast of Africa may lead to greater efforts to establish a more accurate picture of mediaeval China trade in due course.

The following researchers and institutes are carrying out research, or have sources, concerning the theme of the symposium: National Library of Peking; Institutes of Archaeology and History, Academia Sinica, Peking; Chung-shan University, Kwang-chou (Canton), Kwangtung; Fu-tan University, Shanghai; Hsia-men University, Hsia-men (Amoy), Fukien; Institute of History, Academia Sinica, Taipei; National History Museum, Taipei; National Taiwan University, Taipei; Chang T'ieh-sheng, Peking; Chang Wei-hua, Peking; Chou I-liang, Peking University, Peking; Hsiang Ta, Peking; Hsü Yü-du, National Taiwan University, Taipei; Liu Ming-shu, Peking; Pao Tsun-p'eng, Academia Sinica, Taipei; and T'ien Ju-k'ang, Fu-tan University, Shanghai.

Select bibliography

This is limited to works with the emphasis on Chinese sources and researches. Important works relevant to China's historical relations with countries across the Indian Ocean, such as those on Africa by R. Coupland, J. Strandes, G. Matthew, J. S. Kirkman, G. S. P. Freeman-Grenville and H. Deschamps and on Arab seafaring by G. F. Hourani and G. R. Tibbetts, have not been included. Major works on Marco Polo and Ibn Batuta which have contributed materials on this subject have also been left out.

Works in Western languages

DUYVENDAK, J. J. L. *Ma Huan Re-examined.* Amsterdam, 1933.
——. The True Dates of the Chinese Maritime Expeditions in the Early 15th Century. *T'oung Pao,* Vol. 34 (1939), p. 341–412.
——. *China's Discovery of Africa.* London, 1949.
FERRAND, G. *Relations de Voyages et Textes Géographiques Arabes, Persans et Turques Relatifs à l'Extrême Orient du VIIIe au XVIIIe Siècles.* Paris, Vol. I, 1913; Vol. II, 1914.
——. Le K'ouen-Louen et les Anciennes Navigations Interocéaniques dans les Mers du Sud. *Journal Asiatique,* March-April 1919, p. 239–333; May-June, 431–92; July-August, p. 5–68; September-October, p. 201–41.
FILESI, T. *Le Relazioni della Cina con l'Africa nel Medioevo.* Milan, 1962.
FUCHS, W. *The 'Mongol Atlas' of China by Chu Ssupen and the Kuang Yü T'u.* Peking, 1946.
HIRTH F.; ROCKHILL, W. W. (trans.). *Chau Ju-kua: his Work on the Chinese and Arab Trade in the 12th and 13th Centuries, entitled 'Chu-Fan-Chi'.* St. Petersburg, 1911.
LO JUNG-PANG. The Emergence of China as a Sea Power during the Late Sung and Early Yuan Periods. *Far Eastern Quarterly,* Vol. XIV, No. 4, 1955, p. 489–503.
——. The Decline of the Early Ming Navy. *Oriens Extremus,* Vol. V, No. 2, 1958, p. 149–68.
MILLS, J. V. G. (trans.). *Ying-yai Sheng-lan, 'The Overall Survey of the Ocean's Shores',* by Ma Huan. Cambridge, 1970.

NEEDHAM, J. *Science and Civilisation in China.* Cambridge University Press, Vol. 3, 1959, p. 497–590; Vol. 4/I, 1962, p. 279–93; Vol. 4/III, 1971, p. 379–699.
PELLIOT, P. Les Grands Voyages Maritimes Chinois au Début du XVe Siècle. *T'oung Pao,* Vol. 30, 1933, p. 237–452. Additional notes in *T'oung Pao,* Vol. 31, 1935, p. 274–314.
ROCKHILL, W. W. Notes on the Relations and Trade of China with the Eastern Archipelago and the Coasts of the Indian Ocean during the 14th Century. *T'oung Pao,* Vol. 15, 1914, p. 419–47; Vol. 16, 1915, p. 61–159, 236–71, 374–92, 435–67, 604–26.

Works in Chinese

This excludes well-known official records like *Ming Shih,* the various *Veritable Records (Shih-lu)* and other official compilations.

CHANG HSIEH. *Tung Hsi Yang k'ao.* (A study of the eastern and western Oceans.) 1618. Shanghai Edition, 1936.
CHANG HSING-LANG. *Chung-hsi chiao-t'ung shih-liao hui-p'ien.* (A collection of historical data on the relations between China and the West.) 6 Vols., Peking, 1930.
CHANG T'IEH-SHENG. *Chung-fei Chiao-t'ung shih Ch'u-t'an.* (A preliminary study of the history of Sino-African relations.) Shanghai, 1965. Second ed., 1973.
CHANG WEI-HUA. *Ming Shih Fo-lang-chi Lü-sung Ho-lan I-ta-li-a ssu-chuan chu-shih.* (Commentaries on the chapters on Portugal, Spain, Netherlands and Italy in the Ming History.) Peking, 1934.
CHAO JU-KUO. *Chu Fan Chih.* (*Records on Foreign Peoples*; see trans. by F. Hirth and W. W. Rockhill and annotated edition by Feng Ch'eng-chün. Changsha, 1940.)
CHENG HO-SHENG. *Cheng Ho I-shih hui-pien.* (Relics of Cheng Ho's naval expeditions.) Shanghai, 1948.
FEI HSIN. *Hsing-ch'a sheng-lan.* (The overall survey of the Star Raft.) 1436. Annotated Peking edition, 1954.
HSIANG TA I. *Cheng Ho hang-hai t'u.* (The charts of Cheng Ho's naval expeditions.) Peking, 1961.
HSIANG TA II. *Liang Chung Hai-tao chen ching.* (An edition of Two Rutters.) Peking, 1961.
HUANG SHENG-TSENG. *Hsi-yang ch'ao-kung tien-lu.* (Records of the tributary countries in the Western Ocean.) 1520. Yueh-ya t'ang ts'ung-shu edition, Taipei reprint, 1965.
KUNG CHEN. *Hsi-yang Fan-kuo chih.* (Records of foreign countries in the Western Ocean.) 1434. Peking edition, 1961.
LI CHAO-HSIANG. *Lung-chiang ch'uan-ch'ang chih.* (Records of the shipbuilding yards on the Dragon River.) 1533. Edition of National Central Library, Peking, 1947.
LIU MING-SHU. Cheng Ho Hang-hai Shih-chi chih Tsai-t'an. (Further investigations on the sea voyages of Cheng Ho.) *Chung-kuo Wen-hua yen-chiu [Bulletin of Chinese Studies]* (Ch'eng-tu), Vol. 3, 1943, p. 131–70.
LIU MING-SHU. Sung-tai Hai-shang T'ung-shang Shih tsa-k'ao. (Miscellaneous studies on the seafaring and commerce of the Sung Period.) *Chung-kuo wen-hua yen-chiu [Bulletin of Chinese Studies]* (Ch'eng-tu), Vol. 5A, 1945, p. 49–84.
MA HUAN. *Ying-yai Sheng-lan.* (The overall survey of the ocean's shores; see translation by J. V. G. Mills; and annotated edition by Feng Ch'eng-chün, Shanghai, 1935). Reprint, Peking, 1955.
MAO YUAN-I. *Wu Pei Chih.* (Treatise on armament technology.) 1628. Edition of 1843.
PAO TSUN-P'ENG. *Cheng Ho Hsia Hsi-yang chih Pao-ch'uan k'ao.* (A study of the 'great treasure ships' used in Cheng Ho's voyages in the Western Oceans.) Taipei and Hong Kong, 1961 (in a Chinese and an English edition).

T'IEN JUK'ANG. Shih-ch'i shih-chi chih Shih-chiu Shih-chiu Shih-chi chung-yeh Chung-kuo Fan-ch'uan tsai Tung-nan Ya-chou Hang-yün ho Shang-yeh Shang ti li-wei. (The place of Chinese sailing-ships in the maritime trade of South-East Asia from the seventeenth to the nineteenth centuries.) *Li-shih yen-chiu [Historical Studies]*, Vol. 56, No. 8, 1956, p. 1–21. Further notes in *Li-shih Yen-chiu*, Vol. 57, No. 12, 1957, p. 1–11.

WEI YUAN. *Hai-kuo T'u-chih*. (Illustrated record of the maritime nations.) Enlarged edition, 1852.

WANG TA-YUAN. *Tao-i chih-lueh*. (Records of the Barbarian Islands; see translation by W. W. Rockhill in *T'oung Pao*, 1914–1915).

Part II
The settlement of Madagascar and neighbouring islands

Various theses concerning the settlement of Madagascar

Jacques Rabemananjara

The present meeting immediately raises a fundamental problem, which is, on the face of it, a simple one: the geographical significance of the position of Madagascar in relation to both Africa and South-East Asia.

Close to Africa, but separated from it since the Palaeozoic period, Madagascar is by no means an appendage of Africa. Far from it: if we are to believe the geological, biological and ethnological data, we are dealing with another world. It remained much longer joined to India, right down to the Mesozoic, forming, together with Australia, the lost continent of Lemuria. The fauna and flora of the Great Isle are much more Oriental than African in origin, and one writer has gone so far as to say that, despite considerations of distance, it has closer connections with Oceania than with Africa.

Moreover, if one turns one's attention to the origins and history of its inhabitants, one is struck by a similar paradox: men, in the dark ages, came from the East. Down to the present day, indeed, research workers have not found a final solution to this riddle: despite anthropological differences and variations in dialect, from north to south and from east to west the people speak a single language, which indisputably belongs to the Indonesian branch of the great Malayo-Polynesian family.

In these circumstances, does it still make sense to talk of eighteen tribes in Madagascar? A Serer cannot understand a Baoulé. A Malagasy, irrespective of the ethnic group to which he belongs, can travel throughout the island: he will be able to make himself understood everywhere, without the help of an interpreter, whereas the same is not true of his close neighbour, the Comorean.

How is such a phenomenon to be explained? There are two possibilities: either, at some stage in history, one of the tribes was able to dominate the others and impose its leadership and its language, which seems definitely not to have occurred; or the so-called tribes can be traced back to a common stock that branched out into ethnic groups by geographical area, each evolving in a limited region of the country, which itself is very large.

But at this point a fundamental problem arises, called by Hubert

Deschamps 'the biggest riddle in the world': the origins of the Malagasy. Set against linguistic unity is the composite racial character of this people, and this contradiction has sparked off a great many hypotheses, variously interpreted by specialists.

Pierre Vérin, one of the best contemporary experts on Madagascar, summarizes them as follows:

According to A. and G. Grandidier, the island was populated by Indo-Melanesians, followed by Javanese (ancestors of the Merina) and by late African and Islamic arrivals. G. Ferrand, on the other hand, could not agree that the black racial types of Madagascar stemmed from Melanesian ancestry, and gave prominence to the Bantu contribution, while also attributing Javanese origin to the ancestors of the Merina.

H. Deschamps, whom we consider to be the best-informed writer on Malagasy affairs, has just outlined an explanatory theory, affording no doubt a means of reconciling G. Ferrand and A. Grandidier. He believes that at about the middle of the first millennium of our era Indonesians crossed the north of the Indian Ocean and intermarried with the local population on the east coast of Africa. This intermingling gave rise to the Proto-Malagasy, who subsequently intermarried with other Indonesians and with Africans who came with the Arabs or as slaves.

Were there any inhabitants in Madagascar before the Indonesians? According to many Malagasy experts, when the first Indonesians settled on the island they discovered people already living there, known as the Vazimba, whom G. Ferrand considered to be Africans. In fact, these Vazimba were probably the outcome of the earliest cross-breeding between Indonesians and Africans, whom the ancestors of the Merina drove back towards the east at the time of the occupation of the highlands at the beginning of the second millennium of our era. (In this connection, see the works of J. C. Hebert.)

J. Poirier thinks it possible that a Bushmanoid population existed before the Indonesian migrations. In his view, some of the early Behosy and the early Mikea might be the last descendants of these Bushmanoids. So far, we have no archaeological sites that would make it possible to confirm this opinion.

One thing remains certain, however: 'The Malagasy population is the outcome of juxtapositions and syntheses of Indonesian and African elements.' This was acknowledged as early as 1613 by one of the first Europeans to concern himself about the problem, the Portuguese Jesuit Luis Mariano:

All we know of the matter is that the inhabitants of St. Laurence Island (Madagascar) came partly from Malacca (Indonesia) and partly from Kaffraria (East Africa) and that, later, the north-west region saw the arrival of Moors from India and Arabia and, much later, a few Portuguese. Traces of these various nations are still to be found in the local language and customs.

With his usual sense of humour, President Tsiranana used to enjoy proclaiming at international conferences of the Third World: 'We Malagasy are the true Afro-Asians.'

Meanwhile, a contemporary Malagasy writes:

This, then, is Madagascar. A glance at the world map shows us its size: the fifth largest island in the world. Its distinctive geographical position seems from earliest times to have determined its special destiny: somewhat withdrawn from Africa, it seems to be moving cautiously away from it while at the same time stretching out tenderly and nostalgically towards the distant countries of the dawn. It calls to mind a great red beacon placed on the ocean route as if to serve as a natural and delightful link connecting the vast neighbouring continent, the West and Asia. Thus, throughout the ages, seafarers voyaging from many different horizons to sail its waters, blown towards its shores by the trade winds, by the squalls of the monsoons and the violent cyclones, must have seen it as a meeting of many paths—a crossroads of humanity. Each in turn or simultaneously, Malay, Asian, African and European visitors left behind their marks and their features. From this age-old mixture there emerged an intermediate people, difficult to define and yet typically recognizable: the modern Malagasy.

The Malagasy are constantly aware of their multiracial origins. They know, at least, thanks to the evidence of the language and of a body of customs, that this complex is dominated by two elements, Malay and African.

Research workers, as we have seen, have put forward various explanations concerning the arrival of Proto- and Neo-Indonesians in the island.

Relations between Madagascar and East Africa

One point remains to be studied, on which insufficient light has so far been shed: the historical relations between Madagascar and East Africa.

Gustave Julien states categorically: 'It is a fact beyond dispute that there was a steady flow of African immigration to Madagascar from the very earliest times . . . at certain periods it assumed the character of a veritable invasion.'

H. Deschamps seems to lend support to this view, building on the known data concerning winds, currents and ancient navigation techniques in the Indian Ocean:

With neighbouring Africa only about 400 kilometres away and the Comoro Islands forming a stepping-stone, communication does not raise any insuperable difficulties, especially if one comes from the north-west, from the region of Zanzibar. The currents are undoubtedly variable, but they are too weak to be an obstacle to navigation.

Nobody questions the authority of Julien. But his assertion does not appear to rest on any precise facts or events. A research worker like Dr Rakoto Ratsimamanga, in his work on 'Pigmentation and Origins of the Malagasy', while not wholly refuting the hypothesis, nevertheless reduces its impact. Ratsimamanga has analysed four anthropological types, and his claim is precisely that 'the least common type appears to be the Negro-African: black skin, crinkled hair, prognathism, platyrrhiny and dolichocephaly, which are found among the Sakalava and especially among the Makoa, who would appear to be pure Negroes of Africa'.

Modern writers share this scepticism, and take the view that, for the time being, the evidence we have is not sufficiently conclusive to enable us to distinguish between the Negro-African and the Negro-Oceanian type.

However, according to J. Poirier,

the Negro-African type, on first examination, seems easy to explain: it probably originates with the former slaves who were brought from the continent in varying numbers throughout the ages. The Makoa are an example of such African Negroes, but protected from cross-breeding, which, elsewhere, has modified the African type to a greater or lesser degree. We also know that the Arab expeditions carried off very large numbers of East African Negroes in their ships.

H. Deschamps states: 'As regards the African Negroes, forced or voluntary voyages brought them to the Comoro Islands and to Madagascar.' Ibn Magrid, in the sixteenth century, declares that Komr (Madagascar) is the second largest island in the world; it is set apart and beyond it lies the southern darkness. Saleiman al Mahari (early sixteenth century) recognizes four islands between Madagascar and Africa. He gives wind-directions and latitudes, and indicates the principal ports, which are, from north to south: on the west coast, Lanojani, Saada, Manzladji (Masselage, Mahajamba) Bender Bani al Nub, Malwin, Bender Kuri and Bender Hit; on the east coast (seldom visited) beyond Cape Rasal Milkh, Bender Bani Ismail, Bimaruh (Vohémar) Anamil and the Amber Isle (Antongil, Nosy Mangabé), Noshim (Nosy Ibrahim, Sainte-Marie), Manakara, Bender Haduda, Walada and Bender Kus. The indication of islands to the south-east, thirty-six hours away, leads one to suppose either that the Arabs knew the Mascarene Islands, or that they based themselves on the Portuguese discoveries. At all events, it is certain that the Arabs knew both coasts, especially in the north west and the north east.

But the age-old supremacy of the Indonesian, Indian and Arab fleets in the Indian Ocean was soon to come to an end: European ships took their place. When Vasco da Gama sailed around the Cape of Good Hope in 1498, he opened up the Far Eastern route to seafaring.

In 1500, the Portuguese squadron of Pedralvares Cabral was scattered by a storm off the coast of southern Africa, and one of its captains, carried far off course to the east, came upon a coast which was none other than that of Madagascar. Henceforward the Portuguese, the Dutch, the French and the English incessantly sailed around or landed on the coasts of Madagascar and thereby kept up contacts between this isolated country, neighbouring Africa and the rest of the world.

Trade in various commodities was an essential preoccupation of both the indigenous population and foreigners. But the slave trade stood out above the rest:

Deportation of slaves in the sixteenth century by the Portuguese and the Dutch [writes H. Deschamps] was only episodic. But when the Dutch settled in Mauritius, Jakarta and then the Cape, slaves became useful to them. They bought them in the south-east and in the bay of Antongil before 1650, and then on the west coast, where they found themselves in competition with the Portuguese, the Arabs and the English. In the eighteenth century, with the needs of the West Indies and the Mascarene Islands, the English and especially the French were to outstrip the Dutch. Bombetaka, Boina, St. Augustin, Tuléar, Fort-Dauphin, Matitana, Tamatave, Foulpointe and Antongil were the principal ports of departure . . . Curiously enough, although Madagascar was a source of slaves, it also imported slaves from the coast of Africa (the Makoa and the Masombiky). We have very scanty information about this traffic, which was in the hands of the Arabs. It also seems that one of the aims of the Betsimisaraka raids on the Comoro Islands and on the African coast (the town of Iho was attacked three times and the island of Mafia captured) at the end of the eighteenth century was to obtain slaves.

Perhaps it should also be mentioned that, at the end of the seventeenth century and the beginning of the eighteenth, on the coast of Madagascar and particularly on the islet of Sainte-Marie, pirates were to be found who had been driven out of the Caribbean and the Atlantic. They roved the ocean and also made forays on the east coast of Africa: here they captured slaves for trading purposes, and immediately returned to their Madagascar hideout.

There is even a story, related by H. Deschamps, that one of them, by name Mission, a native of Provence and an educated man who had turned his back on society, joined forces with his companions Caraccioli (Italian) and Tom Tew (English) to found the International Republic of 'Libertalia', very probably in the bay of Diego Suarez. In this republic all races intermingled, and prisoners were freed, irrespective of their origins; but its too dazzling display of wealth aroused the envy of the Malagasy, who plundered it and massacred those who sought to defend it.

With the abolition of slavery, followed by the colonization of the island for more than sixty years by France, the history of relations between Madagascar and Africa was practically broken off.

Since Madagascar regained its independence, the Malagasy leaders have seemed anxious to renew relations with the neighbouring great continent: such, it would seem, was the purpose behind the official visit to Tananarive and Tamatave paid by M. Banda, President of the Republic of Malawi, and that of President Tsiranana to Blantyre and Zomba. A similar interpretation should be placed upon the State visit to Madagascar by the Prime Minister of Lesotho and the football matches held in Tananarive and Maseru between the teams of the two States.

Apart from political and trade purposes, the establishment of diplomatic relations between Madagascar, Kenya and the United Republic of Tanzania fits into the same pattern.

Role of the islands in cultural exchanges

In the course of its history, Madagascar has not had contacts with Africa alone: a whole crescent of islands surrounds it, and we have noted the violent impact of its relations with the Comoro Islands.

The latter, in fact, were already inhabited before the westerners put in an appearance. The same is not true of those other lands in the Indian Ocean, the Mascarene Islands.

The settlement of what were to become Réunion, Mauritius, Rodriguez and the Seychelles was due solely to the initiative of bold European seafarers, especially the Dutch, the French and the English. They turned these desert islands into countries which tourists nowadays praise to the skies for their charm and beauty.

Did these islands have a role to play in cultural exchanges with Madagascar? Apparently not. However, the existence in the Great Isle, particularly in Tamatave and in certain towns of the east coast, of a sizeable colony of Réunion islanders and Mauritians has not failed to make its mark: inevitably, people living side by side for several decades mutually influence one another. Nor should the important fact be overlooked that the Réunion islanders, the Mauritians and the Seychellois have ancestors from all the continents, from India, China, Africa, Europe and Madagascar. Each brought crafts and culture, and centuries of day-to-day coexistence have gradually ironed out the differences and turned these lands into a crossroads of civilizations where customs, religions, languages and modes of artistic expression have taken shape in a harmonious synthesis. There can be no doubt that the Malagasy have made their own specific contribution to this process.

Better still, the West, perhaps without realizing it, has succeeded in fostering understanding among the islands: use of the same language, whether English or French, means that, for example, the Malagasy, the Réunion islanders, the Mauritians and the Seychellois share the flavour and the riches of one and the same culture. Leconte de Lisle, Baudelaire and Parny are as highly appreciated in Tananarive, Port Louis and Mahé as the poets J. J. Rabeavivelo, J. Rabemanajara, Robert Edouard Hart, Marcel Cabon and Edouard Maunic.

The language of the colonial power enables its former subjects to communicate across the ocean, take stock of their wealth and exchange this among themselves, just as they trade in material goods, but with the distinguishing note that in the field of human relations nothing is of more value than intellectual and spiritual communion.

As these countries all belong to a single geographical area, their authorities are aware of the need for closer collaboration in all fields. The desire to bring this about gave rise to the establishment of the ATOI (Association Touristique de l'Océan Indien), a body whose members are Madagascar, the Comoro Islands, Réunion and Mauritius, and which uses tourism to pursue the specific objective of encouraging cultural and folk-art exchanges among the islands, and knowledge of one another's way of life.

Conclusion

We cannot end this brief report on the settlement of Madagascar and its relations with East Africa and neighbouring islands without feeling impelled to place a number of suggestions before Unesco: picking out lines of research amounts to emphasizing the gaps to be filled in our present state of knowledge and the questions to which this conundrum gives rise.

The sea has always been a cradle or a vehicle of civilization. One can hardly fail to mention the role played by the Mediterranean basin in the birth and expansion of the outlook, philosophy, ethics and technology of the West.

Can the Indian Ocean be an exception to this rule? One is entitled to suppose that for centuries civilizations have blossomed either on its shores or in its islands, that of Madagascar being one of the last links in the chain.

An undertaking worthy of Unesco would be to seek to identify these and to search for or plot the traces of the famous continent of Lemuria, which we hear so much about.

As regards Madagascar itself, the often contradictory theses of research workers warrant deeper probing by the use of modern and improved methods and tools of research.

H. Deschamps writes: 'The origin of the Malagasy is the biggest riddle in the world. In order to solve it with certainty, one would need teams of specialized research workers: anthropologists, linguists, ethnologists, technologists, musicologists, archaeologists and sociologists, who would carry out research and compare notes in Madagascar, Indonesia, South-East Africa and perhaps elsewhere.'

Furthermore, J. Poirier states emphatically: 'It is clearly first and foremost by means of archaeology, with the help of philosophy, glossochronology and comparative ethnology, that progress will be made towards solving this problem.'

He adds: 'However, there are other possible approaches, which call upon such disciplines as botany, geology, toponymy, agronomy, palaeography and demography and which, above all, combine their results, so that new working hypotheses and perhaps even provisional conclusions may be arrived at.'

Everyone seems to take one point as certain: that the earliest arrival of Indonesian immigrants in Madagascar took place between the third and sixth centuries of our era. The fundamental importance of this Indonesian cultural mould is too obvious to be overlooked.

But some persons have recently taken the view that the essence of Madagascar, anthropologically speaking, is African: a comparative study is therefore called for on the difference between the Negro-Oceanian type and the Negro-African type.

An oral tradition (*lovan-tsofina*) is handed down from generation to generation among the Betsimisaraka of the north, in the noble caste of the Zafi-Rabay of Maroantsetra: they claim direct descent from the earliest Malay immigrants; the dhows of the latter, the famous outrigger canoes, driven far across the ocean by the monsoon, are said to have found refuge in the bay of Antogil, and they are said to have disembarked at Nosy Mangabé, where the tomb of the Anti Mangabé (the villagers of Mangabé) is still to be found. Systematic and scientific excavation on this islet might well bring some surprises to light, especially since this island, together with the island of Sainte-Marie a little further to the south, was also a lurking place for a good many pirates in the seventeenth and eighteenth centuries.

Other problems remain open to investigation: there is a need to throw light on the presence of a pre-Malagasy substratum, the origins of the Vazimba, the extent of contacts with black Africa and the influence of the close proximity of the Mascarene and the Comoro Islands. All these are subjects which should on no account be glossed over, and which may guide and inspire the future work of research workers.

Our conclusion is that of J. Poirier:

The basic components of this Malagasy racial and cultural complex combine to form a powerfully distinctive whole which a great many men of learning and research workers have been drawn to study. This distinctive character itself bears witness to the osmosis which has taken place among the various components. But how can one fail to see that the intrinsic qualities of the cultural patterns, at all levels of material and social existence, remain—as one would say in prehistory—within the Indonesian tradition? These are the styles and standards which cut across the Arab and African patterns: the dwelling on a hill protected by ditches, the four-sided hut and the symbolic layout of its interior, the existence of megalithic monuments, navigation by outrigger canoe, irrigated rice-growing and its highly complex esoterism which is only now beginning to yield up its secrets, food, the importance, where certain rites are concerned, of matrilineal succession, masked by the officially recognized pre-eminence of patrilineal succession, the vocabulary and syntax of the language, the types and themes of the literature, the system of values and its ethic of courtesy conceived as a strategy of interpersonal relations, the ontology and conceptualization of the individual, and, lastly, the essence of magic and religion—both as regards the various rituals and as regards this synarchic relationship between men and their ancestors (its central aspect lying in the conception of death), whose themes, rites and symbols are, with the exception of the 'cult' of the royal snake and the Sakalava *dady*, Indonesian in style.

From the data outlined in this report, one feature emerges with remarkable clarity throughout the ages: the Indian Ocean. Its waves have always borne men on their most daring adventures. The principal religions and philosophies of the world have chosen to send out their missionaries across it to make converts and preach their gospel: Hinduism, Buddhism, Islam and Christianity.

From the tiny boats of the Malays, the Indians and the Arabs, the outrigger canoes and the monoxylic canoes made from a mere hollowed-out tree trunk to the impressive European ships and even the mammoth tankers of our time, the Indian Ocean has borne them all alike on its bosom so as to enable Easterners and Westerners to meet, to get to know one another and thereby to reap mutual benefits.

In our view, this great sea route, the most used of all, warrants a front-ranking place in the world-wide research being undertaken by Unesco.

Bibliography

Basic works of reference

CALLET, R. P. *Tantaran'ny andriana eto imerina.* Tananarive, 1908. (Trans., Académie Malgache, 1953–58.)
DESCHAMPS, H. *Histoire de Madagascar.* Paris, 1960.

DESCHAMPS, H. *Les Migrations Intérieures à Madagascar*. Paris, 1959.
ELLIS, W. *History of Madagascar*. London, 1838 (2 Vol.).
GRANDIDIER, A. *Collection des Ouvrages Anciens Concernant Madagascar*. Paris, 1950 (9 Vol.).
GRANDIDIER, A.; GRANDIDIER, G. *Bibliographie de Madagascar (des Origines à 1955)*. Paris and Tananarive, 1905–1957 (4 Vol.).
——. *Ethnographie de Madagascar*, 1908–1928 (5 Vol.).
——. *Histoire Physique, Naturelle et Politique de Madagascar*. Paris, Impr. nationale, 1872, etc.
ILACOURT, E. de. Histoire de la Grande Ile de Madagascar. Paris, 1658. In: Grandidier (ed.), *Collection des Ouvrages Anciens Concernant Madagascar*, Vol. VIII, 1913.
ISNARD, H. *Madagascar*. Paris, A. Colin, 1955.
KENT, R. K. *Early Kingdoms in Madagascar, 1500–1700*. New York, 1970.
LEROI-GOURHAN, POIRIER, J. Madagascar. In: *Ethnologie de l'Union Française*, Vol. II, Paris, 1953.
MALZAC, R. P. *Histoire du Royaume Hoya*. Paris, 1912.
NUCÉ, M. S. de.; RATSIMANDRAVA, J. *Bibliographie Annuelle de Madagascar*. Tananarive, Bibliothèque Universitaire et Bibliothèque Nationale, 1964.
RALAIMIHOATRA, E. *Histoire de Madagascar*. Tananarive, 1965–66 (2 Vol.).
ROBEQUAIN, C. *Madagascar et les Bases Dispersées de l'Union Française*. Paris, 1958.
RUSSILLON, H. *Un Petit Continent*. Paris, 1933.
THOMPSON, V.; ADLOFF, R. *The Malagasy Republic, Madagascar Today*, Stanford, Calif., Stanford University Press, 1965.
VALLETTE, J. Bibliographie Méthodique des Etudes Relatives aux Sciences Humaines, *Bulletin de Madagascar*, Sept. 1963.

Origins of the Malagasy people

AUBER, *Histoire de l'Océan Indien*. 1955.
BAUMAN, WESTERMAN, *Les Peuples et les Civilisations de l'Afrique*. 1948.
BERNARD THIERRY, S. *Emprunts Sanscrits en Malgache* (unpublished dissertation).
BIASUTTI, et al. *Razze i Popoli della Terra, II Asia, III Africa*. Rome, 1955.
BIRKELI, E. Les Vazimba de la Côte-Ouest. *Mémoire de l'Académie Malgache*. 1936.
CHAMIA, M. C. Recherches Anthropologiques sur l'Origine des Malgaches. *Mémoires du Museum*. Paris, 1958.
COEDES, G. *Les Etats Hindouisés d'Indochine et d'Indonésie*. Hanoï, Impr. d'Extrême-Orient, 1944.
COPLAND, R. *East Africa and its Invaders*. Oxford, 1938.
DAHL, O. *Malgache et Maarijan*, Oslo, 1951.
DAMA-NTSOHA, *Histoire Politique et Religieuse des Malgaches*. Tananarive, Impr. de Madagascar, 1960.
DECARY, R. *Sainte Marie de Madagascar sous la Restauration*, 1937.
DESCHAMPS, H. J. *Les Pirates à Madagascar aux XVII et XVIIIe Siècles*, 2nd ed. rev. Paris, Berger-Levrault, 1972.
DEVIC, L. M. *Le Pays des Zendj d'après les Ecrivains Arabes*. Paris, 1883.
DUBOIS, R. P. Les Origines des Malgaches. *Anthropos*, 1926, p. 22; 1927, p. 80.
FAUBLEE, J. *Ethnographie de Madagascar*. Paris, 1946.
FERRAND, G. *Essai de Phonétique Comparée du Malais et des Dialectes Malgaches*. Paris, P. Geuthner, 1909.
——. L'Origine Africaine des Malgaches. *Journal Asiatique*, 1908, p. 353–500.
——. Les Voyages des Javanais à Madagascar. *Journal Asiatique*, 1910, p. 281–330.

GAUDEBOUT, P.; VERNIER, E. Note sur une Campagne de Fouilles à Vohémar: Mission Rasikazy, 1941. *Bulletin de l'Académie Malgache*, 1941, p. 100–14.
——. Les Rasikajy dans la Presqu'ile de Masoala. *Bulletin de l'Académie Malgache*, 1942–1943 p. 187–91.
GIOTTANELLI, V. *Pescatori dell'Oceano Indiano*. Rome, 1955.
GRAVIER, G. *La Cartographie de Madagascar*, 1896.
GUILLAIN, C. *Documents sur l'Histoire, la Géographie et le Commerce de l'Afrique Orientale*. Paris, A. Bertrand, 1856–57.
HEINE GELDERN, R. VON. Prehistoric Researches in the Netherlands Indies. In: *Science and Scientists in the Netherlands East Indies*. New York, 1945, p. 129–67.
HORNELL, J. Indonesian Influence on East Africa Culture, *Journal of Royal Anthropological Institute*, 1934, p. 305–32.
——. *Water Transports, Origins and Early Evolution*. Cambridge, 1946.
HOWE, S. *L'Europe et Madagascar*, 1936.
JULIEN, G. Pages Arabico-Madécasses. *L'Annale de l'Académie des Sciences Coloniales*, 1929, p. 1–125; II, 1933; Challamel, III, 1942. Grandidier bibliography.
KAMMERES. *La Découverte de Madagascar par les Portugais*. Lisbon, 1950.
MALZAC, R. P. Philologie Comparée du Malgache. *Bulletin de l'Académie Malgache*, 1910–11.
MILLOT, M. Les Ruines de Mahilaka. *Bulletin de l'Académie Malgache*, 1912, p. 283–88.
PANIKKAR, K. M. *Histoire de l'Inde*. Paris, A. Fayard, 1958.
PERRIER DE LA BATHIE, H. Les Plantes Introduites à Madagascar. *Revue de Botanique Appliquée et d'Agriculture Tropicale*, 1931–32.
RABEMANANJARA, J. *Nationalisme et Problèmes Malgaches*. Paris, Présence Africaine.
RAKOTO RATSIMAMANGA, A. Tache Pigmentaire Congénitale et Origine des Malgaches. *Revue Anthropologique*, Paris, 1940, p. 6–150.
RAZAFINTSALAMA, J. *La Langue Malgache et les Origines Malgaches*. Tananarive, 1928.
SACHS, C. *Les Instruments de Musique à Madagascar*. Paris, Institut d'Ethnologie, 1938.
SOUCHU DE RENNEFORT, U. *Histoire des Indes Orientales*, 1688.

Malagasy civilization

ANDRIAMANJATO, R. *Le Tsiny et le Tody dans la Pensée Malgache*. Paris, Présence Africaine 1957.
BLOCH, M. *Placing the Dead*. London, Seminar Press, 1970.
CHAPUIS. Quatre-vingts Années d'Influence Européenne en Imerina. *Bulletin de l'Académie Malgache*, Vol. VII.
CHEVALIER, L. *Madagascar, Populations et Ressources*, Paris, Presses Universitaires de France. 1952.
CONDOMINAS, G. *Fokonoloma et Collectivités Locales en Imerina*. Paris, 1960.
DECARY, R. *Les Ordalies et les Sacrifices Rituels chez les Anciens Malgaches*. Paris, 1959.
——. *La Mort et les Coutumes Funéraires à Madagascar*. Paris, 1962.
FAUBLEE, J. *Les Esprits de la Vie à Madagascar*. Paris, 1954.
LINTON, R. Culture Areas in Madagascar. *American Anthropologist* (Menesha, Wis.), 1928, Vol. XXX, No. 3, p. 363–90.
MOLET, L. *Le Bain Royal à Madagascar*. Tananarive, 1956; Paris, 1955.
MONDAIN, G. *Des Idées Religieuses des Hovas avant l'Introduction du Christianisme*. Cahors, 1904.
RUAD, J. *Taboo, a Study of Malagasy Customs and Belief*. Oslo and London, 1960.
VAN GENNEP, A. *Tabou et Totémisme à Madagascar*. Paris, 1904.

Tribes of Madagascar

COTTE, R. P. *Regardons Vivre une Tribu Malgache.* Tananarive, 1953.
DECARY, R. *L'Andry.* Tananarive, 1930–35, 2 Vol.
DESCHAMPS, H. *Les Antaisaka.* Paris, 1938.
DESCHAMPS, H.; VIANES, I. *Les Malgaches du Sud-Est.* Paris, 1959.
DUBOIS, R. P. *Monographie du Betsileo.* Paris, 1938.
ENGELVIN, R. P. *Les Vezo.* Paris, 1937.
FAUBLEE, J. *La Cohésion des Sociétés Bara.* Paris, 1954.
FRERE, I. *Panorama de l'Androy.* Paris, 1954.
LINTON, R. *The Tanala, a Hill Tribe of Madagascar,* 1933.
MATTEI, L. Les Tsimihety. *Bull. Académie Malgache,* No. XXI, 1938, p. 131–96.
MICHEL, L. Moeurs et Coutumes des Baras. *Mém. Acad. Malgache,* Vol. XL, 1957.
MOLET, L. *Le Bœuf dans l'Ankaizina.* Tananarive.

Malagasy law

FROTIER DE LA MESSELIÈRE. *Du Mariage en Droit Malgache.* Paris, 1932.
JULIEN, G. *Institutions Politiques et Sociales de Madagascar.* 2 Vol. Paris, E. Guilmoto, 1908–09.
POIRIER, J. *Études de Droit Africain et de Droit Malgache.* Paris, 1964.
THEBAUT, E. D. *Traité de Droit Civil Malgache. Les Lois et les Coutumes Hovas.* Paris, 1951, 2 parts.
——. *Le Code des 305 Articles.* Paris, 1960.

Periodicals

Bulletin de l'Académie Malgache.
Revue de Madagascar.
Bulletin de Madagascar.
Madagascar, Revue géographique.
Civilisation Malgache.

Annales de l'Université de Madagascar.
Terre Malgache—Tany Malagasy.
Cahiers du Centre d'Études des Coutumes.
Revue économique de Madagascar.
Tahola.

The settlement of Madagascar: two approaches

Charles Ravoajanahary

The peopling of Madagascar is one of those riddles that have aroused the curiosity of scholars, particularly historians, and the most contradictory theories have been put forward on the strength of more or less reliable evidence. In varying degrees, traces of all the Indian Ocean civizilations are to be found in Madagascar, but despite the widely differing theories it must be recognized that there is a certain common basis that bears witness to an undeniable cultural unity.

Let us try to summarize the various hypotheses:

Over the centuries, travellers who have visited Madagascar have had the impression that there were three different 'races' there: the first, very black, with short, fuzzy hair, seemed to be of Bantu African origin (Julien, 1909) or of Indo-Melanesian origin (Grandidier, 1908). The second, with swarthy complexion and long, straight hair, occupied the interior of the island, and was presumed to have come from the Malay world because of the resemblance of the physical features to those of the inhabitants of that region. Lastly, the third was thought to be simply made up of Arabs.

Set forth in this way, the problems of the peopling of Madagascar seem simple. In reality, this is not so, and no author has written of them in such a clear-cut caricatured fashion. 'This or that race' cannot be confined to this or that region. Internal migrations are not unusual in the course of history: many oral traditions explicitly refer to them.

In point of fact, the disagreement centres round what we have called the 'common cultural basis' rather than round the origin of the migrations, though in Part I, Vol. IV of his *Ethnographie de Madagascar,* Grandidier speaks of Jewish, and even Japanese and Chinese, migrations, a theory many authors are most reluctant to accept.

It is in an effort to explain this 'common basis' that some people maintain that there was a large Bantu migration prior to our era, and that this migration was followed by two Indonesian waves, one between the second and fourth centuries, and the other later, about the tenth century (Ferrand, 1908, 1910; Julien, 1909). Others however, like Grandidier, believe that the number of Bantu who came was extremely small, arguing that they were never a seafaring people; such scholars stress the successive waves of Malays who came from the Malay archipelago (Grandidier, 1908; Hornell, 1934). The fact is that Madagascar lies between the Indonesian and the Bantu worlds, and through those two worlds its culture has been subjected to very strong Indian and Arab influences, to mention only the most important ones. The resultant problem is so complex that in order to solve it we must draw not only on prehistory and history, but also on anthropology—social, political, cultural and physical—on geography, aided by all the resources of technology and ethnobotany, and lastly, perhaps most of all, on linguistics and the study of available written and oral traditions.

An attempt at an overall approach

This high degree of complexity stems from the fact that the islands and archipelagos of the Indian Ocean were directly influenced by the great centres of civilization through the religious and philosophical ideas of Hinduism, Buddhism and Islam. Subsequently, with the appearance of the Portuguese at the end of the fifteenth century, European influences became considerable, completely altering the previous political balances with the introduction of firearms.

In attempting to shed some light on the origin of the Malagasy, we must first of all turn to social, cultural, religious and political anthropology to untangle the different influences on Madagascar. The historical circumstances that brought a composite people to this island, its geographical position just at the juncture between the Indo-Pacific and the African areas, the respective domains of societies having 'elementary structures' (Oceania, Indonesia, South and East Asia) and societies having 'complex structures' (Africa, Europe), in the sense in which Claude Levi-Strauss uses these terms—all these account for a complexity that can be explained by the plurality of its Indonesian, Arab, Bantu and Indian heritages. A glance at Curt Sachs's book about Malagasy musical instruments will show that this is so (Sachs, 1938).

Material culture

In the field of material culture, with the exception of 'African enclaves' in the southern, western and northern regions, the basic pattern almost everywhere seems to be definitely Indonesian. But if we take a closer look at the two main activities, rice-growing and cattle-raising, we find the complexity mentioned above.

Even a cursory reading of works from the past shows that widely varying types of rice cultivation have been practised in Madagascar at different times: the shifting cultivation of cleared forest land, characteristic of the eastern coast and perhaps of certain parts of the uplands in ancient times; cultivation of rice by direct seeding in swamp lands, with no preparation of the soil other than trampling by oxen (this was practised in the low-lying parts of the eastern coast); and a more highly developed form of rice cultivation, in which oxen are used to trample the soil, but the soil is also dug, and while irrigation may not be practised there is a certain degree of control of flood waters. This form of rice cultivation was practised in certain parts of the western coast at an early stage.

Of these three types of rice cultivation, only the second one seems to have been unknown in East Africa, at comparable times (Raison, 1972). The first type also existed in Borneo and the Celebes Islands, and the third might equally well have been a normal technical development from the second. But a detailed examination of the techniques and vocabulary used in rice cultivation in Madagascar seems to indicate that it came from southern India. On the other hand, the importance of rice as a food varies considerably from one region to another, as does its production. In the seventeenth century, rice seems to have been rather uncommon on the eastern coast, where the diet is still largely made up of tubers, such as yams, taros, and sweet potatoes. From oral traditions we know that Andrianampoinimerina (late eighteenth and early nineteenth centuries) urged his subjects to cultivate tubers, despite the considerable development of rice cultivation.

There seems to be no doubt that zebu-raising is of Bantu origin. But here again there is a tendency to speak only of the zebu (*Bos indicus*), without going into all the Merina legends about the 'oxen of Rasoalao' and the 'barea' oxen of the Sakalava, which might be the humpless oxen (*Bos brachyceros*) of East Africa (though it should be noted that the word 'barea' is of Arabic origin).

Population movements

We still know nothing about the numerous migrations in every direction that led to the peopling of Madagascar and the other islands and archipelagos of the Indian Ocean. Nevertheless, two major periods may be discerned.

The earliest migrations probably came from Borneo and the Celebes at the beginning of the Christian era. They led to the introduction into the western part of the Indian Ocean—not only Madagascar and the Comoro Islands, but undoubtedly the eastern coast of Africa, corresponding to the ancient kingdom of Azania—of the cultivated plants of Indian and Indonesian origin, together with the technique of cultivating and using them

(Murdock, 1959). The real problem in connection with these migrations is that of the impact of Indonesia on Africa (Molet and Ottino, 1972).

The second, later wave seems to have been a series of successive migrations between the ninth and the fourteenth centuries. It was through these migrations that major innovations reached the island, such as the extraction and working of iron, the substitution of irrigated rice cultivation on many parts of the island for the shifting rice plantations on cleared land, the use of the spade, which was now possible, and also the introduction of political and religious models that, beginning in the fifteenth century, were to foster the formation of the earliest Malagasy states. first in the south-east and later simultaneously in the south, the west and the uplands. These innovations gradually spread throughout Madagascar and are said to have strengthened cultural unity. The truth of the matter is somewhat different. From the point of view of social anthropology alone, it is clear that in their family and matrimonial regulations, as in their system of inheritance and succession, the peoples of the central uplands exhibit a type of organization that is clearly 'Indonesian', based upon the unity of the married couple and on the autonomy of families and of villages, which are already included in a state system. On the other hand, a type of family relationship based upon the solidarity of brothers, which is definitely evocative of the Bantu world, is found among the peoples of the south and west (Ottino, 1972).

We must now turn to the problem of the Vazimba, who are reputed to be the first Malagasy. On the strength of arguments of a linguistic nature, some believe that the Vazimha came from Africa (Julien. 1909). But if that were the case, as Grandidier says, how is it that 'in four or five centuries a few thousand or rather a few hundred foreigners were able to impose their language on all the previous inhabitants of the country, especially considering that, since they were confined to a small district in mountains and shunned by all their neighbours until the end of the eighteenth century, they did not and could not have any authority or influence on the other tribes, with whom, for that matter, they have never had any relations to this day' (Ferrand, 1910).

Others, on the contrary, think that the Vazimba constitute the 'Indonesian' element, which was sufficiently powerful to preserve a certain culture, especially language, from the many later invasions. The change therefore must have come about as a result of a transformation in the ways of production, which in turn led to a shift in power relations (Boiteau, 1958). All the legends are in agreement about the fact that the Vazimba were not familiar with metal working, the cultivation of rice by irrigation or the domestication of cattle.

According to a third hypothesis, which is not to be discounted, the Vazimba, whether of Bantu or Indonesian origin, are the ancestors, who were not familiar with irrigation, metallurgy or cattle-raising, as opposed to those who adopted these new techniques later. That would explain their ambiguous status: they were feared and worshipped, and at the same time the term used to designate them was somewhat derogatory.

It is necessary to stress the importance of the Bantu origins of Madagascar since, unlike the 'Indonesian' heritage, they have been almost systematically minimized or even ignored. Kent, in a recent work, has tried to supply this deficiency, though a tendency to exaggerate mars his achievements. We now have quite sound evidence of the existence of 'seafaring Bantu' (*bantous marins*), to use P. Verin's expression. This can be seen from Birkeli's collection of Vezo traditions (Birkeli, 1926 and 1936) or even by studying the culture of the Antevolo, who are the Vezo of the north. The Department of Malagasy Language and Literature has gathered together a quantity of conclusive evidence on this subject. It bears witness, on the one hand, to the importance of the African contribution and, on the other, to the fact that, contrary to the assumptions of many authors (Hornell, 1934), the Bantu of Madagascar were not the serfs of the Indonesians, any more than they were slaves imported by Arab or Swahili slave traders, as was later the case with the Makoa down to the end of the nineteenth century. The hypothesis of organized migrations is not to be excluded. The key to this problem is to be found on the African littoral from Mozambique to the southern part of Somalia.

Religion and politics

Almost no mention is made of Arab influences, which have never been inventoried, let alone studied. So long as this is not done in a systematic way, studies of Madagascar and the western part of the Indian Ocean in general are likely to remain at a standstill. Another area—that of 'Indian' influences—which has been relatively overlooked or romanticized deserves particular study. The existence of such influences in the philosophy and systems of ideas and values underlying the social hierarchy seems undeniable, and also, as Boiteau pointed out, in the model of the Indian royal *linga,* distinguishing the cultured Brahman from the *Ksatriya,* the warrior, political leader or king. In the Antaimoro culture, the distinction goes as far as the division of the aristocratic class into two hierarchies, one of which has religious and magical functions and the other political functions as such (Rombaka, 1958; Kasanga, 1956).

Arab traits are very numerous in matters of magic, divination and services to the king. They were perhaps introduced by the Antalaotra, who, beginning in the thirteenth century, settled part of the Comoro Islands and a number of places west, north, and south-east of Madagascar. From the fourteenth century onwards, new ideas in the field of political power and the division of kingdoms into homogeneous territorial units were introduced by the Zafin-dRaminia dynasty (of Arab-Indian origin) and later by groups known today by the name of Temoro (Mahefamanana, 1965). So far as it is possible to judge, these groups were not homogeneous from the outset. They were partly made up of people who came directly from the Arabian peninsula, the 'Ontanpasemac', which literally means 'those from the sands of Mecca' (Flacourt, *Ouvrages anciens,* Vol. 8) and partly of another group. Kent suggests that the latter were of Ethiopian origin (Kent, 1970), though he does not furnish any convincing argument, whereas G. Ferrand supposes them to be of Sumatran origin, which is virtually certain. The Temur of Sumatra, also known as the Simalungun-Batak, which are a subdivision of this latter group (Batak), live to the east of Lake Tobar (Stohr and Zoetnulder, 1968), and their customs are closely related to those of the Temoro in Madagascar.

The solution of these problems is essential to an understanding of the history and societies not only of Madagascar but of all the western part of the Indian Ocean. In this region, the role of these Islamized (or pre-Islamized) groups from the Arabian peninsula, whether of Shirazi Arab or Sumatran origin, was decisive. By introducing new political and religious ideas, they originated the Swahili city-states on both sides of the Mozambique Channel and the first Malagasy dynasties, political structures which, from the fourteenth century onwards, replaced the previous clan organization. In a recent work, P. Ottino shows, on the one hand, that these common influences explain the amazing resemblances between the political and religious institutions of the various countries that experienced them and, on the other hand, that in Madagascar these resemblances have created the illusion of a profound homogeneity that has tended to conceal the reality of the twofold 'Indonesian' and 'African' origin (Ottino, 1972).

An attempt at a regional approach

This general presentation of the problem is somewhat disappointing, though it does enable us at least to grasp the overall complexity that we referred to above. A regional approach might give us more accurate answers to certain questions and at the same time reveal the gaps in our knowledge, thereby enabling us to identify themes for further research.

This involves treating the Indonesian and Bantu facets of Malagasy culture on a regional basis and perhaps pointing out other noteworthy influences.

Our knowledge is still limited and often vague, but if we consider, for example, the hierarchical systems, concepts linked to power, Malagasy and Swahili myths and their relations to ritual and other aspects of social life as well as their connection with Indonesian, Bantu or Arab myths, we may be able to shed more light on certain problems.

The central and south-eastern parts of the island

We shall now look at Indonesian Madagascar, an area strongly influenced by political and ritual models of Arab and Sumatran origin.

We know little of this region as yet, but it can be stated that the second Indonesian wave overran it and subsequently gave rise to the North Betsileo, Zafimaniry and Bezanozano, Vakinankaratra and Merina pseudo-ethnic groups, which are found in the central area between latitudes 17° and 21° south. Some isolated groups like the Zafimaniry or the Antaiva, living in the wooded cliff region, who have kept to an archaic way of life, are of exceptional interest in this regard. The old symbolism is preserved amongst them better than elsewhere. It seems an established fact that there is a similarity of historical relations and cultural background between the peoples of the uplands and those of the south-eastern coast, especially the Antaimoro coast between Mananjary and Farafangana, whence came the political and ritual ideas that were introduced into Imerina and fostered the extraordinary expansion of the Merina kingship and kingdom (Kasanga, 1956). The Department of Malagasy Language and Literature has collected enough oral traditions to throw new light on this question, but of course much remains to be done, and we still have to find out how Madagascar and Sumatra are connected through the Antaimoro (Ferrand, 1910; Kent, 1970).

In order to carry out this task it would be necessary:

To search as thoroughly as possible through what has been written on this region, not omitting the Sorabe—documents written in Arabico-Malagasy characters.

To bring together all that is known of Imerina and Betsileo, and to that end publish or republish certain works that have become difficult to find.

To try to establish historical evidence and bring to light similar cultural traits found in both the peoples of the uplands and those of the south-eastern coast. In this connection, Ludwig Munthe is at present making a very thorough study of the Sorabe.

To determine the connections between Madagascar and Sumatra through the Antaimoro. The main difficulty springs from the fact that while the customs and the social and political organization of the Temoro implicitly point to Temur groups of Sumatra ('Temur' being pronounced in the same way), certain Malagasy traditions explicitly mention Saudi Arabia (Mahefamanana, 1965).

Centre of Madagascar: Imerina

Mille's exhaustive studies of the historic sites of ancient Imerina have made it possible to see exactly where the Merina lived. On the basis of his archaeological work, P. Vérin has been able to establish that the Merina, Sihanaka, Vakinankaratra and North Betsileo peoples have cultural features in common. Certain comparisons can be made between the political, social, religious and family institutions of Imerina and those of the Antaimoro. The ancient Merina territorial organization and its socio-political sub-division into 'demes' is still observable today. It has been maintained by a strict rule of endogamy within the demes, which was instituted in the fifteenth or sixteenth century.

A similar organization, using the same terms to designate socio-territorial units, exists in the central parts of Timor among a people that came from Sumatra (Van Wouden, 1978; Grijzen, 1904).

Merina society is subdivided into three classes (slaves being excluded since they are not considered to be part of the people), each class being subdivided into subclasses, organized for the most part in endogamous demes. The sovereign, at the top of the hierarchical pyramid, sees to it that this system is adhered to. At various ritual ceremonies he receives from each class the *hasina,* a complex symbol of recognition and confirmation of the royal power, a power which comes to him from God and his ancestors, and partly also from the people. In this connection, we must note the importance of the dynastic feast of the 'royal bath', which has its exact counterpart among the Antaimoro (Kasanga, 1956) and throughout most of the Malay archipelago, particularly in the regions that have remained Hinduized (Bali). Similar festivals are found, for the same reasons, among the Thai and the Khmer peoples who have likewise been strongly influenced by Hinduism (Razafimino, 1924).

On the other hand, the highly elaborate customs of paying tribute and making offerings to the sovereign, which are sometimes considered to be of Swahili origin, are almost certainly Arabian, having been imported directly from the Arabian Peninsula or the Persian Gulf.

One of the fundamental aspects of the Indonesian facet of the central Madagascar cultures is that relating to death, to double funerals (in Hertz's sense) and eschatological beliefs. These ideas, which are quite confused and fragmentary in Madagascar (or at least they seem so), become quite clear when they are compared with their equivalents in Sumatra (Warneck, 1909), Borneo (Schärer, 1946; Stöhr, 1959) and the Celebes (Downs, 1956). There is still much work to be done on this central region in Madagascar. The large amount of material on Madagascar in France (Paris, Aix-en-Provence, etc.), Great Britain (at the headquarters of the London Missionary Society and elsewhere), Norway (Oslo and Stavanger) and the Netherlands on all matters relating to Indonesia must be inventoried and made available to scholars. This is only a provisional list. Next, the Malagasy and other texts must be published and translated with explanatory notes. Lastly, the origin of political, social, religious and family institutions of Imerina and Betsileo must be determined, and at the same time systematic comparisons must be made with corresponding Temoro institutions. A comparative study of Madagascar and Indonesia should be made on the basis of models of kinship and marriage, the rules of matrimonial residence and the ideology of procreation. It seems that certain Merina aristocratic demes, Andiantompokoindrindra, for example, observe very ancient customs that are reminiscent of those found in Indonesia.

The south and the western coast of the island

More historical, linguistic and anthropological research and studies on Madagascar as a whole need to be undertaken, but the situation as regards the south is particularly unsatisfactory. Although scholars have taken a greater interest in the western coast of the island in the last decade, their achievements mainly show how much is still to be done.

First of all, Portuguese accounts of the whole of this region should be re-examined, using the original texts. Nothing less than an exegesis is required in order to determine exactly what the authors meant by certain key words such as *muro, negro, bugue* (from the Swahili *buke*, 'Malagasy') or *cafre*. For example, the term *cafre* as opposed to *muro* is translated as 'Negro' or 'African', whereas it undoubtedly means 'pagan', i. e. non-Muslim in the Arabic sense of 'kafir'.

In studying the similarities between certain institutions such as solemn alliance pacts (*fatidra*) and possession ceremonies, as found in eastern Africa and the western coast of Madagascar, Kent brought to light the cultural affinity between these two regions (Kent, 1972).

Symbolism and its philosophical bases, royal power characterized by a blend of the sacred and the political, the role of the king's advisers and their influence during interregnums, all these are more reminiscent of Bantu Africa than of Indonesia. The power founded on control over the coasts and trade with foreigners, particularly the trading of slaves for arms, is very different from that of the kings in the centre of the island, who were irrigators, and whose behaviour followed Sumatran and Javanese models. The distinction is too clear cut to be explained simply by a difference in the economic conditions of the two regions.

Other major lines of research on the island as a whole

Linguistic studies may provide important material concerning the island as a whole, but if such studies are to be useful they must be as exhaustive as possible. The constituent components, including the lexicology, of every language spoken in Madagascar must be dealt with first. Then a comparison of the various languages must be made, in order to reveal or at least get some idea of the contacts there may have been between the various linguistic groups in the course of history. Lastly, an attempt should be made to establish whether there is a scientific connection with the languages of the various countries of the Indian Ocean thought to have contributed to the peopling of Madagascar. As regards the first two phases, the Department of Malagasy Language and Literature has already started its research work, but it is far from finished. A thorough study has been made by Simeon Rajaona on the syntactic structure of contemporary classical Malagasy, a study that is the fruit of long research and lays the scientific foundation for further studies (Rajaona, 1970). The eminent scholar, Otto C. Dahl, has made a definitive contribution with respect to the third phase (Dahl, 1951 and 1973).

The study of all forms of traditional literature should help to solve many problems. The systematic collection of everything of this kind that is available should make it possible to reconstitute the mythical, mythological, philosophical and religious world of the ancient Malagasy and to compare it with that of the peoples who had been in contact with Madagascar while it was being peopled. Such a study, which has also been undertaken by the Department of Malagasy Language and Literature, should be continued methodically until completed.

Lastly, the exhaustive collection of the oral traditions concerning local history at the level of each socio-cultural group throughout the territory should at least make it possible to decide what direction research work should take and to prove or perhaps disprove working hypotheses, even though it may not lead to the establishment of indisputable historical facts concerning the peopling of Madagascar. In any event, it is important for the sake of other disciplines to know how these socio-cultural groups view their past and how it affects their lives today.

Finally, we must stress the interdependence of the various lines of research and the absolute need for interdisciplinary studies. By this we mean not only that the results of research should be collated, but also—indeed, this is of prime importance—that specialists of various disciplines studying the same materials or the same subjects should work as a team. If we have given the impression that we regard anthropology as being of special importance, it is because its research themes are a fresh contribution to solving the problems of the peopling of Madagascar and because it has achieved striking results so far. These results, however, cannot be considered definitive until they have been corroborated by the findings of other disciplines. Even similar cultural facts may stem from substantially different or even fundamentally different concepts. Such facts therefore indicate lines of research rather than establish immutable bases for reflection, and our paper should be considered as an argument in favour of this approach.

Bibliography

ANDRIANI, N.; KRUYT, A. C. *De Barée-sprekende Toradja's van Nidden-Celebes*. Batauá, 1950–51 (3 Vol., 2nd ed.) (Summary by Downs.)
BIRKELI, E. *Marque de Boeufs et Tradition de Race*. Oslo, 1926.
———. Les Vazimba de la Côte Ouest. *Mémoire de l'Académie Malgache*, 1936.
BOITEAU, P. *Madagascar, Contribution à l'Histoire de la Nation Malgache*. Paris, Éditions Sociales, 1958.
CALLET, R. P. *Tantaran'ny Andriana eto Madagascar*. Tananarive, 1878. French trans. by G. S. Chapus and E. Ratsimba: *Histoire des Rois*, Tananarive, 1958 (4 Vol.).
COEDES, G. *Les États Hindouisés d'Indochine et d'Indonésie*. Paris, 1948.
DAHL, O. *Malgache et Maanjan. Une Comparaison Linguistique*. Oslo, 1951.
———. *Proto-Austronesian*. Student Litteratur. Lund, 1973.
DELIVRE, A. *Interprétation d'une Tradition Orale à l'Histoire des Rois de l'Imerina*. Paris, 1967. (Unpublished thesis.)
DESCHAMPS, H. *Histoire de Madagascar*. Paris, 1960.
DEZ, J. Quelques Hypothèses Formulées par Linguistique Comparée à l'Usage de l'Archéologie. In: *Annales de l'Université de Madagascar*, Taloha, Vol. I, Archéologie.
DOWNS, R. E. *The Religion of the Barée-speaking Toradja of Central Celebes*. The Hague,1956.
FERRAND, G. *Les Musulmans à Madagascar* (3 Vols.). Paris, 1891–93.
———. L'Origine Africaine des Malgaches. *Journal Asiatique* (Paris), 1908, p. 353–500.
———. Les Voyages de Javanais à Madagascar. *Journal Asiatique*, 1910, p. 281–330.
FREEMAN-GRENVILLE, G. S. P. (ed.). *The East African Coast*. Oxford, 1962.
GEVREY. *Essais sur les Comores*. Pondichery, 1870.
GRANDIDIER, A.; GRANDIDIER, G. *Ethnographie de Madagascar*. Paris, 1908–28 (4 Vol.).
GRANDIDIER, A.; CHARLES-ROUX; DELHORBE, C.; FROIDEVAUX, H.; GRANDIDIER, G. *Collection des Ouvrages Anciens concernant Madagascar*, 9 Vol. Paris, 1903, etc. (Especially Volumes 1, 2, 7, 8 and 9.)
GRIJZEN, H. J. Mededeelingen omtrent Beloe of Hidden-Timor. In: *Verhandelingen van het Bataviaasch Genootschap van Kunsten en Wetenschappen*, 1904.
GROTTANELLI, V. L. *Pescatori dell'Oceano Indiano*. Rome, 1955.
GUILAIN, M. *Documents sur l'Histoire, la Géographie et le Commerce de la Partie Occidentale de Madagascar*. Paris, 1845.
GUTHRIE, M. *The Classification of the Bantu Languages*. London, 1948.
HARRIES, L. *Swahili Prose Text*. London, Nairobi, 1965.
HERTZ, R. *Sociologie Religieuse et Folklore* (2nd ed.). Paris, 1970.
HORNELL, J. Indonesian Influence on East African Culture, JRAI, Vol. LXIV, 1934, p. 305–32.
JULIEN, G. *Institutions Politiques et Sociales de Madagascar* (2 Vol.). Paris, E. Guilmoto, 1909.
KASANGA, F. *Tantaran'ny Antemoro-Anakara teto Imerina tamin'ny andron'Andrianampoinimerina sy Ilaidama*. Tananarive, 1956.

KENT, R. K. *Early Kingdom in Madagascar 1500–1700*. London and New York, 1970.
LEITÂO, H. *Os Dois Descobrimentos da Ilha de São Lourenço Mandados Fazer Pelo Vice-Rei D. Jeronimo de Azevedo nos Anos de 1613 à 1616*. Lisbon, 1970.
LOMBARD, D. *Trend Report on the Project for the Study of Malay Culture*. 1972.
MAHEFAMANANA, MOSA. *Ali-Tawarath sy Madagasikara*. Tananarive 1965.
MARIANO, L. R. P. In: *Ouvrages Anciens* and Leitâo.
MOLET, L.; OTTINO, P. Madagascar entre l'Afrique et l'Indonésie. *L'Homme, Revue Française d'Anthropologie*, Vol. XII, 1972, Cahier 2 p. 126–35.
MONTEIL, V. (ed.). *Voyages d'Ibn Battuta*. (Bilingual: Arabic-French, 4 Vol.), Paris, Editions Anthropos, 1968.
MURDOCK, G. P. *Africa, its Peoples and Their Culture History*. New York, McGraw-Hill, 1959.
OTTINO, P. Compte-rendu de l'"Ouvrage de Lavondès: Bekoropoka'. In: *Archipel, Études Interdisciplinaires sur le Monde Insulindien*. Paris, 1971, p. 244–53.
——. Quelques Brèves Remarques sur les Études de Parenté et d'Organisation Sociale à Madagascar. In: *Asie du Sud-Est et Monde Insulindien*. Bulletin du CeDRASEMI, Paris, 1972, Vol. III, No. 2, p. 10–133.
——. La Hiérarchie Sociale et l'Alliance dans le Royaume de Matacassi des XVIe et XVIIe Siècles. 1973. (Unpublished.)
——. A Propos de Deux Mythes Malgaches du Début du XVIIe Siècle. *Taloha*. Tananarive, 1973.
OTTINO, P. *et al*. L'Océan Indien comme Domaine de Recherche. 1973.
POLOME, ED, C. *Swahili Language Handbook*. Washibgton, D.C., 1967.
PRINS, A. H. J. *The Swahili-speaking Peoples of Zanzibar and the East African Coast* (Aradb, Shirazi and Swahili). London, International African Institute, 1961.
RAMILISON, E. *Ny Loharanon'ny Andriana Nanjaka teto Imerina*. Tananarive, 1951.
RAINITOVO. *Tantaran'ny Malagasy Manontolo* (3 Vol.). Tananarive, 1932.
RAISON, J. P. Utilisation du Sol et Organisation de l'Espace en Imerina Ancienne. In: *Mélanges de Géographie Tropicale Offerts à P. Gourou*. 1972.
RAJAONA, S. *Structure du Malgache*. Tananarive, 1970.
RAZAFIMINO, C. *La Signification Religieuse du Fandroana ou de la Fête du Nouvel An en Imerina*. Madagascar, 1924.
ROMBAKA, J. P. *Tantaran-dRazana Anteimoro-Anteony*. Tananarive, 1958.
——. *Fomban-dRazana Antemoro*. Fianarantsoa, 1970.
SACHS, C. *Les Instruments de Musique à Madagascar*. Paris, 1938 (Travaux et mémoires de l'Institut d'Ethnologie, No. 28).
SCHÄRER. *Die Gottesidee der Ngadju-Dajak in Sud Borneo*. Leiden, 1946.
STÖHR, W. *Das Totenritual der Dajak Ethnologica*, New series, Vol. I, Köln, 1959.
STÖHR, W.; ZOEMULDER, P. *Les Religions d'Indonésie* (trans. from German: *Die Religionen Indonesiens*). Paris, 1968.
TEMPELS, R. P. *La Philosophie Bantoue* (trans. from Dutch). Paris, 1948.
TRIMINGHAM, J. S. *Islam in East Africa*. Oxford University Press, 1964.

Cultural influences and the contribution of Africa to the settlement of Madagascar

Pierre Vérin

In the present state of our knowledge the question of Malagasy origins can be summed up as follows: they are of mixed Indonesian and African ancestry and the predominantly Indonesian nature of the language in no way entitles us to deny the part played by Africa in settling the island. The vast neighbouring continent makes its presence felt in the form of the biological elements, major linguistic borrowings and numerous features in the cultures and in the traditional social and political systems.[1]

Without wishing to present an exhaustive review of our predecessors' speculations, we need to recall briefly the theories bearing on the African contribution to the peopling of Madagascar, before going on to an objective assessment of the sources, and exhibiting the research prospects.

Review of the principal theories

The theorists, in fact, hesitate between two extremes, either to accord excessive importance to the South-East Asian contribution (neglecting Africa) or the reverse, with, it is true, a few aberrant views, like those of Briant when arguing for an important Hebraic element in the origins of the race, or Razafintsalama, who believed, on the basis of several thousands of doubtful etymologies, that the Great Isle had been colonized by Buddhist monks.

Alfred Grandidier had assigned a prominent role to Asia, holding that all the ancestors of the Malagasy, apart from recent Makao arrivals, came from South-East Asia, including the blacks termed, for the purpose of his argument, Melanesians. Gabriel Ferrand took up this challenge to geography and, to a certain extent, to common sense, stressing the more African aspects of Malagasy origins. Ferrand argued for the following phases:
A possible pre-Bantu phase.
A Bantu period prior to our era.

---

1. We should note that this hybrid situation does not occur in the Comoro Islands nor on the East African coast, where Indonesian penetration has also been suspected.

A pre-Merina Indonesian stratum, from the second to the fourth centuries, originating in Sumatra, during which the new arrivals subjugated the Bantu.
Arrivals of Arabs, from the seventh to the ninth centuries.
A fresh emigration of Sumatrans in the tenth century (whose descendants are the Indonesians of the highlands).
Lastly, Persians and, towards 1500, Swahili, including the Zafikasinambo of the south-east.
Not everything should be rejected in this hypothetical construction of Ferrand's. Its linguistic arguments, in particular, do demonstrate a duality in the Malagasy language corpus of African origin corresponding to the contributions of the first settlers on the one hand, and recent influences from the fifteenth century onwards on the other.

Gustave Julien also conceded an important place to Africa in the peopling process, whereas Malzac believed that the Merina from the highlands (whom he termed the Hova) had taught their language to all the Bantu in Madagascar. It certainly cannot be denied that the Bantu of the Great Isle speak an Indonesian language, but it would be going too far to assert that they learned it exclusively through contact with the people inhabiting the highlands.

After these studies dating from the end of the nineteenth and beginning of the twentieth centuries, the question was reopened in three works that for a long time were virtually unnoticed: first, Birkeli's research on certain isolated ethnic groups in the west, the Behosy in particular, among whom the author demonstrates interesting survivals of African languages and culture; next, Mellis's gleanings, which, in a curious document entitled *Volamena et Volafotsy*—a mingling of wheat and tares—present material concerning the societies in the north-west, from which we see that these societies owe much to East African social organization. Lastly, in an article published in a Norwegian journal, Otto Dahl demonstrates the existence of a Bantu substratum common to the phonological system of all the Malagasy dialects.

In 1960, Hubert Deschamps sought, in his *Histoire de Madagascar*, to exhibit the Afro-Asian symbiosis in the settlement of the island. He established a list of what he considered to be Asian and African contributions and set out a historical schema to explain these in terms that deserve quoting word for word: 'Coming from India, the proto-Malagasy, Indonesian in origin, made a stay on the coast of Africa, where they mixed with or married with Africans and then went on with them to Madagascar.' Kent also argues for a large-scale Indonesian impact in Africa followed by colonization of Madagascar.

Since 1964 thorough archaeological research undertaken by the Institute of Art and Archaeology, University of Madagascar, has begun to provide new facts for the record. In my work *Les Echelles Anciennes du Commerce sur la Côte Nord de Madagascar,* I give the tentative findings of the investigations to date:

The populations of African origin in Madagascar are Bantu. It is likely that they began to arrive in the island from at least the beginning of the ninth century, like the Indonesians, but the migrations from Africa probably did not continue beyond the start of the historical period (sixteenth century). It is arguable that a large proportion of the Africans arrived at the same time and in the same way as the Islamized peoples or the non-Islamized Swahili.

In support of this point of view a series of arguments can be put forward drawing on each of the main sources of documentation. It will be seen that archaeology, physical anthropology and, more especially, linguistics have made a degree of progress that help us to work out the details of the migratory outline set out above. Today the debate is not, as in the time of previous authors, about whether the ancestors of the Malagasy were Indonesian African; they were both, with a marked predominance of Indonesian elements on the plateaux and a very pronounced Bantu substratum on the coasts. The question is to decide how these migratory flows were blended and juxtaposed and under what conditions; above all a meticulous chronology of these events must be sought.

Main African cultural contribution as revealed by present sources of documentation

Language influence

We have seen above that the Malagasy language's membership in the Indonesian family (Hesperonesian subgroup) cannot in any case cause us to lose sight of the reality of the Bantu contribution. It is true that as regards the corpus of the basic vocabulary, the proportion of Indonesian words is overwhelming (93 per cent). The lexical corpus is present in the same way as in the Creole of the West Indies, where there is an essentially French-derived vocabulary (95 per cent) and African elements. The Bantu contribution is on two planes in Malagasy: primarily at the level of vocabulary, but also at that of word structure. Attention has several times been drawn to the words of the Bantu vocabulary in Malagasy, by L. Dahle as far back as 1876, and later by G. Ferrand, G. Julien, O. Dahl and J. Dez. Ferrand has demonstrated that the Bantu words in Malagasy are divided into two categories: those of ancient roots, which are found everywhere, and recent borrowings from Swahili that occur more especially in the north-west. The existence of these Bantu words in all the dialects confirms that the Africans cannot be regarded as latecomers in the peopling process. Their participation must extend back to the very start of the Malagasy civilization. Confirmation of this discovery by Ferrand has been provided by research in glottochronology (lexicostatistics) conducted in 1968 by Vérin, Kottak and Gorlin.

In fact, an examination of the Bantu (basic) vocabulary in Malagasy dialects when processing the glottochronological lists shows us that this contribution is shared by Malagasy dialects to the same extent. It might have been expected that the proportion would be less in regions where people of Indonesian descent are numerous. But this is not the case at all. A fact of this kind amply confirms that one or several Bantu languages[1] were spoken at the very outset of the African-Indonesian symbiosis.

Exploration of the Bantu vocabulary using *Wörter und Sachen* techniques reveals here again a dichotomy in the Malagasy lexical corpus. In every dialect there are words deriving from the archaic period of symbiosis. For example, *omby* (ox), *ondry* (sheep), *akanga* (guinea-fowl), *akoho* (hen), and so on, show as we might expect, that the Bantu contribution to the introduction of animal husbandry in Madagascar is important. There are, furthermore, more recent borrowed Bantu words that occur only in the north-west: *mahogo,* the first, for example (*mangahazo* in the central region and *balahazo* in the south), and nautical terms.

The toponomy also follows this rule. There are few place-names of Bantu origin in Malagasy, or rather they are hardly recognizable or indeed rare (Kaday, Kasijy, Mazy). On the north-west coast, however, there is a series of toponyms introduced more recently by the Swahili traders: Kivinja (encampments), Kandrany (point-like: *Kanda*), Ankomany (where there is seaweed), Langany, Karakajoro (like a raised finger), Sangajira (sandy path), Kongony (where there are bugs), Kisimany (where there is a well), Bandany (where there are houses), Djangoa (unfrequented place flooded by a stream), and so on.

But study of vocabulary is not our only source of information of a linguistic kind in this search for origins. O. Dahl demonstrates very clearly that in Malagasy 'the changing of the (Indonesian) consonant endings into vowel endings has been caused by a Bantu substratum. And, in this case, this change took place shortly after the establishment of the Indonesians among the Bantu during the period when the latter were adapting themselves to the new language'.

---

1. Swahili is the most likely. But towards the tenth century it was in its formative period and there are considerable disparities between the Somali and Mozambique forms.

Lastly, the Indonesian element recovers its predominant position at the grammatical level, but no study has attempted to establish what elements might have been inherited from Africa.

Knowledge of African-Malagasy relations through Arabic and Arabic-Malagasy manuscripts

Certain Norwegian, British, French and Italian libraries plus the book stocks of the Académie Malgache and the University of Madagascar hold manuscripts written in the south-east. These documents contain genealogical information as well as family traditions and recipes for medicines. Some have been translated and published by scholars of non-Malagasy (Ferrand, Gautier, Julien) or Malagasy origin (Rombaka, Kasanga) but the majority remain unexploited, doubtless because of the desire, a premature one, to make a synthesis of the information they contain and the fact that the specialists in the field are working separately, in ignorance of each other's efforts.

It can already be asserted that the Arabic-Malagasy alphabet was to all appearances, an independent invention inspired by 'stimulus diffusion'. The Malagasy vocabulary of Arabic origin deals with divination and astronomical terms, while Swahili has passed on a large number of nautical terms.

As regards manuscripts of a more general nature, Ferrand has provided research workers with many Arabic, Persian and even Turkish texts in his anthology (now unobtainable) of geographical texts. This collection of documents is supplemented by translations by Sauvaget (of Bozorg Ibn Chariyar), Chunnovsky and Grosset-Grange.

Through Bozorg Ibn Chariyar we learn that during the tenth century the Indonesians who could use Madagascar as an advanced base raided the Island of Pemba. As from the eleventh century, the Swahili emergence experienced by the Zenj coast also embraced Madagascar, designated by the ambiguous term 'Waqwaq', and later 'Komr'.

The moment we study the manuscripts of the first geographers of Islam we run into difficulties as regards both the form and the substance. The problems in interpreting these documents have been well brought out by Neville Chittick, who notes:

They can habitually be interpreted in more than one sense, and mistakes are easy to make in Arabic manuscripts, above all by the omission or shifting of a *nukta* (dot). Interpretation is further complicated by the fact that almost all geographers believed, with Ptolemy, that the southern part of Africa bulged out towards the east, to join up with parts of the Far East. Waqwaq, for example, is sometimes situated in Africa, sometimes in Asia. There is also confusion with regard to the islands of Indonesia and those off the south-east African coast.

Ferrand was the first to appreciate the difficulties created by these Arabic homographs. He points out, more particularly, that the consonants K-M-R can indicate Khmer in Cambodia, but also Komr or Komor, the island of Madagascar and neighbouring isles, and, in addition Kamar, the mountain of the moon in East Africa from which the Nile was supposed to spring.

It is only for the fourteenth and fifteenth centuries, i.e. during the period immediately before the arrival of Europeans, that documents written in Arabic become more precise, above all the writings of Ibn Majid and Suleyman el Mahri, for whom the land of Komr included both Madagascar and what is today termed the Comoro Archipelago. These authors give us reason to assume that the relations between Madagascar and Africa were on a considerable scale, since they give the latitudes of certain Malagasy ports and of the African or even Asian towns that lie opposite them. We shall see below that archaeology offers confirmation of the Islamized peoples' maritime knowledge, for it was at about this time that Swahili from Africa founded the great Malagasy towns of Langany and Kingany.

Oral traditions and additional facts from the historical writings of foreigners

These two sources are not to be despised, but contribute in more limited fashion to our knowledge of African Malagasy relations. This is because, first of all, the European intrusions represent a late episode in the history of the settlement of Madagascar, which at the times they occurred was already completed in its main lines, and, secondly, because group memories of traditions diminish very rapidly and cannot go back further than three centuries.

Subject to these reservations, it may be noted that certain Malagasy populations of predominantly African physique deem themselves of overseas stock, and adduce certain customs in support. Not only the Vezo and the Kajemby from the west and the north-west but also the Antandrano from the Sambirano locate their cemeteries in the sand dunes of the narrow beaches, regard themselves as *tompo-jia* (masters of the sands) and control for their exclusive profit the gathering of marine produce and turtles. Even populations in the interior consider themselves as 'offshoots' of these coastal groups, as for example the Sandangoatsy, descended from the Kajemby, who now live in the interior, near Lake Kinkony. This has not always been the case, as Portuguese maps and records at the beginning of the seventeenth century mention *Sarangaço* or *Sangaço* (a distortion of Sandangoatsy) on the shores of the Marambitsy bay. Over the last three and a half centuries the Sandangoatsy have turned their backs on their coastal origin. The same thing happened no doubt with the Vazimba.

This latter name seems to have designated a collection of very diverse populations, who may however have formed part of the first migrations of Africans. Guillain mentions them in the Baly hinterland, where they still exist. In this region they were conquered by Andriamandisoarivo at the end of the seventeenth century. They were numerous at the mouth of the Tsiribihina, and Drury lived among them at the beginning of the eighteenth century. They still exist in the Betsirivy area and the region of Malaimbandy. According to Hebert, who collected their traditions, 'The Vezo are probably themselves Vazimba who have remained on the sea-coast'. This is basically the same process as operated with the Kajemby and the Sandangoatsy. A cultural argument for the ancestors of the Vezo-Sara and of a certain number of Vazimba groups being of the most ancient Bantu stock can be drawn from the absence of circumcision. This East African Bantu custom was introduced by the Islamized peoples and became normal practice. Those who did not adopt it are perhaps Africans who left the east coast before the Islamic influence developed.

The establishment of the colonists of sea-Bantu stock in the west was accompanied by a progressive adoption of the Indonesian language as a lingua franca. The accounts of Mariano and Paulo da Costa show us that a veritable linguistic checkerboard still existed on the west coast at the beginning of the seventeenth century.

The traditions collected in Imerina by Callet, Ramilson and Rainandriamampandry, in particular, mention the existence in the highlands of Vazimba who were progressively displaced or absorbed by the historical highland dynasties. There is still argument as to whether these Vazimba were of African or Indonesian origin. Heine-Geldern, who knows Indonesia well, but not Madagascar, took them to be emigrant populations from South-East Asia. Ferrand, equating their name with the East African term 'Zimba' (population) saw in them an African stratum in the settlement: he was also inclined to favour the etymology of 'Zimu', 'spirit', to which Ralaimihoatra has reverted in a recent contribution. We owe an ingenious theory to Hebert. He suggests that the Vazimba are quite simply the peoples of the interior with whom the last arrivals (the Merina) and also the Sakalava established alliance on a joking level (*ziva*) implying privileges of which the gratuitous insult is not the least curious (even today 'to insult' is rendered by *manazimba*). Thus, Hebert was the first to link the concept of Vazimba not with one race but, rather, with a group of populations occupying the central and western parts of Madagascar. It is difficult to doubt the largely African origin of these populations when we look at the Vazimba of today, but, as in the case of other groups, they must have had close contacts with the Indonesians.

The account of the pirate Cornelius (early eighteenth century), which deals with the alliance of the Europeans and the Sakalava against the Vazimba, spells the name of these original masters of the land as 'Vanjimbo'. But according to Prins the term 'Vanjimbo' was formerly used currently on the Kenyan coast by the Swahili to denote persons of low economic status. In Madagascar therefore it could well be a term imported from Africa, doubtless by the Islamized groups, to designate the people living in primitive conditions in the back country.[1] The tracing of the word 'Vazimba' to an African term in no way destroys Hebert's ingenious explanation. There is perhaps a paronymic attraction[2] of a word not fully understood towards the meaning 'bound by a joking kinship relationship' that has persisted up to the present time.

When we explore the corpus of oral traditions of the peoples of west, north and north-east Madagascar, we find that the coastal Swahili (called the Antalaotse) and their non-Muslim neighbours in the interior share the same myth about a territory that was probably the first home of their ancestors. This territory was an island called Mojomby vaguely located between the African coast and the Comoro Islands. According to the myth, the people lived by trading and the Muslim religion was known then. When impiety and dissension became rife in the island, Allah resolved to punish them. The island was engulfed by a raging sea, with a few of the righteous escaping retribution. Some say that they were miraculously spared, others claim that God sent a whale to carry them away. The Kajemby and the Antalaotse are descended from the ranks of the righteous, but over and above this moralizing history lesson there remains an invaluable indication of the vehicular role of the Swahili in emigrations to Madagascar.

Kent and more recently Ottino rightly stress the African contribution in the establishment of Malagasy social systems. In the view of these authors the end of the seventeenth century saw a new formula, termed the 'Antaimoro system', characterized by a royal succession by pureness of descent (the Volamena from the west) and the combination, in the conduct of state affairs, of magic based on writing and the royal relics (*sampy, dady*). This new socio-political datum was to secure the lightning expansion of the Maroseranana in the west in the eighteenth century and strengthen the development of the Merina State at the end of the eighteenth century. Antaimoro diviners aided kings Andrianampoinimerina and Radama I, but

1. The same applies in the case of the word 'Masikoro', which in the south-west denotes the Sakalava if the Fiherenana interior and comes from a work still used in the United Republic of Tanzania meaning peasants from the interior.
2. Another example of paronymic attraction has been pointed out by Ferrand. For him, 'amboalambo' (pig-dog), which the Sakalava derisively termed the Merina in former times, originated from a Bantu word 'Ba-lambu', i.e. 'yellow men' (a word that does not appear in the Sacleux dictionary).

this influence might have been much earlier (importation of the *sampy* from the Matitanana by Ikalobe).

This common denominator of the Malagasy socio-political systems inherited from East Africa towards the seventeenth century has concealed from most ethnologists the diversity of the social organizations of Madagascar. The highlands possess a social structure closely resembling that of Indonesia (the *foko*, the social unit Bloch calls the deme, is found in Timor under the name of *fukun*), while the coast is reminiscent in many particulars of what is found in neighbouring Bantu Africa.

It would be unfair to assert that the oral traditions and historical notes show us unidirectional relations only, from Africa to Madagascar. Gulwich has reported a story of a group of Africans established at the mouth of the Rufiji river whose ancestors would appear to have left Madagascar because of an acute famine. We also know that between 1785 and 1822 fleets of Sakalava and Betsimisaraka canoes periodically ravaged the Comoro archipelago and the East African littoral between Bajone and Zanzibar. Further traces of these two-way contacts are found in the discoveries of archaeology (see below).

Ethnographic data

These data are the best known, as the old authors—and Grandidier in particular—were much given to comparing the cultural features of Malagasy societies with those of the inhabitants of areas with which the Great Isle might have had relations or contacts. In our view these comparisons are of value essentially in the domain of material culture, and of the techniques of navigation, ethnobotany and ethnozoology. Even here, often all that they do is to confirm what we suspect, from using the *Wörter und Sachen* linguistic method.

Among the parallels with East Africa, Deschamps lists the following: 'growing of millet; importance of cattle as a token of wealth, notching of the ears of cattle; cotton spinning; long robes; pottery; serrated sickles; silos; spear; round shield; sculpture on wood (long-billed birds, breast motif on doors), disk on forehead; circumcision; filing down of teeth'. However, the author of the *Histoire de Madagascar* observes, realistically, that apart from Sachs's[1] investigation of musical instruments, these comparisons have not yet been the subject of systematic and meticulous study.

It is, of course, not without interest to note, for example, that the

---

1. Sachs distinguishes instruments of African, Asian and Arab origin with great precision but his work should be reconsidered in the light of Jones's discoveries—in his view, the musical systems of South-East Asia have extensively influenced those of Africa.

Malagasy have adopted both the outrigger canoe of Indonesian origin and the Swahili dhow, or, again, that certain plants imported long ago into Madagascar sometimes have an Indonesian and sometimes an African name, or occasionally the two together.[1] Borrowing plays its full part in this domain. We know that East Africa also has the outrigger canoe and the dhow. It is advisable always however not to generalize. In the sphere of ethnobotany Haudricourt notes, for example, that the existence of a name of Indonesian or African origin is not a definite indication that the plant has come from one or the other region, as emigrants may have recognized among the local flora plants similar to those in their mother country and given them the same name.

While not devoid of interest, ethnographic comparisons are risky when they fix on this or that single trait. On the other hand, physical anthropology adopts a more general stance for elucidating the problems with which we are concerned.

The African contribution, as physical anthropology sees it

The initial studies have confirmed that the Malagasy come from both Mongoloid and Negroid stock. Rakoto Ratsimamanga played a pioneering role in this regard, and in his study of the distribution of the pigmental spot (more frequent among the inhabitants of the highlands) he distinguishes four morphological types, distributed as follows in the population: Indonesian-Mongoloid type, 37 per cent; Oceanian-Negro type, 52; African-Negro type, 2; Europoid type, 9.

We have mentioned Grandidier's explanation of the Oceanian origin of a large part of the Negroid element. Later, on the basis of craniological studies, M. C. Chamla suggested that three types be distinguished: (a) light brown type, Asian, closely related to the Indonesians; (b) black type with African rather than Melanesian characteristics; and (c) mixed type, which seems the most frequent.

Haematologic studies are naturally the most likely to throw fresh light on the question. As was clearly seen by Pigache, whose researches represent a considerable advance in our knowledge of Malagasy population groups, the importance of certain blood characters lies in their all having a known genetic origin, and hence their hereditary transmission can be determined with perfect accuracy and is relatively unaffected by environmental conditions if we consider a fairly limited period of time, as seems to be the case in Madagascar.

1. The banana tree is known by an Indonesian name on het west coast of Madagascar *(fontsy)*, while in the highlands its name is of Bantu origin *(akondro)*.

As regards the general distribution of A, B and O blood groups, Pigache's studies, covering 50,000 persons in all regions of the Great Isle, reveal a fairly large degree of homogeneity as regards the different groups.

The O group is dominant everywhere, with 40 to 50 per cent of the subjects.

The A-B group is low everywhere, with 5 per cent of the subjects.

As regards the distribution of the A and B groups, an interesting cleavage is to be noted between the centre and west on the one hand, and the rest of the country on the other.

For the time being we are not in a position to compare the distribution recorded in Madagascar with that within the Afro-insular group in which Kherumian includes the people of South-East Asia and Africa. The R_o chromosome of African origin is widely distributed in the west and the south, while the R_1 chromosome, which has a high frequency rate among the Indonesians (60 per cent), is extremely widespread in the highlands. Since R_1 has a high frequency and R_o a low frequency rate among the Melanesians, the coastal Negroid types among whom R_o is widespread obviously come from Africa and not South-East Asia.

The S haemoglobin responsible for the presence of sickle cells is a genetic defect with the particular feature of giving the heterozygotic individual increased resistance to malaria. The sickle-cell belt extends from West Africa to Sri Lanka but does not include South-East Asia. In Madagascar the S haemoglobin is found among 10–20 per cent of the coastal population and 5 per cent of the inhabitants of the highlands. As the mutation from which this defect derived did not originate in Madagascar, the defect came from elsewhere—Africa, India or Sri Lanka. As a result of its African origin, which is the most likely, it has affected the coast-dwellers more than the people in the highlands. Greater accuracy in determining the African and Asian contributions to the peopling of Madagascar will be gained by systematic study of the glucose 6-phosphate dehydrogenase deficiency, as described later in the section on prospects for research.

African cultural contributions and archaeological evidence[1]

Excavations carried out in 1941–42 at the Vohemar necropolis in the north-east of the island revealed the existence of the Rasikajy civilization to the world. Since then we have learned that the establishment in this

---

1. Although in the Great Isle we do not find, as in some areas of the immense neighbouring continent, the same profusion of masks, statues and decorated dwellings, this does not

region of a trading city was part of the expansion of the Islamized peoples in the north of Madagascar and that it was founded in the fourteenth century to disappear in the eighteenth.

Since 1962, the programme of excavations carried out in Madagascar has covered Indonesian and African sites without distinction. As regards the latter, we can now identify five civilizations, territorially complementary but overlapping in time. Examining them one by one, we have the following.

Swahili of the archaic settlements

They established themselves first of all in the extreme north and in the north-west. We find them as early as the ninth century at Irodo and in the twelfth century in Ampasindava Bay, Mahilaka and the Ambariotelo islands. Their culture has many analogies with that known on the East African coast between the Lamou and Kiloa islands. The domination of trading at the turn of the fourteenth century by a dynasty of Hadrami origin also had repercussions in Madagascar.

The founders of these settlements had a vehicular or promotional role for the migrations of non-Islamized Bantus, which began at that time and continued until the dawn of the historical period.

Ancient coastal civilizations of fishermen in the west and south

Their preferred territory was on the coastal fringe running from the mouth of the Betsiboka at the southernmost point of Madagascar up the west coast through Maintirano, Lamboarana, Sarodrano, Bevoalavo, Talaky and Analapasy. Although this migration certainly dates back to an era contemporary with that of the earliest Swahili settlements, no sites of this culture earlier than the twelfth century have been discovered as yet.

The manner of life of these populations, which has a certain analogy with that of the Antavelo and Vezo of today, depended very largely on fishing and the consumption of shellfish. Iron objects and grooved pottery

---

warrant our repudiating, as certain authors have done, the very existence of Malagasy art. The last exhibition on Madagascar at the Neuchâtel Museum revealed to an international public evidence of extremely important artistic achievements in the form of funerary objects and craft techniques applied to furniture. The figurative or geometric motifs have been analysed, but the convergence of styles does not make it easy to separate external influences from local invention. It would, however, be interesting to make an accurate comparison between Sakalava statuary and that of the Makondé in Mozambique. We know, in fact, from discoveries such as the Kingany stele (fourteenth century) that Swahili art had a profound influence on the geometric decoration used in north-west and east Madagascar.

abound in these sites. And it was from these settlements that the interior was settled.

Herdsmen and hunters of the inland settlements in the west and south (thirteenth to sixteenth century)

These sites are distinguished by a complex set of features, of which the following are the main examples:

Presence of imported objects of which larger quantities are found in the archaic or classical Swahili sites; the inland settlers therefore had at their disposal objects purchased by the trading posts with which they retained direct or indirect relations.

Obvious relationship and sometimes even similitude between the styles of pottery from these sites and those of the coastal Swahilis or the old civilizations of the fishermen.

Frequent occurrence in middens of subfossil bones, associated with other kitchen waste and artefacts. In Madagascar, subfossil means animals that have become extinct in very recent times through the direct or indirect action of man. These animals include *Testudo grandidieri, Aepyornis (maximus, medius) muilerornis, Hippopotamus lemerlei, Cryptoprocta ferox spelea* (larger than the present species).

Presence of large quantities of cattle bones. There can be no doubt that cattle rearing was an increasingly important factor in this civilization of the interior in the sixteenth century, when game disappeared or became scarcer. The burning-off of areas to create pastureland gradually reduced the zones where the hunting way of life could be carried on and, above all, produced a succession of major ecological transformations.

These Bantu groups, who were familiar with metal working and agriculture, but who also depended for their subsistence on hunting and food-gathering and on their livestock, occupied the interior of Madagascar in widely scattered groups between the sixteenth and the eighteenth centuries. The most notable sites are those of Rezoky and Asambalahy in the Bara country, and those in the High Valley of the Lambomaty in Androy.

At the end of the seventeenth and beginning of the eighteenth centuries the development of States with a political structure, based on the Antaimoro model, marked the end of these rulerless groups with self-sufficient economies.

It is probable that the Vazimba of the west and the highlands belonged to this civilization, which was based more on food-gathering than on agriculture, and depended very largely on utilization of the resources of the natural environment. Only a few very isolated groups, the Mikea and the Behosy, were to maintain, up to the twentieth century, this manner of living based on food-gathering, hunting, fishing and the collection of honey. Drury, who visited the Vazimba of the Tsiribihina, describes them as river fishermen. Excavations of supposed Vazimba sites in Imerina have disclosed large quantities of fresh-water shellfish which had been consumed, notably *pila cecillei* in Ankatso (whereas in Rezoky *Helisophanta vesicalis* is abundant).

Eastern chlorite-schist-working civilizations

These were, at the outset, a variant of the Swahili civilization of the archaic settlement, but between the eleventh and the fourteenth century, their area of settlement lay on the north-east coast. Later, rapid 'Malgachization' took place, and the settlements spread along the whole of the east coast down to Matitanana and Fort Dauphin. As in the case of the north-west trading posts, these towns maintained regular relations with the East African coast, the Persian Gulf, Southern Arabia and North-West India. They exported their carved chlorite-schist or soapstone vessels all over the Indian Ocean zone as well as to the cities in north-west Madagascar. Several dozens of chlorite-schist workshops have been found in the Vohemar back country, but the finishing operations were carried out in the ports on the east coast. These civilizations on the east coast of Madagascar did not (except in Mahanara) produce stone buildings, as was done by the classic and historical Swahili civilizations in the north-west.

The Antalaotse trading posts (classical Swahili civilization of the north-west)

From the fourteenth century onwards a veritable Swahili renaissance, of African derivation, occurred in north-west Madagascar. The urban centres of Langany at the mouth of the Mahajamba and Kingany on Boina Bay were founded and became active trading posts. Towns established on the small islands had bonded stone monuments decorated with carved coral and afterwards stucco (mosque, chieftain's house, tomb). These buildings are in every way comparable with those on the East African coast and the Comoro Islands, of which they are the carbon copies after a fifty-year interval.

Whereas in Africa the Portuguese intrusion brought about a marked decline, trade in Madagascar remained active up to the nineteenth century, for the inhabitants of the Great Isle were never proclaimed subjects of the King of Portugal.

The historical evidence in our possession concerning these settlements enables us to assert that Swahili was spoken more than Malagasy, and that the Moslem religion, continually reinforced by fresh elements from East Africa, flourished.

Prospects for research

Among all the lines of research described above some have proved more productive than others. In each of the disciplines concerned it is possible to propose complementary information to be sought or realignments to be effected. However, it would be most useful, in our view, to concentrate on archaeology and historical linguistics, and it is in this order that we shall now offer recommendations and arguments in support of them.

The systematic archaeological explorations undertaken for some ten years past in Madagascar should be pursued. Apart from the study of the coastal civilizations in the north-west and the survey of the fortified villages in the Imerina, most of the excavations have been done on a piecemeal basis, and their results do not as yet permit of synthesized conclusions, particularly as huge regions of Madagascar are still *terra incognita* from the archaeological point of view. These untouched zones include the east coast between Mananara and Matitanana, the Betsileo, and the west coast between Maintirano and Lamboharana. Yet this latter region, where the Vezo-Antavelo culture was born and flourished, certainly saw the arrival of African migrants at a remote point in time.

It is already possible to define certain styles in ceramics, of which some have Indonesian (Sa-Huynh culture) but others African affinities. A degree of interpenetration of these styles can be seen in north Madagascar, which would lead one to think that this part of the island was where the Malagasy culture's African-Indonesian symbiosis was worked out. The real problem does not consist merely in the determination of the respective contributions, but even more in grasping the symbiosis process, its epoch, and its mechanism. More archaeological excavations and positive dating (radiocarbon 14) will gradually make it possible to fill in the blanks in this puzzle.

Simultaneously, research should be increased in the countries from which the ancestors of the Malagasy may have come. This requirement is all the more urgent as we are beginning to touch the furthest limits of Malagasy proto-history and need to go back in time beyond that point. It is not possible to trace this or that style of ceramics to an outside cultural area when we know nothing whatever about the latter's archaeology. The Indonesian culture of the first millennium of our era, in particular, is completely unknown to us, like that of the Comoros of the eighth century A.D., though it must have been this archipelago that served as a transit zone for a great many African migrants to Madagascar. Only eighth-century Swahili culture is well known to us, thanks to Chittick's work, and we have seen what these data have contributed towards the determination of the Swahili facet of Malagasy culture.

Apart from the Comoro Islands, we recommend the intensification of archaeological research on the Bantu civilizations of Mozambique, on whose probably long-standing links with Madagascar[1] Kent has insisted.

Historical linguistics must advance in line with archaeological research. In particular, as soon as we have the results of a glottochronological survey covering both the Indonesian languages and Malagasy, it will be well to examine more deeply the problem of the interferences between Malagasy and the Bantu languages. This should not be confined to the lexical domain, but should include the phonological and grammatical aspects. Since Ferrand, no Malagasy or Malagasy scholar has made a serious study of the problem of the Bantu substrata. This is no doubt due to the fact that the weight of Grandidier's researches, with their excessive South-East Asian bias, is still too great.

We know little of what tenth-century Swahili was like; when the Indonesian ancestors of the Malagasy made contact with Bantus they found a language very different from that of today. While it may be desirable to find out which Indonesian languages are the closest to Malagasy, it is equally necessary to discover the Bantu language or languages involved in the contact. According as the comparisons pointed more to the Chimbalazi of Barawa, standard Swahili from Zanzibar or Mwani from the Kerimba islands, the archaeological research strategy would be correspondingly quite different.[2]

In Madagascar itself, the precisest possible inventory also needs to be made of any survivals of the former linguistic checkerboard in the west or elsewhere, comprising an examination of the toponymy, etymologically focused extraction of the terms cited in the seventeenth-century accounts (particularly in those of Paulo da Costa, which have been published recently); lastly, thorough ethnological surveys of the Behosy, continuing the pioneer work of Birkeli, would be useful. The deciphering of Arabic-Malagasy manuscripts and the search for new manuscripts primarily in the Fort Dauphin area but also in the north-west appears absolutely necessary. No single researcher, Malagasy or foreign, however competent he may be,

---

1. The Maldives, Ceylon and Indonesia represent other key areas for an understanding of the Malagasy peopling process. But they can be no more than mentioned in a report that is confined to Africa.
2. The possibility of considerable surprises in these comparisons must be taken into consideration. It was recently discovered, as regards Anjouan island, that its language basis was linked with Pokomo on the Kenyan coast.

can seek to make this kind of work his exclusive preserve, for it involves concerted effort and mutual aid on a considerable scale.

It is vital to republish the writings in Arabic on the Indian Ocean. Ferrand's book, although fundamental, is incomplete and, what is more, unobtainable. It is unfortunate that this distinguished Arabic scholar was unable to translate the manuscripts of Suleyman el Mahri and Ibn Majid which he brought to notice in the form of reproductions of the original texts. For the present, all that are available are the Arabic, Russian or Portuguese editions of Ibn Majid. Incidentally, a recommendation for the translation of this too-little-known material is proposed periodically by the International Association of the Indian Ocean at its congresses.

Comparative ethnology can contribute a great deal provided that it does not restrict itself to isolated traits. An evaluation of the aesthetic, sociopolitical or social organization systems of Madagascar compared with those of Bantu Africa would provide a wealth of information.

Physical anthropology could, in our view, make a useful contribution: the study of ancient osseous remains in Madagascar should help our understanding of the course of the mixings and, more especially, of the fusion between the African and Indonesian elements: did it happen in the island or elsewhere? The almost total lack of skeletons found in an archaeological context has, up to now, prevented the assembly of information of this order.[1]

Physical anthropology is also a most promising approach, for anthropobiology directs its attention to traits with a known genetic origin in somewhat the same way as the linguist uses the living dialects derived from the same language to reconstitute the original proto-culture. We have seen the initial results obtained by Pigache with regard to the Rhesus sub-groups and S haemoglobin. This author has also drawn attention to the need to pursue research on the glucose 6-phosphate dehydrogenase deficiency. This enzyme deficiency, important in metabolism, is spread throughout the whole world. It has been shown that this enzyme is not unique, but corresponds to two types, A and B, of different electrophoretic mobility: type A is represented in Africa and type B in Asia. In Madagascar, the deficiency is found in 15 per cent of the population. It would be interesting to determine the relative proportion of the two types in the Malagasy ethnic groups.

---

1. The work on the bones found in the Vohemar excavations has been the only exception so far. Even so the osteological studies have not been linked with the context of each tomb.

Select bibliography

General

BIRKELI, L. *Les Vazimba de la Côte Ouest de Madagascar. Notes d'Ethnologie.* Tananarive, Mémoires de l'Académie Malgache, XXII, 1936.
BRIANT, J. *L'Hébreu à Madagascar, Aperçus, Suggestions.* Tananarive, Pitot de la Beaujardière, 1945.
DAHL, O. [The Proto-Malagasy Phonological System]. *Norsk Tidsskrift for Sprogvidenskap* (Oslo), 1937.
DESCHAMPS, H. *Histoire de Madagascar.* Paris, Berger-Levrault, 1961.
FERRAND, G. L'Origine Africaine des Malgaches. *Journal Asiatique*, Vol. X, No. XI, 1908, p. 353–500.
GRANDIDIER, A.; GRANDIDIER, G. *Histoire Physique, Naturelle et Politique de Madagascar.* Vol. IV, Ethnographie T.1, Les Habitants de Madagascar, Paris, Imprimerie Nationale, 1908.
JULIEN, G. *Institutions Politiques et Sociales de Madagascar.* Paris, E. Guilmoto, 1908, 2 Vols.
KENT, R. *Early Kingdoms in Madagascar 1500–1700.* New York, Holt, Rinehart & Winston, 1970.
MALZAC, R. P. *Histoire du Royaume Hova depuis ses Origines jusqu'à sa Fin.* Tananarive, Imprimerie Catholique, 1912.
MELLIS, J. *Nord et Nord-Ouest de Madagascar, Volamena et Volafotsy.* Tananarive, Imprimerie Modern de l'Emyrne, 1938.
VERIN, P. *Les Echelles Anciennes du Commerce sur les Côtes Nord de Madagascar.* Lille, Université de Lille, 1975, 2 Vols. 1016 p.

Arabic and Arabic-Malagasy manuscripts

CHITTICK, N. The Coast of Africa. In: P. L. Shinnie (ed.). *The African Iron Age*, p. 108-41. Oxford, Clarendon Press, 1972.
CHUMNOVSKY, T. *Tres Roteiros Desconhecidos de Ahmad Ibn Majid, o Piloto Arabe de Vasco da Gama.* Academy of Sciences of the USSR, 1962.
FERRAND, G. *Instructions Politiques et Routiers Arabes et Portugais des XIVe et XVe siècles.* Paris, Geuthner, 1923–28, 3 Vols.
——. *Relation des Voyages et Textes Géographiques Arabes, Persans et Turcs relatifs à l'Extrême-Orient du VIIIe au XVIIIe siècle.* Paris, Leroux, 1913–14, 2 Vols.
GAUTIER, E. Notes sur l'Écriture Antaimoro. *Bulletin de Correspondance Africaine* (Publication of the École des Lettres d'Alger, Paris, Vol. 25), 1902.
GROSSET-GRANGE, H. Translations of Texts of Ibn Majid and Suleyman al Mahri. *Azania* (review of the Institute of History and Archaeology, Nairobi.)
JULIEN, G. Pages Arabico-Madécasses. *Annales de l'Académie des Sciences coloniales, 2.* Paris, Challamel, 1929, p. 1–123.
ROMBAKA, J. Tantaran-drazanany Antaimoro. *Revue du Foyer*, Fanilon'ny Tanora. Tananarive, April 1930 to October 1931.
SAUVAGET, J. Les Merveilles de l'Inde. *Mémorial Jean Sauvaget.* Damascus, Institut Français de Damas, 1954, p. 189–309.

Oral traditions and ethnography

BARE, J. F. Hiérarchies Politiques et Organisations Sociales à Madagascar. In: *Malgache qui est-tu?*, p. 43-67. Neuchâtel, 1973.
BIRKELI, L. See 'General' section.
BLOCH, M. *Placing the Dead.* London, The Seminar Press, 1970.
CALLET, R. P. *Tantaran'ny Andriana nanjaka teto Imerina.* Tananarive, 1908.
DANDOUAU, A. *Contes Populaires des Sakalava et des Tsimihety de la Région d'Analalava,* Algiers, 1922. (Story No. 75, p. 380-5, mentions Darafify's journey from Vohemar to the south.)
DESCHAMPS, H. See 'General' section.
FERRAND, G. Articles on Madagascar in *Encyclopédie de l'Islam.* Paris, 1936.
——. Les Iles Ramny, Lâmery, Wakwâk, Komor des Géographes Arabes et Madagascar. *Journal Asiatique*, Vol. X, 1907, p. 433-500.
——. Le K'ouen Louen et les Anciennes Navigations Interocéaniques dans les Mers du Sud. *Journal Asiatique*, 1919.
——. *Les Musulmans à Madagascar et aux îles Comores.* Paris, 1891-1902.
GRANDIDIER, A. See 'General' section.
GRANDIDIER, G. See 'General' section.
GUILLAIN, C. *Documents sur l'Histoire, la Géographie et le Commerce de la Partie Orientale de Madagascar,* 1845.
GULWICK, Indonesian Echoes in Central Tanganyika. *Tanganyika Notes and Records,* 1936, p. 60-6.
HEBERT, J. C. La Parenté à Plaisanterie à Madagascar. *Bulletin de Madagascar*, March 1958, p. 175-216; April 1958, p. 268-85.
HEINE-GELDERN, R. Prehistoric Research in the Netherlands Indies. In: *Science and Scientists in the Netherlands Indies,* p. 129-67. New York, Riverside Press, 1945.
HORNELL, J. Indonesian Influence on East African Culture. *Journal of the Royal Anthropological Institute*, 1934, p. 305-32.
KENT, R. See 'General' section.
LEITAO, H. *Os dois Descobrimentos de Ilha de São Lourenço.* Lisbon, Centro de Estudos Históricos Ultramarinos, 1970.
MELLIS, J. See 'General' section.
PRINS, A. *The Swahili-speaking Peoples of Zanzibar and the East African Coast.* London, International African Institute, 1961.
RAINANDRIAMANPANDRY. Collected Manuscripts Deposited in the Archives of the Malagasy Republic, Tananarive.
RALAIMIHOATRA, E. Le Contexte et la Signification du Terme Vazimba dans l'Histoire de Madagascar. *Bulletin de l'Académie Malgache,* N.S. XLVII, 1969, p. 183-4.
RAMILISONINA. Ny Kajemby sy ny toerampandevenany. *Taloha 3*, 1970, p. 179-81.
RAMILSON. *Ny Loharanon'ny Andriamamilaza.* Imprimerie Volamahitsy, 1951-52.
SACLEUX, P. *Dictionnaire Swahili.* Paris, Travaux et Mémoires de l'Institut d'Ethnologie, 1939-1941.
VERIN, P. Histoire Ancienne du Nord Ouest de Madagascar. *Taloha 5.* N.S., 1973. (For the Malagasy incursions into Africa, see p. 153-63.)
——. Mojomby, la Ville Disparue. *Bulletin de Madagascar,* Nos. 293-4, 1970, p. 256-8.

Ethnobotany

HEBERT, J. C. *Les Noms Vernaculaires de Plantes à Madagascar*. Manuscript. (Quotes Haudricourt: L'Origine des Plantes Cultivées Malgaches.)
MURDOCK, G. P. *Africa, its People and Their Cultural History*. New York, 1959. (See Ch. 6, 'The Ancient Azanians', p. 204–11, and Ch. 7, 'Cultural Impact of Indonesia', p. 212–70. Also the summary of Chapters 6 and 7 by W. G. Solheim in *Asian Perspectives*, Vol. 4, 1961, p. 61–2.)
PERRIER DE LA BATHIE, H. Les Plantes Introduites à Madagascar. *Revue de Botanique Appliquée et d'Agriculture Tropicale*, 1931–32.
——. La Végétation Malgache. *Annales du Musée Collection* (Marseilles), 1921.

Linguistics

DAHL, O. *Malgache et Maanjan*. Oslo, Egede Institutet, 1951. (Discusses Ferrand's material).
——. See 'General' section.
DAHLE, L. The Swahili Element in the new Malagasy English Dictionary. *Antananarivo Annual*, Vol. III, 1889, p. 99–115.
DEZ, J. Quelques Hypothèses Formulées par la Linguistique Comparée à l'Usage de l'Archéologie. *Taloha 2*, 1965, p. 197–214.
FERRAND, G. See 'Oral Traditions and Ethnography' section.
JULIEN, G. See 'Manuscripts' section.
VERIN, P.; KOTTAK, C.; GORLIN, P. The Glottochronology of Malagasy Dialects. *Oceanic Linguistics*, Vol. VIII, 1969.

Physical anthropology

BAKOTO-RATSIMAMANGA, A. Tache Pigmentaire et Origine des Malgaches. Thesis reproduced in *Revue Anthropologique*, January/March 1940, p. 6–130.
BOUCHEREAU, A. Note sur l'Anthropologie de Madagascar, des Iles Comores et de la Côte Orientale d'Afrique. *L'Anthropologie*, Vol. 8, 1897, p. 149–64.
CHAMLA, M. Recherches Anthropologiques sur l'Origine des Malgaches. *Mémoires du Muséum* (Paris), 1958.
CHAMPION, C. La Tache Pigmentaire Congénitale à Madagascar et aux Comores. *Journal Société des Africanistes*, Vol. 7, No. 1, 1937, p. 79–92. (One map, four bibliographical tables, p. 91–2. Survey concerning the nature of the pigmentation mark, distribution by population, beliefs, customs.)
DAVID, R. Contribution à l'Étude des Groupes Sanguins à Madagascar. Nouvelles Observations chez les Mahafaly du Sud-Ouest de l'île. Records of meetings of the Société de Biologie, 9 July 1938, p. 987; also in *Journal de la Société des Africanistes*, 1939, Vol. 9, No. 2, p. 119–52.
——. Le Problème Anthropologique Malgache. 1. La Répartition des Groupes Sanguins et son Aspect Ethnique dans le Centre et l'Est de Madagascar. 2. Observations Anthropométriques et Sérologiques chez les Mahafaly du Sud-Ouest de Madagascar. *Bulletin de l'Académie Malgache*, Vol. 23, 1940, p. 1–32. (3 maps, 2 tables, 2 photo plates, bibliogr., p. 29–31.)
GOULESQUE, J. Eléments d'Etude pour une Anthropologie Malgache. *Taloha 3*, 1970, p. 165–74.
GRANDIDIER, A. Ethnographie 2: 1–19. *Aspect Physique des Malgaches*, 1914.
HARTWEG, R. Les Races de Madagascar. In: Faublée, *Ethnographie de Madagascar*. p. 129–35. Paris, Ed. de France et d'Outre-Mer, 1946,

——. Observations Odontologiques sur les Crânes Provenant des Anciennes Sépultures Arabes de Vohémar. *Bulletin de l'Académie Malgache*, Vol. 28, 1947–48, p. 50–8.
HERIVAUX, A.; RAHOERSON, R. Les Groupes Sanguins chez les Malgaches de l'Emyrne. *Bulletin de la Société de Pathologie Exotique et de ses Filiales*, Vol. 24, 1931, p. 247–50.
HIERNAUX. Bantu Expansion: the Evidence of Physical Anthropology Confronted with Linguistic and Archaeological Evidence. *Journal of African History* (London), Vol. LIX, No. 4, 1968, p. 505–15.
MARQUER, P. Étude Anthropométrique des Ossements Provenant des Sépultures 'arabes' de Vohémar. *Bulletin de l'Académie Malgache*, Vol. 28, 1947–48, p. 68–80.
PIGACHE, J. P. Le Problème Anthropologique à Madagascar. *Taloha 3*, 1970, p. 175–8.
ROUQUETTE, M. Anthropométrie des Races Autochtones de la Province de Fort-Dauphin. *Bulletin de l'Académie Malgache*, Vol. 1, 1914, p. 37–71. (28 tables, 1 map.)

Archaeology

Atlas de Madagascar, 1970–71. See map and notes concerning archaeological sites. Plate 19.
BATTISTINI, R. Conditions de Gisement des Sites Littoraux de Subfossiles, et Causes de la Disparition de la Faune des Grands Animaux dans le Sud-Ouest et l'Extrême-Sud de Madagascar. *Taloha 4*, 1971, p. 7–18.
BATTISTINI, R.; VERIN, P. Irodo et la Tradition Vohémarienne. *Revue de Madagascar* and *Taloha 2*, 1966.
BATTISTINI, R.; VERIN, P.; RASON, R. Le Site de Talaky, le Contexte Géographique et Géologique, Premier Sondage, Note sur les Habitants Actuels. *Annales de la Faculté des Lettres et Sciences Humaines de l'Université de Madagascar*, No. 1, January 1963.
CHITTICK, N. The Shirazi Colonization of East Africa. *Journal of African History* (London), Vol. VI, No. 3, 1965, p. 275–94.
COWAN, W. D. The Stone Elephant at Ambohisary. *Antananarivo Annual*, Vol. 4, 1885, p. 525–6.
DANDOY. Découverte Archéologique à Fénérive. *Bulletin de Madagascar*, No. 264, 1968, p. 457–66.
DOMENICHINI, J. P.; RAKOTOARISOA, J. A. Les Fouilles de Matitanana. In: *Taloha 6*.
GARLAKE, P. The Early Islamic Architecture of the East African Coast. Nairobi, *British Institute of History and Archaeology in East Africa*, No. 1, 1966.
GAUDEBOUT, P.; VERNIER, E. Notes à la Suite d'une Enquête sur les Objets en Pierre de la Région de Vohémar. *Bulletin de l'Académie Malgache*, Vol. 24, 1941, p. 91–9. (Description and map of the 'Rasikajy' workshops.)
——. Notes sur une Campagne de Fouilles à Vohémar, Mission Rasikajy 1941. *Bulletin de l'Académie Malgache*, Vol. 24, 1941, p. 100–14.
GEVREY, A. *Essai sur les Comores*. Pondichéry, Seligny, 1870.
HEURTEBIZE, G.; VERIN, P. Archéologie du Lambomaty. *Journal de la Société des Africanistes*, 1973.
KIRKMAN, J. The Coast of Kenya. In: *Sociétés et Compagnies de Commerce en Orient et dans l'Océan Indien*, p. 247–53. Paris, SEVPEN, 1970.
MILLE, A. Anciens Horizons d'Ankatso. *Taloha 4*, 1971, p. 117–26.
MILLOT, L. Les Ruines de Mahilaka. *Bulletin de l'Académie Malgache*, Vol. 10, 1912, p. 283–8.
OLIVIER, R. Discernible Developments in the Interior, 1500–1840. In: Oliver and Matthew (eds.), *History of East Africa*, Vol. 1. London, 1963.
SLEEN, W. C. N. Van der. Les collections du Musée de Nîmes (France). *Le Naturaliste Malgache*, Vol. 12, 1960, p. 183–91, Tananarive-Tsimbazaza.
——. Ancient glass beads with special reference to the beads of East and Central Africa and the Indian Ocean, *Journal of the Royal Anthropological Institute*, 88, 1957, p. 203–17.

VERIN, P. Les Antiquités de l'île d'Anjouan. *Bulletin de l'Académie Malgache*, N.S. XLV-1, 1967, p. 69–79.
——. Notes Préliminaires sur les Sites Islamiques du Mozambique. *Azania V*, 1970, p. 184–90.
——. Recherches sur le Sud-Ouest de Madagascar Suivi des Anciens Sites de Rezoky et d'Asambalahy ainsi que les Recherches sur la Côte Vezo. *Taloha 4*, 1971, p. 3–53.
——. See 'General' and 'Oral Traditions' sections.

The role of trade
in the settlement of Mauritius

Auguste Toussaint

Originally, Mauritius was uninhabited. The Dutch attempted in vain to establish themselves there in the seventeenth century, but it was not until 1721, with the takeover by the French Compagnie des Indes, that the settlement of the island began.

In 1767, control passed to the French Ministère de la Marine. In 1810, the island was captured by the British and became a Crown Colony, until its accession to independence in 1968. At the end of the French occupation, the population numbered some 70,000; today the figure is nearly 835,000.

1721–1810

At first no more than a port of call, the island was only opened up to the outside world after 1767. Very early on, however, the 'Compagnie' sought to develop a saleable commodity. Coffee, cotton and sugar were all tried, thereby necessitating the introduction of settlers and slaves, the latter being considered essential for cultivating the crop.

The first settlers came from Britanny and Normandy. Very few were farmers. Most had but one aim: to make quick fortunes and then return home. From the beginning, the gambling spirit predominated.

The slaves were initially drawn from Madagascar. In 1740, slave-trading expeditions were dispatched to Mozambique, and from 1767 on, Africa became the main source of supply.

The opening of the port under the French navy's administration produced an influx of traders from every province in France, but predominantly Bretons, Bordelais and Provençals. Between 1769 and 1810, the list comprised 751 merchants, ship-owners, brokers, mercantile agents, exchange brokers, without counting the still more numerous 'market men', shopkeepers and retail traders. Of the 674 persons of professional level shown by the census in Port Louis in 1808, 365 were engaged in commerce.

This commercial class represented a dynamic element that gave the island's life a seawards start and got it into the international mercantile circuit.

Its principal activities were trade with Europe and America, the Indian coastal trade, import trade from Madagascar, Negro-slave trading, and privateering in wartime, for commercial as much as military ends.

The traders also promoted cash-crop farming, leaving the subsistence farming to the Ile Bourbon, then a mere 'dependency'. It was the merchants who furnished the farmers with slaves, equipment and capital, and 'commercialized' their produce.

To get rich quickly and return home continued to be the objective, but it was a pipe-dream only. Most of the newcomers settled down, married and had families. In 1809, the island's population included 6,227 persons born in Europe or of European stock, more than most of the other European trading-posts in the Indian Ocean could boast.

Trading activities were accompanied by an acceleration in the movement of shipping. The maritime traffic in and out of Port Louis maintained a floating population of seamen, and their transitory liaisons with women of the free 'coloured' population were a factor in increasing the numbers of free non-whites (587 in 1767, 7,133 in 1809). In the Ile Bourbon, where there was little movement of shipping, the 'coloured' element increased much more slowly.

The consequences of the commercial expansion were even more pronounced in the case of the slave population. Totalling 15,027 in 1767, their numbers rose to 55,422 in 1809. The chief period of slave trading was between 1767 and 1793. Interrupted, or rather slowed down, during the French Revolution, the trade picked up again in 1803. Filliot reckons that between 1769 and 1810 Mauritius and its dependencies imported 115,000 slaves. The writer's own estimate for Mauritius alone, for the period 1773-1810, is approximately 51,000 from the African coast and some 12,000 from Madagascar, allowing for losses.

To this must be added an undetermined number of slaves imported from Asia. In 1817, d'Unienville estimated those of Indian or Malaysian stock as representing one-seventeenth of the slave population (79,493 souls).

Precise information is lacking concerning the free Indians (Hindu or Muslim) who entered Mauritius under French rule. As early as 1781, a suburb of Port Louis was known as the 'Camp des Malabars', but these people were not merchants. The censuses taken in the eighteenth century reveal that the mercantile class included no Asians. There were no 'coloured' merchants and very few 'Creoles' (Europeans born in the island).

1810–1900

After the British conquest, Port Louis was closed to foreign vessels. In 1813, the slave trade was abolished. The war had killed the Indian coasting trade. These developments generated a reorientation of the island's life. The port was reopened in 1820, and the slave trade continued clandestinely for several years, but during the second decade of the century the island made the transition from a maritime to an agricultural economy, with sugar as its staple, indeed its only produce. Actually the agriculture was always concentrated on cash crops.

The change was fostered by the British traders who were arriving in Mauritius at that time. Though few in number, they possessed the capital that the colonists lacked. Their influence was decisive, above all from 1825 on, when Great Britain agreed, as a result of their representations, to purchase Mauritian sugar at the same price as West Indian sugar.

There followed a veritable stampede away from all other crops in favour of sugar-cane. At the same time, the old mercantile class was gradually supplanted by the sugar-planters. But the 'get-rich-quick' spirit remained.

The euphoria did not last long. After the slave trade, it was the turn of slavery itself to be abolished, in 1835. Sugar-cane, however, required an abundant supply of labour for its cultivation. As soon as they sensed the threat to the slave system, the sugar-planters turned to another source, namely the voluntary immigration of indentured Indian labourers.

The first contingent arrived from Madras in 1829. In 1834, two further contingents arrived from Calcutta and Bombay. In 1835, several recruitment agencies were set up in these three ports, from where they dispatched an increasing number of indentured labourers to Mauritius.

This operation was baptized the 'coolie trade'. And a trade it was, indeed, much reminiscent of the old trade in Negro slaves.

The British capitalists had a considerable share in this operation. In 1832, Port Louis had thirty-two representatives of British companies engaged in financing the trade. The classic example is that of James Blyth, one of the first to charter ships to bring coolies and rice—their staple diet—from Bengal, thereby making a double profit.

From the outset, the question of provisions loomed large. The Africans ate manioc, which was produced locally. The Indians ate rice, ghee, dholl and flour, while for clothing they required cotton fabrics, all articles that had to be imported. The total cost of imports of these five items rose from £220,069 in 1835 to £420,566 in 1838, and continued to rise thereafter.

In 1839, the abuses to which the indentured-labour system gave rise led to its being suspended. In 1842, it was revived and was continued until 1907, the total number brought in rising eventually to 450,000 (mostly Hindus), of whom only a third returned to India. The result was an artificial growth of population, which was to prove laden with consequences.

The indentured labourers were closely followed by Muslim and Chinese merchants, who came on their own account to share in the lucrative food and textile trade. This was a natural corollary of the system of indentures.

Around 1845, the Cutcheemaimans, natives of Cutch, began to arrive. By 1853, they already boasted five trading houses. In 1860 the first Hallayemaimans, Muslims from Hallar and from Kathiawar, arrived, almost at the same time as the Soortees, who were Muslims from Surat.

These Muslim merchants, wrongly called Arabs, had by 1870 acquired a near monopoly of the provision and textile trade. They also engaged, as shipowners, in the coolie trade, in the exportation of sugar to India and the importation of beef from Madagascar, a trade that developed in importance as the population increased, locally raised livestock being insufficient to meet requirements.

At the end of the nineteenth century a change occurred in the nature of the island's trading, described by one of the governors, Sir Charles Bruce, in the following terms:

The immigration of Asians caused rice to become the staple diet of the entire island; at the same time, the competition from sugar-beet growers in Europe, added to other causes, resulted in India becoming the principal market for Mauritian sugar. Thus the bulk of the traffic in all articles of consumption and everyday use has moved from Europe to India and is controlled by Indian merchants.

Detailed statistics concerning the rise in their numbers are lacking, but the 1901 census put the island's Muslim population at 41,208, equivalent to one-third of the Christian and one-fifth of the Hindu populations.

The Indian merchants were not all Muslims. In 1890, nine of the forty-seven registered Asian trading companies in Port Louis belonged to Hindus (as compared with thirty-two belonging to Muslims and six to Chinese traders). None the less, the predominance of Muslims is patent.

We have scant information concerning the Chinese. The first settlers arrived in the eighteenth century; they were natives of Canton, the only city in China open to European trade, and were for the most part craftsmen. The first shopkeepers appeared on the scene around 1830. By 1880, they were playing a major part in the retail and indeed in the wholesale trade. Numerically, however, the Chinese population was still fairly small (3,509 in 1901).

As the traditional division into whites, blacks and half-castes was abolished in 1830, it is difficult to follow the evolution of these three groups during the nineteenth century solely by reference to the censuses, in which from 1846 on all three were merged together under the head 'general population'.

As far as can be judged, Europe's contribution to the peopling of the island was negligible after 1810. It would appear that there were also two exoduses of French settlers, the first shortly after the British conquest and the second after the abolition of slavery, when the compensation paid to slave owners enabled a number of people to realize their assets and return home.

The flow of French immigrants did not, moreover, dry up completely. Around 1850, immigration was again on the increase. In 1851, the island had 2,000 French-born settlers, excluding Creoles. In this connection, it should be stressed that trading relations with France remained active, and 'French taste' retained its hold for many items (dress, wines, foodstuffs, etc.).

With regard to the British merchants, while they were responsible for launching the coolie trade, they themselves helped but little to populate the island. By and large, the volume of British immigration to Mauritius may be considered negligible. British travellers visiting the island have invariably depicted it as being a French colony within the British Empire.

From 1900 to the present day

At the beginning of the twentieth century, the lines of trade underwent a further change. After the First World War, sugar, the island's only export, was once again channelled to European markets. The importation of indentured labour stopped in 1907, and an attempt to revive it in 1922-23 came to nothing. India's part in the island's trading activities declined, as did its contribution to the population.

Nevertheless, the 'return to Europe' did not prompt a further influx of European immigrants. On the contrary, many Creoles began to emigrate. Some went to Madagascar, occupied by France in 1895, others to South Africa. Towards 1920, a veritable Mauritian 'colony' had established itself in the province of Natal.

Until 1940 or thereabouts, the population remained more or less at the level reached in 1901 (371,023). Malaria, introduced by accident in 1865, served as a kind of regulator and checked the natural increase.

Its elimination at the end of the Second World War triggered off an unprecedented upsurge in numbers, from 419,185 in 1944 to 681,619 in 1962, and to almost 835,000 by the end of 1973.

The present era has thus been one of considerable growth; trade, however, is no longer the factor responsible. The only element, it would appear, whose increase can be directly linked to trade is the Chinese population, which rose from 3,509 in 1901 to 8,923 in 1931, all but tripling in thirty years. Since that date, it has continued to grow, and is today probably in the region of 35,000.

This growth is due to the increasing influx of China-born Chinese women from 1911 on. It was only at that date that the Chinese merchants and shopkeepers were able to import wives from China. The same phenomenon occurred at the same time in other countries situated in the Indian ocean. This mass influx of women sufficed to transform, in Mauritius as elsewhere, the character of Chinese settlement.

A spectacular increase is also observable in the Muslim group (41,208 in 1901, as compared with 110,332 in 1962), which shows a growth rate appreciably higher than those of the Hindu and Christian groups. To what extent, however, is the economic factor responsible? Lack of adequate data precludes our doing more than noting the question here.

Today, immigration has completely stopped, and it is emigration, rather, which is being encouraged, in an effort to relieve population pressure. Present-day emigration is no longer, as at the beginning of the century, a phenomenon confined to a single ethnic group, but is to be observed in almost all of them.

Exchanges of goods present a very varied picture. All in all, however, the economy continues to be dominated, as it was in the previous century, by the sugar-cane monoculture.

Main lines of research

There is still no study of the human geography of Mauritius comparable to the excellent thesis produced by Jean Defos du Rau on that of Réunion. This is a major lacuna.

With regard to the European settlement in the eighteenth century, only partial studies have been made, of the Breton and the Meridional settlers respectively by Henri Bourde de la Rogerie and by Louis Dermigny.

The writer's own research field at the Centre National de la Recherche Scientifique (CNRS) covers the entire trading class from 1769 to 1810. He began by establishing an overall picture, and by describing and analysing the transactions of a typical merchant in an as yet unpublished work (*Le Mirage des Iles*).

In a recent thesis, Jean-Michel Filliot has made a thorough study of the mechanics of the slave trade. It still remains to review the subject from the economic standpoint. In particular, the transactions of the sixty-odd merchants who dealt in slaves call for analysis.

D'Unienville's *Statistique de l'Ile Maurice* contains many errors. A critical re-edition of this compendium is desirable. A complete analytical inventory of parish records and civil registers during the period of French domination is also needed.

Again a complete study should be made on how the 'coloured' element came into being. The transitory liaisons referred to earlier are but one of the factors to be taken into account.

For the British régime, the only major demographic survey is Kuczynski's, which supplements d'Unienville's *Statistique*. An exhaustive study, however, has not yet been undertaken.

Brenda Howell's thesis brings out the part played by British merchants in launching the sugar industry. It also contains valuable material concerning the beginnings of the coolie trade; this latter has never, however, been studied as a commercial undertaking.

The history of Indian immigration, outlined initially in the classic report by Frere and Williamson and in Cumpston's book, is re-examined in the more recent study by the American sociologist Benedict. This is the only scientific work produced to date on the Indians of Mauritius; it is, however, focused more upon the present than the past.

The indentured labour system gave rise to a great number of speculative undertakings by the importers and recruiting agents, as also by the 'distributors', that is, the job contractors and the *sirdars* (foremen) whose role is emphasized by Frere and Williamson. This is an aspect that warrants most careful examination.

The history of the Asian merchants, their success, and the evolution of European trade faced with their competition are all subjects upon which light needs to be shed. We have only one very superficial monograph, by Moomtaz Emrith, concerning the Muslim traders. This describes the present-day situation and provides but little information on their beginnings. The Chinese element still awaits a historian.

Lastly, research is unquestionably called for on the African group (including the Malagasy element), a subject about which very little is known. The 1851 census recorded 48,330 freed men (emancipated slaves) who were not half-castes. How did this group subsequently evolve?

Conclusion

The geographer Pierre Gourou sees the Mascarene Islands and the West Indies as veritable prisons, peopled through the lure of profit. This generalization appears to be fairly close to the truth, though whether, in the case of Mauritius, it is the whole truth remains open to question. The peopling of this island calls, in fact, for more than one further study.

Select bibliography

BENEDICT, B. *Indians in a Plural society. A Report on Mauritius*. London, H.M.S.O., 1961.
BOURDE DE LA ROGERIE, H. *Les Bretons aux Iles de France et de Bourbon*. Rennes, Imp. Oberthur, 1934.
CUMPSTON, J. M. *Indians Overseas in British Territories, 1834–1854*. Oxford University Press, 1953.
DERMIGNY, L. Languedociens et Provençaux aux Iles de France et de Bourbon. *Rev. Hist. des Colonies* (Paris), 1957, p. 369–452.
D'UNIENVILLE, A. M. *Statistique de l'Ile Maurice et ses Dépendances*. Paris, G. Barba, 1838. 3 Vols.
EMRITH, M. *The Muslims in Mauritius*. Port Louis, 1967.
FILLIOT, J.-M. *La Traite des Esclaves vers les Mascareignes au XVIIIe Siècle*, 1970. (Unpublished thesis.)
FRERE, W. E.; WILLIAMSON, V. A. *Report of the Royal Commissioners Appointed to Inquire into the Treatment of Immigrants in Mauritius*. London, William Clowes & Sons, 1875. 3 Vols.
HOWELL, B. *Mauritius, 1832–1849. A Study of a Sugar Colony*, 1950.
KUCZYNSKI, R. R. *A Demographic Survey of the British Colonial Empire*. Oxford University Press, Vol. II, 1948–49. p. 707–885.
TOUSSAINT, A. *La Route des Iles*. Paris, SEVPEN, 1967.
———. *Le Mirage des Iles*, 1973. (Unpublished study.)

The part played by agriculture in the settlement of Réunion

Hubert Gerbeau

The Mascarene archipelago, which had long been known to the Arabs, was discovered by Westerners early in the sixteenth century. Between 1638 (or 1640) and 1671 Réunion was seized on four successive occasions in the name of the King of France. This is indicative of the slight importance attached to the island, which until 1638 was uninhabited, and the first attempts at settlement were sporadic.

However, in the last third of the seventeenth century the population settled down. Accounts by travellers gave Réunion the reputation of another Eden. The inhabitants lived mainly by food-gathering, hunting and fishing, but they were driven by their own needs, those of passing ships and the urging of administrators, to experiment in agriculture, with favourable results from the outset. In addition to growing rice, wheat, maize and tobacco, they began to raise cattle, pigs, sheep and goats. The northern part of the country, the 'Beau pais', was occupied because it seemed more suitable for agriculture (Sainte-Suzanne was founded in 1667 and Saint-Denis in 1669). However, the earliest inhabitants had settled in the only area that offered, if not a port, at least a bay where ships could anchor fairly safely. Many of their successors were to remain faithful to the Saint-Paul district for this reason.

In 1690, Bourbon had 314 inhabitants. (Bourbon was the name of the island from 1649 to 1848, with two interruptions—at the time of the Revolution, when it was called Réunion, and under the Empire, when it was called Ile Bonaparte.) The population was distributed as follows: Saint-Paul district, 166 comprising 125 white and 41 black; Saint-Denis district, 77 comprising 40 white and 37 black; Sainte-Suzanne district, 71 comprising 47 white and 24 black; i.e. 212 white and 102 black.

In 1714 the population totalled 1,157. The white population was still in the majority (623, as compared to 534 black). However, by 1735 the slaves constituted by far the largest group, numbering 6,573 out of a total population of 8,289 (J. Barassin).

Thus, while the majority of the island's population consisted of Europeans right up to the second decade of the eighteenth century, from that time onwards many shiploads of slaves arrived, with the result that from 1735 up to the end of the century the black population accounted for about four-fifths of the total population. This change reflected a change in economic activities.

From 1735 to 1815

In 1735, when La Bourdonnais became governor of the Mascarenes, the most forsaken of the islands seems to have been Mauritius. With a population of 2,000, it was abandoned to the ravages of rats, monkeys and deer, threatened with famine and disturbed by the presence of runaway slaves and deserters. However, this island had the natural harbours its neighbour lacked. It was possible to establish bases for a navy or for merchant shipping, and that is what La Bourdonnais chose to do. His intuition was to have far-reaching results in the future, as A. Toussaint's numerous studies have shown. From then onwards, Bourbon, with its fertile volcanic soils and great variety of microclimates, was systematically oriented towards agriculture.

The idea of La Bourdonnais (1735-46), and also of the royal administrators (1767-89), was that Bourbon should become the granary to feed Mauritius, its squadrons, troops and traders. To grow all this food more slaves were required, and to feed the increasing numbers of workers more land had to be put under cultivation. As a consequence, most of Bourbon's farm land was devoted to food crops, though cereals, vegetables and various grain crops did not displace speculative cash crops.

These cash crops were cultivated chiefly in the windward zone. After tobacco and cotton, the planters took to growing coffee. Fortunes were made with it under the Compagnie des Indes and later, after a lull, under the royal administration (2,500,000 pounds were harvested in 1744, 1,117,000 in 1765, then more than 2 million in 1771 and more than 3 million in 1788).

With the introduction of spice plants in the second third of the eighteenth century cloves were produced (200,000 pounds in 1802) and, in smaller quantities, nutmeg, ravensara, cinnamon and cocoa.

Where did the labour force that worked on these plantations come from?

J.-M. Filliot recounts that when the contingents drawn from Madagascar and the trading posts of Gorée, Ouidah and India proved insufficient, the French in the Mascarene Islands turned to the east coast of Africa. The first consignments of slaves from that area were organized under La Bourdonnais and came from the Portuguese trading posts south of Cape Delgado. After a drop towards the middle of the eighteenth century, there was a brisk revival of this traffic from East Africa. As regards areas under Portuguese control, Sofala, Mozambique and above all Ibo supplied shiploads. As regards territory under Arab control, the Zenguebar coast, which stretches from Cape Delgado to the Gulf of Aden, was systematically exploited when the monopoly of the Compagnie des Indes came to an end (1764). Along the Zenguebar coast, the islands of Quiloa and Zanzibar were those most frequented by the traders from the Mascarene archipelago. It is not possible from the documentation to determine the exact origin of the slave shipments. Many of them seem to have come from the western reaches of Lake Victoria and from the Lake Nyassa region. According to Filliot's estimates, the number of Kaffirs landed in the Mascarene Islands from 1770 onwards was at least five times as great as the number of Malagasy. The prohibition of the slave trade (1794-1802) curbed the traffic, but it flourished once again under Decaen (1803–10). Between 1769 and 1810 the Mascarene Islands would appear to have imported 115,000 slaves. Since, according to A. Toussaint, Mauritius imported about 63,000 slaves during the period 1773-1810, it is plausible to reckon that about 50,000 slaves were imported into Bourbon in the course of forty years (1769-1810).

By 1767 Bourbon's population numbered 21,047 slaves and 5,237 whites. By 1779 the number of slaves had risen to 30,209 and that of whites to 6,464, and there were also 465 'coloured' freemen. By 1788 there were 33,377 slaves, 8,182 whites and 1,029 'coloured' freemen.

On the basis of partial censuses carried out in each commune from 1805 to 1808, an attempt has been made to classify slaves according to 'caste', i.e. place of origin (unpublished study by C. Wanquet). By 1808 there were about 13,500 whites, 2,800 'coloured' freemen and 54,000 slaves. Of the latter, 23,013 were Creoles, 17,476 came from Mozambique, 11,547 were Malagasy and 1,690 Indians or Malays. In the light of this composition of the slave population one might perhaps query, so far as Bourbon is concerned, J.-M. Filliot's hypothesis concerning the high proportion of slave convoys from East Africa after 1770. Possibly the phenomenon was short-lived, and was more pronounced on Mauritius than on Bourbon. In any case, it is evident that the trade in Malagasy slaves in this island was not insignificant in the late eighteenth century and early nineteenth.

From 1815 to 1860

During this short period Réunion's economy relied mainly on sugar-cane growing, which reached a peak in its development, and there was a frantic search for agricultural labour, which resulted in an influx of Africans, Malagasy and Indians.

In a work published in 1828, the comptroller Thomas seemed just as certain as La Bourdonnais had been that the island's prosperity should be founded on agriculture. 'From the earliest times of its settlement', he writes, 'rice, wheat and maize were cultivated by the settlers and grew most successfully, guaranteeing its future prosperity.' A detailed survey of soil utilization in each commune shows that between 1815 and 1860 food crops had to compete with sugar-cane but often held their own. While the decline of rice and especially wheat was irretrievable, maize was still widespread. Along with manioc, 'dry' vegetables, root crops and tubers and a multitude of kitchen garden products, it provided employment for part of the labour force. Between 1834 and 1860, for instance, the area under food crops at Saint-Paul remained unchanged (5,300 hectares) and at Sainte-Suzanne and Saint-Leu increased (from 1,100 to 1,300 hectares and from 1,700 to 2,200 hectares, respectively). Elsewhere there was a more or less pronounced decline.

Sugar-cane ousted the various cash crops more decisively than the food crops. The 1806 and 1807 cyclones and the diplomatic and economic situation (foreign competition, taking of Mauritius by the British, loss of San Domingo, need for sugar) gave the planters an incentive to look for some crop to replace coffee and spices. There are records attesting to the presence of sugar-cane in Réunion as early as the seventeenth century, but until the nineteenth century it was grown only on a small-scale family basis. From 1815 to 1827 its cultivation expanded rapidly, and after a few years' hesitation its dominant role remained undisputed from 1834 to 1860 (21 tonnes of sugar in 1815, 15,200 tonnes in 1829, 30,000 in 1846 and 73,000 in 1860). Out of the 100,000 hectares of land under cultivation in 1860, some 62,000 were planted with sugar-cane. Owing to the high market prices paid for sugar, a further 10,000 hectares were cleared and devoted to sugar-cane between 1857 and 1860 alone.

What is paradoxical in these radical changes in Réunion's agriculture is that they occurred so late. The inhabitants of Réunion discovered long after the inhabitants of the Antilles just how much manpower the 'sugar-god' demanded. By that time the slave trade was compromised. Prohibited by the British authorities as from 1807 and by the French as from 1817, the importation of slaves took the form of smuggling to circumvent the increasingly tight controls. The authorities, while tolerant at first, became strict, and the severity of the 1831 legislation seemed calculated to discourage further attempts. Besides, the authors generally situate the end of the slave trade in 1830 or 1831. A study based on demographic data, police reports, administrative correspondence, records of court cases and private archives shows that the traffic did not end before 1834 and possibly not until later. The inference to be drawn from the study is that about 45,000 slaves were smuggled into Bourbon between 1817 and 1848, the vast majority of them during the period 1817-31.

Where did these slaves come from?

In the rare cases in which their origin is indicated, Madagascar is most often referred to, the exact locality sometimes being given—Tamatave, Fort-Dauphin or Sainte-Marie. Next comes the east coast of Africa with occasional references to Zanzibar or Mozambique. Only once are Malays mentioned (the Alcyon transported 270 Malays in 1830, and 144 were said to have perished during a mutiny).

While these fragmentary data do not convey a clear picture of the ethnic composition of the slave population imported in the nineteenth century, it gives some indication of the circumstances in which slaves arrived in Bourbon. Rebellions were exceptional, but losses of lives seem to have been everyday occurrences. It is estimated that in the thirty-year period immediately preceding the prohibition of the slave trade the rate of loss among slaves from Madagascar en route was 12 per cent and among slaves from East Africa 21 per cent (A. Toussaint). All the evidence points to the conclusion that the mortality rates were higher at the time when the slave trade was clandestine, owing to the need for secrecy, the overcrowding and the absence of sanitary precautions. The landing at night on a beach pounded by breakers was not effected without loss of life, and it was by a forced march that the new recruits were taken, without transition, to the plantation where they received the shock of a world incomprehensible to them.

The massive arrival of these 'savages and pagans' to join the labour force may have contributed to the deterioration of the living conditions of the slaves. Its effects were superimposed on the consequences of the revolutionary period and the British occupation (1810-15), marked by a breath of freedom the inhabitants remembered with dread (threats to slavery, too many emancipations, revolt of the slaves at Saint-Leu in 1811). Above all, the island discovered the demands made by the sugar industry and the need for capitalist concentration. While in the eighteenth century slavery may have seemed more 'paternalistic' in Bourbon than in Mauritius, where the main concern was to make a quick profit, in the nineteenth century there appears to have been a regression, noticeable in such matters as discipline, health, food, marriage and the family life of the slave. The humanitarian regulations laid down under the restored monarchy (1810-48) had more theoretical than practical significance in Bourbon.

However, after the abolition of slavery in 1848 the inhabitants, whose plantations were expanding rapidly, had to rely increasingly on the recruitment of freemen. The first of these had arrived in 1829.

The thesis prepared by J.-M. Filliot makes it possible to study this population movement. A few brief remarks will suffice here: in 1834 the population of the island totalled about 106,000 inhabitants, comprising 34,282 whites and 'coloured' freemen, 69,983 slaves and about 2,000 immigrants (Archives of Réunion, estimates given by the mayors). Estimates of the number of immigrants in 1860 vary according to the source, between 55,000 and 65,000, and of the local population between 123,000 and 135,000. The higher figure is the more plausible. Accordingly, in 1860 Réunion would appear to have had 200,000 inhabitants. Immigrant labour at the end of 1859 was estimated at 37,005 Indians, 27,522 Africans and 443 Chinese (J.-F. Dupon).

The Chinese were brought in as agricultural workers in 1844. There were 728 of them in 1845. This group did not settle: by about 1880 the last of the Chinese had left. Labour was recruited from areas as remote as the Pacific islands (Archives of Réunion, the case of the Sutton in 1857), but preferably in East Africa and Madagascar, the scene of the earlier slave trade. There, the slaves went through the dubious transactions of prior redemption and hiring themselves out as 'volunteers'. This form of recruiting was prohibited in 1859.

As in the case of Mauritius, though on a smaller scale, India was the principal supplier of recruits. As early as 1729 Dumas had introduced a hundred or so Indian workers into Bourbon. Exactly one hundred years later the first free agricultural workers were also brought from India. In 1860, when the sugar-cane industry reached its peak, their camps were concentrated in the sugar zones along the coasts of Réunion, where they were to leave their mark on the population.

From 1860 to date

The competition of beet sugar from 1861 onwards, the borers that attacked the cane in 1863, cholera in 1859 and malaria in 1865 dealt the people of Réunion and their agriculture the first heavy blows. Sugar production dropped from 73,000 tonnes in 1860 tot 23,000 tonnes in 1870. Malnutrition, epidemics and alcoholism pushed up the mortality rates.

The inhabitants did not resign themselves to this stagnation: a slow revival of sugar production (39,000 tonnes in 1890, 45,000 in 1910) was accompanied by the introduction of other crops (vanilla towards the end of the nineteenth century, geraniums early in the twentieth). Manpower continued to be brought in from abroad: 6,994 coolies were brought into the island in 1861, and 4,943 in 1862. Immigrants continued to arrive, though in diminishing numbers, until 1885, in which year the last shipload of Indian immigrants landed. At that time, 117,813 persons had been registered with the Immigration Service. In 1891, out of a total population of 160,000 inhabitants, about 25,000 were Indians. As in the slave population in earlier times, there was a marked imbalance of the sexes. This male community, ill fed, ill treated, ill paid or not paid at all, resorted to delinquency, to running away and to traditional religious practices ('Malabar' rites).

When Indian immigration ceased, agricultural labour was sought elsewhere, with numerically limited results. From 1888 to 1900, some 3,000 Kaffirs were introduced. This was the last wave of workers from Mozambique. In addition, some Malagasy prisoners of war arrived at this time. Early in the twentieth century 173 Tonkinese came to Réunion as 'contract labour' for a specified period, and 808 Chinese from Foochow were decimated there by malaria. Just after the 1914 war about 3,000 Antanandro were recruited in Madagascar and, finally, in 1933, 735 Rodriguez islanders entered Réunion. This was the last of the migrations due to the needs of Réunion's agriculture.

Two groups of immigrants were attracted by the fringe of tertiary activities whose expansion was made possible by sugar. In the second half of the nineteenth century Chinese came from Canton on their own initiative to engage in retail trade. The presence of the first Chinese shopkeeper at Saint-Denis was recorded in 1861. In the ensuing years, his compatriots settled all around the island and in the upland villages. In 1861, Réunion's Chinese shopkeepers numbered 547, including 17 women and 50 children (J. Defos du Rau). Muslim Indians, who had come in the main from Gujarat between 1880 and 1900, concentrated in Saint-Denis and the principal towns. They were known locally as 'Z'Arabes'. They specialized in tailoring and then in the textile trade. The 1921 census records 709 of them, under the heading 'Bombay Indians'.

The establishment of this motley population and certain technical achievements, such as the construction of a railway (1882) and the opening of a port at Pointe-des-Galets (1884), might give the erroneous impression of steady advancement. The economic difficulties and demographic stagnation are evidence to the contrary. From 1902 to 1912, the average mortality rate was 2.4 per cent, the chief cause of death being malaria, which was responsible for 2,000 deaths annually (Réunion Archives). The island's population declined from 175,293 inhabitants in 1912 to 173,190 in 1921. An upward trend is noticeable in 1926 (186,637 inhabitants); and by 1931, the figure for the total population (198,000) was almost back to the 1860 level. In consequence of the higher rate of natural demographic growth the population rose to 220,000 in 1941. However, in 1946, when the colony became a *département* of France, it had only 227,500 inhabitants. Malaria continued to cause the death of 1,000 to 1,500 people annually until 1950. The eradication of this disease and the protection of mothers and children and social legislation were responsible for the strong rise in the population figures: from 275,000 in 1954 to 350,000 in 1961, to 425,000 in 1967 and to 473,000 in 1973.

Sugar production, after the vicissitudes attributable to local conditions and to the world situation (for example, it rose to 110,000 tonnes in 1940 and then dropped to 13,000 tonnes in 1944), passed the 200,000-tonne mark in 1957 and since then has fluctuated between 200,000 and 260,000 tonnes, save in an exceptional year. However, agriculture is no longer, as it was up to the end of the nineteenth century, the magnet attracting settlers. On the contrary, it might be said that people are disenchanted with agriculture: farmers are leaving the land and increasingly are leaving Réunion. The emigration agency arranged for the departure of 623 islanders in 1963; in 1973, the outflow reached the figure of 4,722.

The peasant society based on mixed farming is no more attractive to young islanders aspiring to advancement than was the plantation society. Owing to the archaism of the one and the 'bipolarization' of the other, they look to the French industrial society or to the pseudo-industrial society established by France in this remote *département* (J. Benoist). It could hardly be otherwise now that commerce and services account for so large a share of the gross domestic product. In 1970 these activities represented 57,165 million CFA francs out of a total of 81,702 million, whereas agriculture (including sugar-cane) accounted for 8,514 million and industry (including sugar) for 16,022 million. Regarded as servile, work on the land has lost its economic efficacy without regaining its dignity in the scale of local values. Back in the eighteenth century, and even more in the nineteenth, the inhabitants and the authorities were as anxious to import manpower for agriculture as to export useless mouths. The latter were the 'poor whites', who formed an idle proletariat, apparently debarred by their ethnic origin from working the land. Enlistment in the army and emigration to Madagascar were among the solutions devised to counter their proliferation. What is new today, then, is not the emigration as such, but the fact that it involves indiscriminately descendants of the early French settlers, of slaves and of 'coloured' freemen. Agriculture was at the origin of the inflow. Its inability to ensure a decent living is responsible for the outflow.

Lines of research

While Réunion was the subject of an important geography thesis by J. Defos du Rau, it has not given rise to any historical works of the scope and standard of A. Toussaint's on Mauritius.

Apart from the first few decades, on which the researches of J. Barassin and A. Lougnon have shed light, most of the island's history is almost unknown. The only reference works available are old publications (e.g. Azéma, Betting de Lancastel, Brunet, Thomas), brief surveys (e.g. Scherer) and a few studies on specific aspects written by specialists in disciplines other than history (e.g. H. Foucque, J. Mas, Y. Pérotin, J. Defos du Rau, R. Chaudenson, J.-F. Dupon).

The establishment of a Local History Centre within Réunion's Centre of Higher Studies has made it possible to undertake further research in association with the University of Provence. Since 1970, four dissertations have been submitted by students reading for the master's degree dealing with the political and administrative life of Réunion in the nineteenth century and its economy at the time of the Second Empire. Articles on the eighteenth and nineteenth centuries have been written or are being prepared by teachers at the Centre.

In the next few years State doctoral theses will throw new light on the following subjects: *L'Ile Bourbon, Terre Féodale (1663–1767)* (J. Barassin); *La Réunion pendant l'Epoque Révolutionnaire* (C. Wanquet); *Les Problèmes de Peuplement aux Mascareignes au XIXe Siècle* (J.-M. Filliot) and *Une Société Coloniale devant le Problème de l'Esclavage: la Réunion de 1815 à 1860* (H. Gerbeau).

The geography thesis by J.-F. Dupon (1974) *(Étude Thématique des Aspects de la Dépendance dans l'Ensemble Insulaire Mascareignes-Seychelles)* will be useful to historians, as will be the research carried out by anthropologists (J. Benoist on the Indians, and Denise Helly on the Chinese in Réunion).

However, many areas remain shrouded in mystery.

In some cases it is the research techniques that have been neglected, as, for example, archaeological excavation, which might be attempted in the caves occupied by runaway slaves.

Then again, there are periods that have not yet found their historian, e.g. the period following 1870.

Some subjects demand accurate statistical data: it has been found that the statistics concerning population and the economy from the eighteenth to the middle of the twentieth century are full of mistakes and in some cases purely fictional. What is required is studies such as those of G. Debien on the origin of the slaves in the Antilles. Whether they are realizable is problematical. The problem is the same in regard to the demographic studies that need to be carried out on the slaves, on those who were emancipated in 1848 and on the hired freemen.

The most serious gap, and the most disturbing one in a history of civilizations, concerns the folk culture. The silence of the slaves, the hired freemen and their descendants, seemed unbroken in Réunion. A thesis like R. Chaudenson's on the 'parler créole', the recent investigations made by anthropologists, the preparation of an anthology of stories by B. de Gamaleya, are beginning to show that there was not silence, but rather a screen, and that cultural alienation was not complete.

Conclusion

Réunion, a small island with a surface area of 2,512 square kilometres and a present population of about 500,000, is virtually a microcosm. In the course of a history less brilliant than that of neighbouring Mauritius, it has received its distinctive mark not from sea-borne trade, but from agriculture. In both cases, the economy was dominated by sugar-cane. Over the three centuries of its history, Asia, Africa and Europe met in Réunion through the Indian Ocean. Underneath the superficial gloss left by the French administration, the wealth of cultural contacts and the complexity of 'acculturation' have many surprises still in store for research workers.

Select bibliography

BARASSIN, J.; GERBEAU, H.; WANQUET, C. Cartes historiques et notices inédites pour l'*Atlas de la Réunion*. Paris, Institut Géographique National, 1976.

BENOIST, J. *Structure et Changement de la Société Rurale Réunionnaise*. Saint-Denis, 1974.

CHAUDENSON, R. *Le Lexique du Parler Créole de la Réunion*. Paris, H. Champion, 1974.

DEFOS DU RAU, J. *L'Ile de la Réunion, Étude de Géographie Humaine*. Bordeaux, 1960.

DELABARRE DE NANTEUIL. *Législation de l'Ile Bourbon*. Paris, 1st ed., J.-B. Gros, 1844, 3 Vols.; 2nd. ed., 1861–63, 6 Vols.

DUPON, J.-F. Les Immigrants Indiens de la Réunion. *Les Cahiers d'Outre-mer*, 1967, p. 49–88.

FILLIOT, J.-M. *La Traite Africaine vers les Mascareignes*. Tananarive, ORSTOM, 1972. (Mimeo.)

——. *La Traite des Esclaves vers les Mascareignes au XVIIIe Siècle*. Tananarive, ORSTOM, 1970. (Mimeo.)

GERBEAU, H. *Quelques Aspects de la Traite Interlope à Bourbon au XIXe Siècle*. Saint-Denis, 1972. (Mimeo.)

LEGRAS, R. Note sur l'Immigration à la Réunion. In: *Recueil de Documents et Travaux Inédits pour Servir à l'Histoire de la Réunion*, No. I, Bérac, 1954, p. 53–65.

SCHERER, A. *Histoire de la Réunion*. Paris, Presses Universitaires de France, 1965.

Statistiques sur la Réunion. Direction Départementale de l'Agriculture et Institut National de Statistiques et d'Études Économiques, Saint-Denis.

THOMAS, P. P.-U. *Essai de Statistique de l'Ile Bourbon*. Paris, 1828. 2 Vols.

TOUSSAINT, A. *La Route des Iles*. Paris, SEVPEN, 1967.

——. *Histoire des Iles Mascareignes*. Paris, Berger-Levrault, 1972.

Part III
Indian Ocean studies

A proposal for Indian Ocean studies

J. de V. Allen

It is the object of this article[1] to suggest that the Indian Ocean as an area for academic study is at the moment seriously undersubscribed in terms both of academic personnel and of funds. There is an urgent need for expanded and better co-ordinated research programmes not only because the region deserves to be studied in its own right but also because such research would unquestionably throw a useful light on major problems facing those already studying in areas bordering on it—in South-East Asia, the Indian subcontinent, the Arabo-Persian world and (above all perhaps) East and Central Africa. To speak of the need for expansion is not, of course, to minimize what has already been done. On the contrary, it is largely due to the efforts of those already working in this field that we are able to realize how important the Indian Ocean is; and I should like to start with a tribute to them, although regrettably space prevents me from summarizing their achievements.[2] Much of the paper will instead be taken up with evidence that there has been over a long period what we might tentatively call an Indian Ocean culture—some would even say an Indian Ocean civilization—to which all lands bordering on it owe at least something, although a good deal of this evidence has still to be posed in the form of unexamined parallels and untested hypotheses. And I shall conclude with a few very provisional proposals for bringing about the suggested expansion and co-ordination of future researches.

The case for Indian Ocean studies is not easily perceived or documented in a short article. But as well as having done research for some years in South-East Asia and for several more in East Africa, I have been fortunate to attend in recent years two conferences, the Conference on East Africa and the Orient convened by Robert Rotberg and Neville Chittick in Nairobi in March 1967, and the Fourth International Conference on Asian History

1. This article is a revised version of a paper presented to the University of East Africa Social Sciences Council Conference, held in Makerere University College, Kampala, in January 1969.
2. One name, that of Auguste Toussaint, is outstanding, and his elegant history of the Indian Ocean published in its English version in 1962 must long remain a classic introduction.

sponsored by the International Asian History Association and held in Kuala Lumpur in August 1968; and from both formally presented papers and informal discussions on these two occasions have gained much material for the arguments put forward here. I should extend my thanks to the organizers and participants in both conferences and hope that they will have no objection to my reproducing the gist of many of the points made where I have been unable to seek permission from the authors for express quotation. Since it is a large part of my argument that Indian Ocean studies are undersubscribed and have suffered by being partitioned between other area studies, it is perhaps not inappropriate that I should have to draw heavily on the views of these eminent scholars from adjoining areas as evidence for the existence and importance of the Indian Ocean area.

A definition of the Indian Ocean as a study-area is no easier than a definition of say, South-East Asia in the same context, probably even more difficult; but for the moment we may envisage it as including the following: the coastlands of all East Africa from the Limpopo to Djibouti or even Suez ('coast-lands' stretching far inland in some places such as the hinterland of Sofala and the Tana River); the Arabian Peninsula and most of modern Iraq and Iran; the southern part of Pakistan and the Gujarati-speaking areas around Bombay; at least the southern part of the Indian subcontinent, including Calcutta; the Krah Peninsula and the whole of the Malay Peninsula, including the east coast, which does not touch the Indian Ocean, but not, in general, Thailand nor Indo-China; and most of the Indonesian Archipelago, including Borneo and at least the southern, Muslim districts of the Philippines but excluding Papua New Guinea. For some purposes the west and north-west coast of Australia might be included[1]. And of course Madagascar and the other islands and archipelagoes in the ocean would be central, with the conceivable exception of Sri Lanka.

The rationale for this definition would be as follows: most of the areas mentioned have been for many centuries Muslim, retaining on the whole close links with the mainstream of Islamic thought and civilization, and with the great Arab centres of the Muslim world. It is true that large Muslim areas such as North Africa are excluded, but I believe we can posit a distinction between Muslim maritime civilization, or at least those regions where the advent of Islam was closely associated with trade, and the Muslim land empires, conquered mainly by the sword; although the Arabian Peninsula would, in the nature of things, have to be included as key to both. If Sri Lanka were excluded, it would be because it has seldom in its history been

---

1. It has been suggested to me by Dr Colin Jack-Hinton, of the University of Western Australia, that submarine archaeology on this coast might produce useful information about early trading routes, types of vessel and so on.

particularly outward-looking in terms of trade and culture, nor Islamic.[1] The same would apply to most of Burma and Thailand. At first sight, for instance, fishing villages in East Africa, Borneo, Sumatra and the east coast of Malaya resemble each other much more markedly than any of them resemble fishing villages in Sri Lanka or the Gulf of Siam. Those in the Arabized part of Madagascar around Majunga would also conform to this general type. Indeed throughout most of the Indian Ocean area as I have defined it the Arab or pseudo-Arab, whether merchant or imam, would be an astonishingly constant phenomenon, wearing much the same clothes and conducting himself in much the same way wherever he was found.

But the Indian Ocean has not always been predominantly Muslim, and it is because of what it was before the Prophet, and because of the singularly enduring and pervasive nature of the culture of that particular region even since, that Indian Ocean studies cannot really be contemplated without including (largely non-Muslim) south India. Hindu rituals in Bali; Indian influences in the languages and literature, architecture and music of many ostensibly Arabo-Muslim or Malayo-Muslim societies; very long-established trading or migratory links between south India (including Goa) and all parts of the Indian Ocean, west and east, as well as the enormous movements of Indians to the islands and coastal areas that have taken place in more modern times, some of them under imperialist auspices—all these things make it quite unthinkable that one should exclude India, and particularly the (relatively little-studied) Dravidian south India, from the Indian Ocean world. To do so would be like trying to write a history of Christendom without any mention of ancient Greece.

There is a third major source of unity in the Indian Ocean area as I have defined it, albeit a less important one than the other two, and that is the Malay race.[2] What must seem to be one of the major migrations of the last two millenniums, but one about which we still know practically nothing, was the movement of Malay-speaking peoples across the Indian Ocean to Madagascar and the eastern shores of Africa. Opinions as to when and how such a movement took place differ widely, but it is generally assumed that they occurred before the Hinduization of South-East Asia was completed, but not long before—say between A.D. 400 and 1000—and that some at any rate of the migratory waves must have been quite large ones. They may well

1. I do not wish to exaggerate the isolation of Sri Lanka from the Indian Ocean worlds. It had important contacts with Srivijaya—a Chronicle of Srivijaya, written in Sinhalese on rocks at Anuradhapura was reported by S. Paranavitana at the 1963 Asian History Conference. There are also Malay populations who may have been there for some time; and of course in Portuguese and Dutch times Sri Lanka was central.
2. Throughout this paper I use 'Malaya' in its geographical sense to refer only to the Malay Peninsula, 'Malaysia' in its former non-political sense covering the entire Malay world.

have been related to simultaneous migratory waves of other Malay races into South-East Asia and Malaysia itself.

There are other movements of peoples that must also have contributed in large measure to Indian Ocean unity. Apart from Indian migrations already mentioned, we may particularly note the so-called 'Shirazi' colonization of East Africa's coastline and the export of large numbers of Africans sent as slaves back to the Middle East regions from which the Shirazis purportedly came—such large numbers that already by A.D. 694, and again from 868 to 883, they were responsible for rebellions on a massive scale in Mesopotamia. But the Malay migrations both within South-East Asia and from thence to Madagascar and Africa must be held to eclipse these other ones in significance, even if not necessarily in the actual number of migrants.

We thus have, in the Indian Ocean area, what might be envisaged as three layers of unity, although of course not all three layers are to be found in all districts. First, there is racial unity of a sort provided by Malay and other migrations; secondly, cultural unity radiating out from the Indian subcontinent; and thirdly, the religious unity provided by Islam, which of all religions has probably been the most successful in subduing, though not necessarily eliminating, political, racial and cultural differences among its adherents. These three layers, as I have called them, were regularly refreshed and reinforced, at least until very recently, by a constant intercourse between most of the lands concerned. Traders from the Indian subcontinent and the Persian Gulf, teachers, holy men, dynasts and would-be dynasts from Arabia, fishermen, pilgrims and nakhodas from South-East Asia were still to be met in practically any port you cared to mention in large numbers at the beginning of this century. Many still circulate, but the growth of national, regional and continental sentiment and the corresponding increase of bureaucratic and other obstructions has reduced the number of them considerably of late.

Of such ingredients, and many others besides, is Indian Ocean unity composed. Perhaps the easiest way, on this occasion, to provide tangible evidence of this unity, and at the same time to stress the need to investigate it further, will be to list the kinds of problem that await investigation, and the types of source available for such investigation, by each academic discipline in turn: history, geography, archaeology, ethnomusicology, ethnobotany, ethnobiology, linguistics, Islamic and comparative religious studies, sociology, nautical science, oceanology and so on. I make no apology for beginning with history. Not only is it my own subject, it is also, so it seems to me, the most obvious parent for all other disciplines in this area, since most of the factors that have united the Indian Ocean area go back a long way in time. I would go further and suggest that one of the main reasons why Indian studies have been relatively more successful as an area study than African studies is that in Indian studies two long-established and well-founded disciplines, history and linguistics-literature (since, alas, divorced) have been fairly widely accepted as parent disciplines under whose aegis scholars in other fields have been content to play their own distinctive roles. If any discipline has been the senior one in African studies, I suppose it has been social anthropology; and the basic assumptions of social anthropologists have become so unacceptable to many that they have failed to provide a firm basis for students of other disciplines to work on. However, this is, and must for some time remain, an open question.

The historian turning to the Indian Ocean area is faced with a far larger amount of documentary evidence than is often realized. There are, for instance, a fair number of Greek, Roman and Byzantine sources, apart from the well-known *Periplus of the Erythrean Sea,* and the geographies of Ptolemy and Strabo. Some work, for instance, is at the moment being done by a British scholar on the Roman spice trade;[1] and it is to be hoped that this provide valuable information about the Indian Ocean in the early centuries and about Rome. Greek and Byzantine accounts of early explorations and of the exploits of Alexander the Great and Middle Eastern empires should also be scrutinized for data relevant to Indian Ocean history. Geographers have an important role to play here and elsewhere in the study of place-names and location of ancient sites. There may also be some room for geologists, since there is here and there evidence that the coastline may have changed considerably in relatively recent times.[2] At the other end of the Indian Ocean, and not only at the other end, Chinese documentary sources (especially useful because of their rigidly correct chronology) have been shown to be of the greatest value. We can now see that Duyvendak's pioneering work, *China's Discovery of Africa* (1947), was only a beginning. It turns out that the Chinese knew of two snow-capped mountains in East Africa, of a series of great inland lakes and of a great river running north from them long before Krapf, Speke and Co. 'discovered' these things for Europe.[3] A caveat should however be added: it is regrettably clear that it is highly dangerous for non-Sinologists to attempt to interpret Chinese sources, especially from translations, without a detailed knowledge of the rules and conventions governing Chinese diplomacy and official history. The long-standing myth, duly imbedded in many textbooks, that Chinese sources 'prove' that the first two Emperors of Malacca were the same man, recently

1. Innes Miller, formerly of the Malayan Civil Service.
2. In Manda Island in the Lamu archipelago recent excavations by Chittick show that the ninth-century ruins are below the present sea level.
3. See the paper presented to the East Africa and the Orient Conference by Paul Wheatley. The papers presented at this Conference have been published under the title *East Africa and the Orient*, New York, Africana Press, 1975.

exploded with little difficulty by the first Sinologist to turn his attention to the subject,[1] provides an object-lesson in this.

Both the Graeco-Roman world and the Chinese empire were marginal to the Indian Ocean. The Arabs and Persians, on the other hand, and the great empires of south India, were most of them fairly central to it (even if it was not necessarily central to them) and it seems a fair *prima facie* assumption that the literature of these regions, properly examined by scholars with an adequate background knowledge, should provide an even richer yield. The Arab geographers in particular promise well. Of special interest is the fact that most of them assumed that the south-west end of the ocean was linked by land with the north-east end, and that they referred to Madagascar and to the Malay and other lands of South-East Asia by the same name, (usually) Qumr, a word evidently linked with the name of the Khmer empire and which reappears in the name of the Comoro Islands. Just one example of the sort of thing that emerges from these sources: Buzurg ibn Shahrivar, writing between 930 and 947, records that in 945–46 the far eastern Waq-Waq invaded the coast and islands of East Africa in a thousand ships. (Waq-Waq are commonly identified with Qumr: Idrisi, d. 1154, identified Ard al-Waq-Waq as the mysterious area stretching from beyond Sofala to the far-eastern islands.) They spent over a year on the voyage and pillaged and conquered villages of Sofala and Zanj, and when asked why they had come replied that they sought products useful to their country—tortoise-shell, ambergris, ivory and leopardskins and also slaves, for the people of Zanj, on account of their physique, made good slaves and were much sought after.[2] Some time before the thirteenth century, people of Qumr are reported to have conquered and for a while ruled Aden, arriving in outrigger canoes; but it is generally assumed that these people, although they may have been of Indonesian stock, came from the Comoros or at furthest Madagascar since 'they came in one season and in one voyage'.[3] Apart from the light they throw on Malay migrations, Arab sources seem certain to be of value in tracing movements of peoples to and from East Africa and Arabia-Mesopotamia; and an examination of them by someone well-acquainted with other relevant literature concerning the peopling of the East African coast might well reveal something of value.[4]

Apart from documentary sources derived from great empires, most of which are fairly ancient, it seems at least possible that there are in existence a great number of what I may call local documents of more recent

1. See Wang Gungwu, 'The First Three Rulers of Malacca', *Journal of the Malaysian Branch, Royal Asiatic Society*, Vol. XLI, i, 1963.
2. See J. Spencer-Trimingham's paper to the East Africa and the Orient Conference, 1967.
3. See D. B. Dee's paper to the same conference.
4. See J. Spencer-Trimingham's and A. W. J. Prins' papers, 1967 conference.

date not yet exploited. An example is the apparently rich hoard of documents, mostly in Arabized Swahili but some in Arabic, discovered in Lamu by J. W. T. Allen in 1966[1] Unfortunately these have not yet been examined in any detail, but it appears that some are of literary and some of commercial interest, and it is not out of the question that some may be explicitly historical. Lamu, Pate and Kilwa are all already known to have their own chronicles although only the last has yet been found in any form of antiquity (and that has proved controversial enough) and it might not be too outrageous a supposition that at some time the people of Majunga, the Comoros, Mogadishu and elsewhere attempted similar works: certainly in the Malay world there are the Malacca Chronicle, Hikayat Johor, Hikayat Atjeh, Hikayat Riau, etc. The precise value of these local documents—the Atthidography of the Indian Ocean—is debatable: but one thing is certain, and that is that they cannot be entirely ignored by historians, especially as they often deal with periods about which we otherwise know nothing, even if they obviously cannot be taken at their face value. I frankly do not know what sort of written material might be discovered in south India and in the Maldives, Laccadives, Nicobars, Andamans, etc. But it seems conceivable that, even if there are no chronicles, there may exist in some of these places records of the great merchant houses and concerns over several centuries, shipping records and so on. In this respect, as in so many, India at the moment represents a large and inexcusable lacuna in our knowledge.

And last but not least in the list of documentary sources, conveniently filling in many gaps, is the Portuguese and Dutch literature on the area. It is fashionable to sneer at such sources, but it is as well to remember that, provided they are not used uncritically nor exclusively where other materials exist, they have proved generally more useful than indigenous sources in, say, South-East Asia;[2] and they have the undoubted advantage that there is probably a larger supply of scholars ready-equipped to make use of them and who have some experience of when and how to read between the lines. The impact of Portugal and the Netherlands on the Indian Ocean is undoubtedly important in certain spheres (though not all), and the 'Portuguese Indian Ocean' and 'Dutch Indian Ocean' would inevitably form two separate aspects of Indian Ocean studies that would merit individual attention. Moreover, both these European nations made their presence felt from the end of the fifteenth to the middle of the twentieth centuries, and observed and recorded a good deal. All-important is the fact that the Dutch, in particular, were wont to describe in great detail one thing of vital importance to Indian

1. J. W. T. Allen's papers, 1967.
2. Even in East and Central African history Portuguese sources can sometimes prove quite invaluable. Those who doubt this should examine the paper on the Malawi Empire and the Yao given to the 1967 Conference by E. A. Alpers.

Ocean research: the volume of trade. Trade was of course the life-blood of all Indian Ocean civilizations, and we have ample evidence of it from earliest times: the relief carvings at Deir al Gebrawi, Egypt, dating from the Sixth Dynasty; the *Periplus* and the account, for instance, of Socotra as an island peopled by a mixture of Greeks, Indians and Arabs mainly engaged in commerce; Persian and Chinese pottery littering beaches throughout the area; the record of ships from Malindi in the harbour of sixteenth-century Malacca, and so on. But anything like statistics for trade, unless it comes from the unexplored documentation of India, would be very hard to come by until the Dutch, with their passion for recording such matters, make their entrance. As well as Dutch and Portuguese literature there is, of course, British and French for the last two or three centuries. But with one or two notable exceptions[1] this would be of less interest, since it was as a result of British and French activities that the Indian Ocean's basic unity began to disintegrate as imperialism constructed great, landward-facing empires from its component parts.

For the more orthodox historians who require documents, then, there is ample fare; but there are plenty of non-documentary sources too. And for archaeologists in particular the Indian Ocean offers probably more bread and butter than almost any part of the world except for the Mediterranean and the Middle East. Bread and butter, but not much jam: that is to say, there is a great volume of potsherds and many ruins dotted about but much less has survived whole, or nearly whole, than in the sands of Egypt or Mesopotamia or the gentle climate of the Mediterranean. Yet one can walk along the sandy beaches of the Lamu Archipelago and pick up without much difficulty, merely from the surface, literally dozens of pieces of ninth-tenth-century Persian 'Sassanian' ware, thirteenth-fifteenth-century Chinese celadon, Indian and Arabian glazed pottery, and perhaps even the occasional sample of Malagasy stoneware. From time to time one may even buy, in one of the villages, a seventeenth- or eighteenth-century Chinese bowl. If one then has the opportunity to cross to South-East Asia one may come across an identical bowl in a Dayak longhouse in Borneo or unearth a tenth-century Persian sherd in one of the islands off south Thailand that is, at least to the amateur's eye, the exact replica of what is being discovered in the earliest ruins in East Africa.

The volume, date and origin of these pieces are very significant because, through most of the area, pottery and porcelain seem to have been the main registers of prosperity and status: as still in Borneo, so earlier everywhere, imported pots and plates were placed on show in houses and public places

---

1. The work of the early nineteenth-century French traveller Guillain is an outstanding exception.

as evidence of wealth and luxury. There is therefore a close correlation between the amount of imported pottery discovered and the degree to which, and time when, a civilization flourished. In places like East Africa, particularly, where there was no major tradition of locally glazed pottery, if ruins yield no imported sherds it is not likely to be because the inhabitants were spending their wealth on something else; it would be because they had no wealth to spend.

Potsherds apart, there is a good deal else that the archaeologist or the social anthropologist may turn his eye to: certain types of domestic utensils, lamps, etc.; the origin of the supposedly phallic pillar-tombs, of the outrigger canoe and of the game known in Uganda as mwesso; beads and glassware (a massive recapitulation of the evidence in this sphere might produce vast additions to our existing knowledge, or might produce nothing); styles in metalwork and silverware (here the art historian has an important role to play); and even architectural styles and fashions in mosques and domestic dwellings. Those who doubt the value of this sort of research I can only refer to the dictum of Kirkman: describing the patterns in ceramics and utensils through the centuries, which archaeology in East Africa has revealed, he notes that they are 'comparable with patterns from other parts of the Indian Ocean (and) evidence of an Indian Ocean cultural unity which covered large distances and varying, often antipathetic cultures'. The same patterns and the same unity, he observes, may also be traceable in the humbler buildings and mosques, although this subject has unfortunately never been studied.[1] Certainly the little that has been done in some areas by way of studying architectural methods and styles has proved important: it is largely, at least, on evidence deduced from masonry and building techniques that Chittick has constructed his demolition (if you will excuse the mixed metaphor) of the Kilwa Chronicle and suggested a new date for the foundation of the 'Shirazi' dynasty in Kilwa, 'the 1066 of East African history'. This may be an appropriate moment to stress the significance of the fact that on the coast of East Africa there have been two major assaults on the version of events based on documents by scholars working from non-documentary sources.[2] Perhaps it may turn out (I would not for the moment put it more strongly) that, if Indian Ocean history has a sound skeleton of documentary matter, it has an even more ample flesh and sinew

---

1. J. Kirkman's paper to the 1967 conference.
2. As well as attacking the accepted date for the Shirazi colonization of Kilwa, Chittick has seriously criticized the orthodox account of the founding of Pate based on the evidence of the Pate Chronicle as a result of archaeological evidence. See his 'The "Shirazi" Colonization of East Africa', *Journal of African History*, Vol. VI, III, 1965, and his report on excavations in Pate in the second number of *Azania*; cf. his paper on 'The Peopling of the East African Coast' at the 1967 conference.

of artefacts of various types which, if looked at overall and not piecemeal, will allow us to recognize that it has a quite different shape from what we have hitherto believed. Or, to put it another way, perhaps it will turn out that 'cultural historians' in the broadest sense of that term, will have at least as important a part to play as their more orthodox 'documentary' colleagues.

Three somewhat specialized branches of knowledge have, as has long been recognized, a particularly important part to play in unravelling the problems of lands adjoining the Indian Ocean by means of research within its bounds. It will save time if I refer to them, not by their titles, but by the symbols of the chief problems they have to unravel; the xylophone, the banana and the cow. Along with them I think we should consider a fourth branch of knowledge upon which all must to some extent rely—linguistics. Now, I have not been unduly modest so far in dealing with topics of which I know little: but the xylophone and the banana in particular have engendered so much academic heat, particularly in this part of the world, that even I hesitate to say much about them. Nevertheless, a token point or two must be made.

Let me start with xylophones. It was not Jones but Wachsmann who drew attention to the fact that we find in Uganda a technique of xylophone playing, known as Amakonezi (the allocation of the two top keys of the instrument to a special player), which was reported by Curt Sachs in Madagascar and is also shown in a fourteenth-century relief in a temple at Panataran in Java. And it was Wachsmann, too, who noted that the bosses carved on some xylophone keys in Uganda were curiously like the bosses on the Java xylophone.[1]

Put alongside this the quite emphatic statement of M. D. Gwynne at the 1967 Nairobi conference that 'the great inland banana plantations of Uganda and west Kenya... must have been derived from ancestral material originating in Malaysia' and he would be a brave, perhaps even a foolhardy scholar who shrugged off the possibility of early links between the two areas. But what route did these links follow? Gwynne continues to note the '(the bananas) need not have come immediately from Malaysia for there could have been one or more intermediate sites, e.g. Arabian coast and Madagascar'.[2]

And again the fact that one of the three major types of cattle found in Africa, the humpless shorthorn, which is still found in Socotra and south Arabia, is mentioned as having existed relatively recently in Mafia, Pemba and Madagascar.[3] Let me record, finally, that I have heard it fiercely argued

1. 'Musicology in Uganda', *Journal of the Royal African Institute*, Vol. LXXXIII, No. 1, 1953, p. 54–6.
2. M. D. Gwynne's paper to the 1967 conference.
3. M. D. Gwynne's oral contribution to the same conference.

by a linguistics expert that the relationship between one of the Malgache words for sheep and the word for the same beast in Madi, north Uganda, proves conclusively that Madagascar must once have been peopled by ancestors of the Madi. Whatever reservations people may have about the certitude of some or all of these statements (and I myself have many), it must be conceded that they cannot be dismissed out of hand and must receive some immediate attention of scholars from all parts of the Indian Ocean (and East and Central African) area in all relevant disciplines working closely together. It is simply unscholarly to say that there is no evidence of East Africa owing a heavy debt to South-East Asian imports. This evidence may not yet be conclusive, but it exists in great abundance—what I have here mentioned is only the tiniest tip of the iceberg. We need not assume wholesale colonization or cultural imperialism—maybe there is some other explanation. But East and Central African history can only lose if we pretend the problem does not exist.

Let me suggest just one or two avenues that might profitably be explored in quest of a solution to this particular problem (which is, after all, only one of many such to which the answer lies in the Indian Ocean area). Jones himself has pointed out that Marcelle Urbain-Faublee finds the closest parallels to Malagasy art in the Celebes and claims that xylophonic evidence leads him to the same part of Indonesian archipelago.[1] Now one of the main problems as between Madagascar and Indonesia so far is that it has not proved possible to link the Malagasy language more closely with any one Indonesian dialect than with all the others: here is a pointer, surely, for linguists? The students of dimple-based pottery in East Africa, on the other hand, might consider the hypothesis of Wilhelm G. Sollheim II linking it with what he calls pottery of the Sa-Huynh Kalanay tradition in South-East Asia—particularly since very unusual burial-jar lids reported from Madagascar are reminiscent of one similar lid found in a Sa-Huynh Kalanay site and others found again on the west coast of Palowan Island in the Philippines, just opposite the Celebes.[2] More research could also be done in the islands which lie across the northern and southern Indian Ocean routes: Socotra, the Maldives and Laccadives, Andamans and Nicobars, Comoros, Seychelles, and Aldabra: what sort of cows, bananas, and xylophones, if any, do we find on these islands? I emphasize again that the answers to some of these questions may already be known, but if so there is an urgent need to communicate them to scholars in East Africa and South-East Asia. Even if findings are wholly negative, or conclusively prove that there were no links in any particular sphere, we shall have achieved something. The litter

1. A. M. Jones's paper to the 1967 conference.
2. W. G. Sollheim's paper to the 1967 conference.

of mistaken hypotheses cannot just be impatiently brushed under the mat: it must be painstakingly studied and then thrown firmly out of the door, or it will return to plague and obscure later work. My own belief, however, is that we shall be able to keep more than we throw away from these hypotheses. All that is needed is a deeper, wider, better co-ordinated academic effort to enable us to do so.

I have dealt all too briefly with the role of linguistics in Indian Ocean studies, but I hope it is so self-evidently important that I need say no more. I also omit, but because it is so obviously vital, not because I underestimate it, the role of Islamic scholars and students of comparative religion.

But what of sociologists and social anthropologists? There is of course a good deal of groundwork to be done and plenty of scope for comparative studies and overall conclusions. It may be, though I am far from sure, that as Grandidier has suggested,[1] we can detect Indonesian origins for certain features of Malagasy social behaviour and custom—the judicial personality of the wife, the father taking the name of his child, the frequency of adoption, the taboo on the king's name after his death, the two-stage burial, the cult of the royal relics, and so on. Even if we hesitate to establish any meaningful link lasting over so many centuries, these topics deserve attention in their own right, as do the ways and customs of the populations of African slave stock now living in the Middle East (the contrast between the amount of attention lavished upon transatlantic slave populations and our ignorance about trans-Indian Ocean ones is embarrassing). To these and similar problems associated with individual societies or groups of societies should be added the more generalized problems such as the impact of Muslim law upon different Indian Ocean societies and the repercussions of doctrinal disputes in the Islamic religion upon different peoples of the region. All these questions demand active fieldwork by sociologists or social anthropologists on the spot.

But there is also, it seems to me, a pressing need for armchair sociologists, theory-spinners examining the minutiae of evidence from all over and excogitating new theories to explain the fundamental problems of the area, such as methods of cultural spread, syncretism of values and harmonization of different civilizations and ways of life. The Indian Ocean would appear to provide a paradise for research workers interested in how one culture infects another—how, for instance, Indonesian music might have deeply influenced African music without extensive colonization (a problem historians cannot pretend to have gone any way towards solving) or how a Hindu 'substratum' has modified the operations of Islam in certain spheres in specific regions. The consequences of large-scale migrations upon both the

1. Cited in M. Deschamps' paper to the 1967 conference.

migrants and upon host societies; the different fate of the institution of kingship at different ends of the ocean; the problem of what constitutes a 'maritime civilization'—recently touched upon by A. H. Prins in his *Sailing from Lamu*—all these broad questions might very profitably occupy the attention of sociological thinkers interested in broadly applicable theories rather than in the facts themselves. One question above all should preoccupy them, and that is one which I have consistently begged throughout this paper: what is a 'culture' or a 'civilization'? And in what sense can the Indian Ocean area be said to have shared a single, collective one as well as the various distinct ones undeniably existing within it?

I have left to the last two disciplines or subdisciplines upon whose findings all the rest are to some extent dependent. For Indian Ocean studies cannot get very far without first acquiring more knowledge than we at the moment possess about the boat-building skills of the area's earlier occupants and the working of ocean tides and currents, winds and monsoons in so far as they affect the capacity of these early boats, once built, to traverse the region. To put it more succinctly, and at the risk of making some specialists shudder, there is need for ten or twenty, maybe even thirty Kon Tikis. One problem in particular will have to be cleared up once and for all: whether it is really necessary to believe—what many Africanists are understandably unwilling to believe—that everything worthwhile came from Asia to Africa and not vice versa: *ex Africa nihil unquam novum*. I have generally accepted this assumption throughout this paper, but I must admit that I do not see yet that it is conclusively established. We know, after all, that the Waq-Waq and their predecessors returned to Indonesia and elsewhere with their tortoise shell and slaves, catching the same monsoon from the East African coast, no doubt, as Persian Gulf dhows catch today back to Arabia and India, and continuing from there by normal, long-established routes. While it seems unlikely that Africans themselves conveyed new things to Asia (although we know that slaves reached not only Arabia but also Java and China), is it so impossible that one or two things—yams, maybe, or pillar tombs or outrigger canoes—found their way back by this route?

But we are slipping here into the realm of surmise and it is the moral of this paper that there has been too much surmise about Indian Ocean matters for too long. I do not pretend to have covered all that can be said about the area as a focus of study nor even to have mentioned all the disciplines which might usefully share in uncovering all the true facts. But I hope I have said enough to what academic appetites and may now move on to a few brief and tentative proposals for the actual organization and co-ordination of an expanded research programme.

It is not unfair, I think, to say that little has happened in Indian Ocean studies so far, if we exclude the valiant efforts of individual scholars, beyond periodic conferences such as the two I have cited held in regions adjoining it and attended by some (but seldom enough) Indian Oceanists and a number of other scholars from the area concerned as well.[1] I should be the last to deprecate the value of these conferences, but it seems to me essential that at least one conference partly devoted to the Indian Ocean area should be held annually, and that a conference specifically devoted to Indian Ocean problems should be held at least once every three of four years. The relevant papers from such conferences, along with reports on work in progress and progress in work, should be collected in a journal or bulletin so that as many scholars as possible in all connected areas may profit by fresh discoveries and conclusions at the earliest possible moment.

This predicates, what is anyway clearly indicated, the establishment of an Institute of Indian Ocean studies, along the sort of lines now fairly well-established and normal, with a director, library, secretarial facilities and a number of academic fellowships available for tenure by would-be researchers over three-to-five-year periods and renewable. I doubt if much impression could be made upon the amount of work waiting to be done by less than twenty-five or thirty research workers, and it might be desirable to ensure that at any one moment at least a certain number of them were working at least partly in one of the four major areas—East Africa and Madagascar, the islands, South-East Asia, and the Asian mainland. Travel and technological funds and facilities would have to be made available, and I should myself consider it essential that in view of the importance of what we may call the 'cultural factor', there should also be attached to the centre a museum housing as many sherds and beads, artefacts, utensils and *objets d'art* as could be collected. At the moment, for instance, scolars wishing to compare such objects from different parts of the Indian Ocean area might manage to do so if they visit Majunga and Zanzibar, Oman and Yemen, Kuwait, Shiraz, Bombay, Madras, Atjeh, Jakarta, Kuching and Singapore, but could not anywhere find them all collected in a single place. (I happen to know that one or two of the leading art museums in the United States are only just beginning to build up collections of East African Islamic arts and crafts.)

It goes without saying that all this would be extremely costly—costlier, perhaps, than most institutes of similar type and size. This should, I think, be taken into account when siting the centre and also in considering what should be its principal language. It would be important that the site should be politically and in other respects acceptable and accessible to governments

1. Some three or four years ago the International Commission of Maritime History, whose headquarters are in Paris, organized in Beirut a conference more or less explicitly on the history of the Indian Ocean; but inquiries made about the aim, scope and results of this conference had at the time of writing received no reply.

or foundations from which most funds are expected to come and that the institute, although it would be hoped that it would draw some at least of its researchers and fellows from the Indian Ocean area itself, should operate in the main languages of the academic world. Without going into all the reasons which led me to such a decision, I should say that, in my opinion, the most propitious site for a centre of Indian Ocean studies would be either Mombasa or Penang or Singapore, and the chief languages should be English and French, although the library should acquire as many holdings in Malay, Swahili, Arabic, Gujerati, Tamil, Dutch and Portuguese as seem relevant. It is important that, since much of the pioneering work in the Indian Ocean was done by francophone scholars, they should continue to feel that they have a place in the region.

There remains little to be said except that perhaps, since the unity of the Indian Ocean area seems to be diminishing in modern times, the formalization and co-ordination of research into this unity is a matter of some urgency. And yet it is not a dying brontosaur I am recommending for study but rather what once has been, and could become again, a living and thriving social and economic unit. I am not suggesting that there is anything wrong with studying brontosaurs, rather that there are good reasons—though we do not yet know whether they will be strong enough—why the former prosperity of the area, based on trade across the ocean and cultural and religious links encircling it, may some day revive; and it is not inconceivable that academic researches might make their own humble contribution to such a revival. Several governments of new States—those of Singapore and Mauritius are only two that come at once to mind—would certainly be extremely interested in anything that promoted stronger links between them and their neighbours elsewhere in those parts of Africa and Asia bordering on the Indian Ocean. While not all governments would be equally interested in such projects, none I believe could fail to welcome anything that promoted better understanding in the region. Perhaps the hope that something of immediate value to the people of the area could result from the efforts of an institute of Indian Ocean studies could best be symbolized in a crest or coat of arms (not an Indian Ocean institution, but one widely adopted throughout it in recent centuries) divided into three parts: in one corner, a dodo, symbolizing interest in the region's unique past; in a second, a roc or garuda, mythical birds reflecting interest in the ideas and spirit of its people; and in the third a phoenix rising from the ashes.

Historical studies on the Indian Ocean

Auguste Toussaint

I hardly need to recall here that the history of colonization is closely bound up with maritime history. *'Point de colonies sans marine',* La Bourdonnais used to say, and rightly so. Indeed, the first colonies all over the world, and ever since ancient times, have been a consequence of navigation. Setting out for distant seas originally to engage in trade, the earliest navigators established trading-posts or 'factories', which subsequently became colonies. This is true not only of the Europeans but also of peoples of Asia such as the Indians and the Chinese—to take just these two examples—who established virtual colonies long before the Europeans did.

I hasten to add that, while colonization is a consequence of navigation, it is not an inevitable consequence. For instance, between 1784 and 1815 the Americans did not need to establish trading-posts along the Indian Ocean coasts in order to carry on trade in those regions. Basically, colonization is perhaps just an accidental phenomenon, but to pursue this theme would lead us too far afield. I shall confine myself here to discussing the study of things maritime and of things colonial.

The historians of Europe have apparently concentrated much more on the study of colonization than on that of maritime expansion, to judge by the considerable number of works dealing with the former, compared with which the bibliography of works dealing with the latter seems rather meagre, especially if we exclude works dealing with naval history, that is, 'battle history'.

Is it that the discredit which has, quite wrongly, attached to colonial history ever since the decolonization process began has affected maritime history? In any case, since the last war, maritime history has experienced a virtual revival. As evidence, I would cite only the publication of the first maritime bibliographies, the establishment of chairs of ocean history in certain universities—Harvard led the way, I think—and above all, the formulation of an International Commission of Maritime History, as a consequence of a decision taken at the Eleventh Congress of Historical Sciences in Stockholm. All this happened in the 1950s, that is, in the post-war period.

At about the same time, archivists from all over the world decided to join forces, and in 1950, in Paris, they held the first International Congress on Archives, which I attended as Director of Archives of Mauritius.

From the outset it was apparent that, while the objectives of archivology were the same in every country, the means and technique employed to attain them could not be the same everywhere. In tropical countries, for instance, the filing, conservation and restoration of documents posed special problems calling for special techniques.

For this reason, after pondering the question at length, I proposed, at the Third International Congress on Archives, which was held in Florence in 1956, that a body should be set up to bring together archivists and historians of the Indian Ocean countries. My proposal was favourably received, and Unesco subsequently agreed to grant us its sponsorship.

The first meeting was held in April 1960 at Tananarive, under the auspices of the Académie Malgache and with the gracious support of the young Republic of Madagascar. The meeting adopted the statutes of an International Historical Association of the Indian Ocean, and my colleagues did me the honour of asking me to act as its chairman. A report of this Tananarive meeting appeared in the review *Bulletin de Madagascar* in July 1960.

If I am not mistaken, this was the second international association devoted to the study of the Indian Ocean. The first, the Pan Indian Ocean Science Association, was founded in 1951 on the initiative of Professor A. D. Ross of the University of Perth, Australia. Its object was to study the Indian Ocean solely from the scientific point of view. For reasons unknown to me it did not last for long. The last meeting took place at Karachi in November 1960 and the association broke up after that.

Shortly after our own group had been set up, an Association of Historians of South-East Asia came into being. I might mention parenthetically that the name was not a very felicitous one to designate what I prefer to call the Indo-Pacific region bordering the Indian Ocean. The first meeting, held in Singapore in January 1961 under the auspices of the University of Malaysia, was a success. Since March 1960, the University of Malaysia has been publishing a biannual review entitled *Journal of South-East Asian Studies*.

However, unlike our own association, that of the historians of South-East Asia does not deal exclusively with maritime history. Actually, it seems to be more interested in the contemporary political history of the region in question.

To revert to our association, our first meeting in Tananarive was essentially of a consultative nature. We tried to reach agreement on certain points of common interest without discussing any particular topic. We also touched on the need for a handbook on archivology in the tropics for the use of archivists in the Indian Ocean countries, a bibliography of ocean history, and lastly, some sort of bulletin to enable members of the Association to keep in touch with each other and with other bodies.

The manual of tropical archivology was brought out in 1966, thanks to the support of Unesco and the French Centre National de la Recherche Scientifique. It was edited by Yves Pérotin, the first professional archivist placed in charge of the Archives of Réunion after the island was made a *département* of France. It appeared simultaneously in French and in English in the series 'Le Monde d'Outre-mer Passé et Présent' of the Paris École Pratique des Hautes Etudes. It is a valuable guide, all the more useful in that most of the countries in the tropical zone do not possess the means of giving their archivists a professional training. Yet surely, if we want to write history, we must first organize the archives.

Owing to the lack of financial resources we were unable to make our *Bulletin* as ambitious a venture as the *Journal of South-East Asian Studies*. We have contented ourselves with a very modest little publication obligingly multicopied by the services of the Archives of Réunion thanks to our first secretary-general, André Scherer, who succeeded Mr Pérotin as the head of the service. The first issue, published in January 1963, contained a small select bibliography on the Indian Ocean, which I compiled myself. It is far from perfect, I know, but it represents a working hypothesis.

Also in 1963 the International Commission of Maritime History undertook the publication of a *Bibliographie de l'Histoire des Grandes Routes Maritimes*, intended to carry forward in time, if not to follow the method, of the bibliography published under the guidance of Eugène Deprez in 1931 for the *Commission d'Histoire des Grandes Découvertes,* whose programme coincided partly with that of the present International Commission of Maritime History.

Several instalments of this work, financed by the Calouste Gulbenkian Foundation and directed by Professor Charles Verlinden, have already come out.[1] In this way, in a few years' time, yet another of the major projects mooted at our Tananarive meeting in 1960 will have been brought to fruition.

Our second congress was held in Lourenço Marques, in the Portuguese territory of Mozambique, in August 1962, along with the Sixth International Symposium on Maritime History. Organized with the assistance of the Scientific Research Institute of Mozambique, this joint meeting had as its theme: trade routes to India, first in the Indian Ocean, then in the Mediterranean. The Mediterranean route was dealt with more specifically at a second session held in Venice in September of the same year.

1. See select bibliography at the end of N. Mallat's article, p. 58.

Until then, as was pointed out by Professor Michel Mollat, Chairman of the International Commission of Maritime History, historians had not attempted to devote two meetings to the study of one single problem as seen from two geographically remote vantage points.

The proceedings of both sessions have been published in full. The papers submitted at Lourenço Marques appeared in a special issue (January 1963) of the Portuguese review *Studia,* the publication of the Centro de Estudos Historicos Ultramarinos, Lisbon. Those submitted in Venice were issued by the Sixth Section of the École Pratique des Hautes Études in 1970 in a special volume entitled *Méditerranée et Océan Indien.*

Meanwhile, in September 1966 the two associations met together again in a third congress, held this time in Beirut, to study jointly the trading companies in the East and in the Indian Ocean. The reason for choosing Beirut was that, after all, Lebanon is none other than the Phoenicia of old and that the Phoenicians were the first merchants to establish a trade link between the Mediterranean and the Indian Ocean; another reason was that in modern times the Levant companies were the precursors of the chartered companies trading with the Indies.

The participants in the Beirut congress were so numerous that we had to divide into two sections, one dealing with antiquity and the Middle Ages, the other with modern and contemporary times. In the first of these sections, twenty-seven papers were submitted, and in the second, thirty. There were altogether 150 participants, representing 28 Eastern and Western countries. The proceedings, published by the Sixth Section of the École Pratique des Hautes Études in 1970, run to a volume of 732 pages.

After the memorable congress in Beirut we had to wait for six years before meeting again. With the exception of South Africa and Australia, the Indian Ocean countries are generally poor and hence hesitant to defray the expenses of a historical congress. South Africa is virtually ruled out owing to its apartheid policy, and Australia is too remote for participants from Europe. The problem is not a simple one.

Finally the Island of Réunion, or rather the French Government, agreed to accept responsibility for the physical arrangements of our fourth congress, which took place in Saint-Denis in September 1972, again in association with the International Commission of Maritime History and with the collaboration of Unesco.

The theme of this fourth congress was the history of migrations in the Indian Ocean from antiquity to our own time. We could not have wished for a better site than Réunion to study such a subject, because the island, originally uninhabited, is peopled entirely by immigrants from Europe, Asia and Africa. Réunion has the further advantage of possessing two institutions that are absolutely essential for the promotion of historical studies: a very modern archives service and an autonomous university centre which gives great prominence to the teaching of history and geography, subjects only too often neglected in other so-called developing countries. At this fourth congress, twenty-five papers were submitted.[1]

We also hope to be able to meet at least every five years in future, preferably in an Indian Ocean country, though for my part I do not see any reason why this ocean should not be studied in a European or even American country, as it was in 1971 on the initiative of an American university.

In March of that year Georgetown University, Washington, D.C., organized in that city an absolutely fascinating symposium on the Indian Ocean. I was invited to make the opening address to the symposium on the clash of powers in that part of the world from the earliest times to the present day, and I followed the discussions with keen interest. The main purpose of this symposium on the Indian Ocean was to identify the essential aspects of the present situation from the political, economic and military point of view.

With the ample resources at its disposal, Georgetown University quickly issued the proceedings of its symposium in a 457-page volume entitled *The Indian Ocean: Its Political, Economic and Military Importance,* which was published in New York by Praeger late in 1972. I can highly recommend it to your attention, for it represents an outstanding contribution—actually the first of its kind—to our knowledge of current Indian Ocean problems.

Whatever doubts may have existed in certain quarters at the time when we decided to set up an International Historical Association of the Indian Ocean in 1960, as to whether that ocean could really be regarded as a single historical entity, have by now, I think, been dispelled, and it is surely commonly conceded that the study of the Indian Ocean was neglected for far too long.

I would go further and say that I am convinced that the study of this ocean will generate more and more interest in future, for historical reasons I shall now briefly review.

The concept of an ocean is a phenomenon of modern times. All that the ancients knew of the Indian Ocean was the part which they called the Erythrean Sea, now known as the Gulf of Oman. In the second century A.D., Ptolemy still imagined this vast stretch of water as a kind of Mediterranean completely enclosed by land. Nor do the Arabs and the Chinese,

---

1. Colloque de la Commission Internationale d'Histoire Maritime (Saint-Denis, 4–9 September 1972). *L'Histoire des Mouvements de Populations dans l'Océan Indien de l'Antiquité à nos Jours*, Paris, Librairie Honoré Champion (in press).

good geographers though they were, seem to have had a very clear idea of the size and shape of the Indian Ocean, even though their navigations ranged far and wide over the ocean. And as regards India, it is far from fitting that its name should have been given to an ocean which admittedly washes its shores on three sides, but which has never been much sailed by Indians, except around the archipelago.

The Europeans were the first to explore the Indian Ocean and later to try to dominate it. 'The most European of all oceans', Admiral Ballard called it.

This claim of alleged European domination is, however, subject to a good many qualifications. Taking the Portuguese first, for they were the earliest, it has by now been demonstrated that, while their fleets were able to oust the fleets of the Easterners in the sixteenth century, they never succeeded in establishing their domination everywhere. What they did accomplish was to draw the first fairly accurate nautical charts, though they remained secret for a long time.

The Dutch, who came next, also have remarkable cartographical achievements to their credit, but they did not really dominate the ocean either. In the seventeenth century and even in the eighteenth, Dutch possessions were limited to a few key positions in the Indian Archipelago. The Dutch had a few outposts elsewhere as well, but all that never amounted to an empire.

The eighteenth century was a sort of interregnum marked by a protracted conflict between the Dutch, the French and the British, which ended with the victory of the latter, but this did not happen until the turn of the century, or more precisely in the first few years of the nineteenth century, for it was not until after 1811 that Great Britain succeeded in eliminating its rivals.

An age of enlightenment, or at least of curiosity, the eighteenth century left its mark on the Indian Ocean region in a different way, for it was then that it really began to be studied systematically.

It was during that period that the great comprehensive works which are classics even today were published—those of Valentin, Hamilton, Abbé Guyon and Abbé Raynal, particularly the latter, whose works were published and translated over and over again. For the first time European scholarship became aware of the ocean world while, on the practical side, hydrographers such as D'Après, Dalrymple and Horsburgh endeavoured to give as accurate an idea as possible of the ocean in superb nautical atlases, and merchants drew up veritable vademecums. The classic example, in French, is Pierre Blancard's *Manuel du Commerce des Indes Orientales et de la Chine*.

It was also in the eighteenth century very soon after their accession to independence that the Americans rediscovered the Indian trade route for their own profit. Between 1786 and 1810 more than 600 United States ships put in at the Mascarene Islands, and contacts with India, the Indian Archipelago and China were on a like scale. One needs to have visited the Essex Institute and the Peabody Museum in Salem, Mass., to realize the full importance of this American eastward push, which was actually the basis of the prodigious economic rise of the United States.

In the nineteenth century the British held the scene almost alone, at least until the Suez Canal was opened. This event resulted in renewed activity on the part of their former competitors and attracted some new ones, with the arrival on the scene of the Germans and the Italians. At the same time the Americans, who had almost disappeared after 1815, returned to the region via the Pacific, where the Japanese too were beginning to make an impact.

The major event of the nineteenth century was not, however, the British territorial expansion in India and neighbouring countries, but the development of shipping in consequence of the substitution of steam-vessels for sailing-ships. Even if the British had not conquered India, there is no doubt that their advance in this respect would have sufficed to give them economic supremacy.

In the twentieth century British domination on land came to an end. Decolonization being the order of the day, the peoples of the Indian Ocean in their turn became conscious of their past, but at the same time they perceived that even freed from territorial occupation, they were still, then as before, terribly weak, terribly vulnerable and—let us not be afraid to say so—terribly dependent.

They had hardly come out of the colonial era when they realized that they might well be threatened with a new hegemony owing to their inability to defend themselves at sea. This explains why they all clamour for a policy of strict neutrality in regard to every sector of the ocean.

But can the ocean be made an absolutely neutral zone? The conclusion reached on this point by the sponsors of the Washington symposium after the March 1971 discussions was positively negative, if I may put it that way. In the light of history, they said, and in view of the forces and interests involved today, any hope of 'neutralization' is sheer starry-eyed idealism.

For this reason I think that the peoples of the Indian Ocean will in future have to take a special interest in things of the sea, while the great powers will be obliged, whether they like it or not, to take the ocean increasingly into account in their plans for the the future. In short, for both, the sea is a reality that cannot now be disregarded.

In this connection, what part can France play, having regard to its present position in this area of the world? I am thinking, of course, solely of the human sciences, especially history and geography, which are my personal concern. In this sphere France is one of the countries that have contributed the most to our knowledge of the Eastern seas and Eastern peoples.

I venture to point out—for it is too often forgotten—that while the French did not triumph over the British in the eighteenth century, they ranged all over the Indian Ocean—and I mean all over—from north to south and from east to west. One has only to open a bibliography of geographical works of the eighteenth century to confirm this. I have already alluded to D'Après, Guyon, Raynal and Blancard, but many other names could be mentioned.

Lastly, I need hardly remind you, in the nineteenth century with the opening of the Suez Canal France performed a feat even more remarkable than Vasco da Gama's discovery of the Cape route. Nor need I remind you that the Messageries Maritimes is one of the oldest steamship navigation lines to ply the Eastern seas.

It is therefore to be deplored, I think, that France has not as yet any review of maritime history comparable to the *American Neptune* or the *Mariner's Mirror*. This is a gap that requires filling, and it is not the only one. There is, of course, the *Revue Maritime,* but it is not exactly a historical review.

It is true that for some years now the École Pratique des Hautes Études has been making a great effort to promote maritime studies, but this is not enough in my opinion. There is scope for other ventures, not only in France but also locally. Here I naturally have in mind that archipelago which I have suggested calling 'Franconésie'. This is not an invention on my part but has a strictly historical basis, since the Mascarene Archipelago was known for a long time as the 'Iles Françaises Orientales'. In point of fact, not until 1825 did the designation 'Mascarene' make its first appearance in geographical literature. Surely, it would not be excessively ambitious to ask for the setting up of a centre for maritime studies in Réunion or Mauritius —and preferably in both. This would make it possible at least to publish a great many completely unknown documents concerning the history of France and that of neighbouring peoples, which, I fear, will not withstand the effects of age and of the climate indefinitely, despite the efforts of the local archivists.

This might also contribute to liberating the inhabitants of these islands from the mystique of the sugar-cane, to reminding them that their ancestors lived literally from the sea and that they themselves can still find abundant resources in the sea.

I do not know to what extent our academy can help in the setting up of centres of maritime studies. Just the same I thought that it was worth while to speak to you about what has been done and what can be done. The international bodies whose activities I have described do not have very large resources at their disposal, despite Unesco's assistance, and I think that they may legitimately expect even greater support at the national level than they receive at present.

Part IV
Meeting of experts

Report on the discussions

Participants in the meeting stressed throughout that one should dispose of the idea that there were peoples, classes or individuals compelled to put up with history written by others, and the meeting was anxious to find means of discovering the historical life of those who have hitherto been denied all historicity. In this as in other contexts it was time to bury the myth of passive peoples and continents, previously regarded as objects of a history acted out by major external protagonists. The influences between the Indian Ocean and Africa should not be studied as a one-way phenomenon, but whenever possible as a reciprocal relationship. Examples concerning the Hadhramaut were mentioned, as showing the extent to which Africa had likewise, in certain instances, contributed to the countries with which it maintained regular relations.

Navigation and maritime techniques

A great deal of research has already been done in these fields, as is shown by the bibliographies attached to several of the reports. It seemed desirable, however, to single out some points for specific mention.

Reference was made to the geographical conditions affecting navigation. In addition to the alternating winter and summer monsoons there are the strong westerly winds in the southern Indian Ocean, which European sailing-ships did not make use of until the eighteenth century. Several experts consider, however, that apart from the monsoon mechanism, which was used regularly from the Arab period onwards, the great westerly winds were perhaps known and used before the eighteenth century by Asian peoples.

As yet, not enough is known about the forms and sizes of the vessels or about the materials used in shipbuilding, even though a number of studies have been published. How, for example, were the outrigger canoes used (if, indeed, they were used) to sail from South-East Asia to the African coasts and the islands close to Africa? What was the size and equipment of the Indian, Indonesian and Chinese boats in the pre-Islamic period? Several experts considered that, on the basis of all available sources, studies of shipbuilding techniques should be carried out in all the countries of the Indian Ocean. Different kinds of wood are required for the hulls, masts, decks and oars. Where did these different woods come from and what trade did this traffic give rise to? Caulking techniques are also worth studying: in Mauritius it would be interesting to identify the composition of one caulking material—Indian stuff.

The earliest sources of detailed knowledge of navigation techniques are the Arabic language route-books. As regards earlier periods, historians are not yet agreed as to the origins and development of these techniques. Natural factors were certainly a much greater constraint between the period of the *Peripli* (coastal guides) and that of the route-books than subsequently; they determined the choice of port of arrival on the African coast. The town of Kilwa, for example, owed its expansion to the fact that it represented the southern-most point of a twelve-month round trip between Asia and Africa. This explains why trading ports further south, which were served by secondary traffic, were dependent on this town. This situation is thought to have lasted until the Arab system was upset by the arrival of the Portuguese.

The view was expressed that it would be desirable to publish further documents concerning Indian navigation in antiquity, to seek and to publish in several languages other Arabic and Portuguese route-books comparable to those already known, and to look for Chinese or Vietnamese documents of the same kind and, lastly, to study the Malagasy *Sorabe,* which might contain references to voyages. It would also be of interest to trace documents concerning the navigation and trade of the Banian merchants.

Archaeology may provide valuable evidence in this as in so many other fields. The experts stressed the technical requirements to be satisfied for the sound comparative utilization of the results obtained through archaeological excavations. They regretted that hitherto these technical requirements had not always been respected everywhere or at all times. The methods used in stratigraphic research, dating and technical investigation of the objects discovered and of their statistical processing should be as similar as possible, and the strictest standards should be applied. Failure to take such precautions may give rise to spectacular but short-lived theories.

It was mentioned, in passing, that the presence of a few inconclusive archaeological remains did not, in the present state of affairs, constitute evidence of the antiquity (sixth century A.D.) of Indian voyages along the East African coast. In general the results of excavations should be interpreted with great caution. One question asked, for example, was whether the existence of goods traffic necessarily meant that the goods had come from the same place as the ship carrying them. The question 'who carried what' could be answered in many different ways, which should be a warning to historians.

With regard to East African 'shipping facilities', the meeting selected various topics for study:

What led to the opening up of the African coasts to seaborne traffic?

What part did Africans play in the crews of boats that crossed the Indian Ocean or sailed along its coasts? Did their part remain unchanged at all periods?

Did Africans receive any training for seafaring through fishing, and under what circumstances?

'Maritime towns' were established in the south of present-day Somalia before the sixteenth century, without in general any protection other than the water surrounding the islands on which they were commonly built. How did these towns develop as communities linked to the sea and to maritime activities?

As from the sixteenth century the Portuguese and the Arabs became rivals; local aggressions occurred later, for example, when the Batsimisaraka and the Sakalaves increasingly threatened the Comoro Islands. Simultaneously large-scale fortifications of different types made their appearance. At the same time, the tonnage of ships increased greatly, with the consequence that the siting of ports of call had to change, and new sites were developed accordingly. In the case of Madagascar, the evidence of this change of sites is well attested; it might be studied more thoroughly than has been the case hitherto on the coast of the African mainland.

The case of the Somali coast is somewhat different: the old-established, stable ports in two known places were equipped with sizeable fortifications.

The shipping facilities also included a series of rules of navigation recognized by communities of varying size. The example of the Maritime Code of Malacca was mentioned, though its precise date was not given during the discussion. No comparable text has so far been reported for Africa or the islands.

The attitude of the coastal or island dwellers with regard to the sea also calls for study.

As regards the exploitation of the sea, research has to start almost from scratch. There should be a comparative study of fishing gear, techniques and vocabulary as well as of the extraction of and trade in salt, ambergris, pearls and coral, for example. This study of the exploitation of the sea and its resources might be carried out, in different forms, on the basis of the diverse available texts.

The importance of fish in the diet of the coastal peoples of the Indian Ocean might form the subject of interdisciplinary comparative studies, possibly supplemented, so far as the later centuries are concerned, by the findings of archaeologists.

The discussion on these topics gave rise to two important comments.

One concerned stowaways, for example the fugitive slaves from the Mascarene Islands who, in the eighteenth and nineteenth centuries, attempted to reach Madagascar. The other was to the effect that, in Volumes V and VI of the *General History of Africa* sufficient prominence should be given to the Indian immigration in Africa.

Botanical and agronomical exchanges

The discussions demonstrated the need for a large-scale international effort to clarify the scientific and everyday terminology relating to plants. Past research has suffered from a good many mistakes due to vagueness of terminology.

Palaeobotanical and ethnobotanical methods of research

Remains discovered during archaeological excavations should be studied by means of the most rigorous laboratory methods. Only then will people cease to claim, on the basis of vague presumptions, that such and such a species is native to Africa or was imported. From just a few examples it can be seen how carefully one has to proceed in this field.

Sweet manioc was cultivated, certainly before 1587, on the coast of Madagascar. This manioc can now be taken to have been the result of the domestication of a local species, and not at all an import from Brazil through the Portuguese, as was believed hitherto. It was also pointed out that the Brazilian bitter manioc planted in Réunion soon turned into the sweet variety in that island, as was noted by nineteenth-century agronomists.

The *qat* plant apparently 'circulated' around the Red Sea between South Arabia and East Africa.

Botanical investigation lends itself particularly well to the study of reciprocal exchanges: plants given by Africa to the rest of the Indian Ocean should not, therefore, be overlooked.

Technical investigation, although indispensable, is not sufficient. Each monograph should be placed by the botanist or historian within a pluridisciplinary context that would show its significance.

The full significance of botanical exchanges becomes visible only when the changes of a dietary or even social kind they brought about can be assessed.

It is generally accepted that in East Africa the change-over from semi-sedentary economies based on hunting and food gathering to agricultural economies was linked in general with the spread of the Bantu-language peoples and marked a stage in the development of the continent.

Other examples of concomitant changes in these agricultural and social structures through the introduction of certain plants were mentioned. In Réunion, a peasant population existed at the end of the seventeenth century who cultivated a variety of food crops. In the eighteenth century, La Bourdonnais instructed these peasants to supply the neighbouring island, Mauritius, and the ships' companies using these ports, with food. This type of cultivation produces a certain type of society. These peasants no doubt improved the plants that had existed in the island before their arrival, and no doubt also they introduced a good many others. Then quite another type of cultivation appeared through the introduction of coffee and the development of sugar-cane. As a result, a different type of society came into being. In this case the introduction of new plants cultivated under certain economic conditions changed the social structures. Conceivably, this was also the pattern in other instances of plant transplants occurring in earlier times.

All specialists, including archaeologists, who may be able to give an answer should be asked the following questions: How did the African or island societies react to the introduction of some particular plant? Was the introduction desired? Requested? Made inevitable by the movement of its consumers? Was it refused? Did it cause any important changes in agrarian or dietary balance? Can the movements of certain groups be traced by means of their specific diet?

Types of investigation desired

The study of the sugar-cane should take the form of a monograph prepared on an international basis. This plant, as is well known, was transmitted by the Muslims in Asia to the Mediterranean. At what dates was it imported—if it was—into the western regions of the Indian Ocean? Some data exist, but a synthetic study still remains to be done.

The possibility is not apparently to be ruled out that sugar-cane occurred in its natural state in Réunion in the eighteenth century.

Sugar-cane seems to have been linked, historically, with two very different types of cultivation. One type consisted of garden cultivation in various forms, in household or village production structures. Sugar-cane was then only one of a number of other items in the local diet. Did this type of production exist in East Africa and in the islands? It seems that in Réunion at least it existed before the nineteenth century. The other type of cultivation, linked with the large estate, implies the use of manpower which, according to the historical evidence, had the status of slaves up to the nineteenth century. This form of cane production was obviously well known in Réunion or Mauritius, and the sugar-cane was an important crop, particularly in the nineteenth century, when the sugar from these islands no longer suffered from the earlier strong competition from sugar from Batavia and Santo Domingo. What was the situation in remoter periods throughout the whole Indian Ocean area, and what were the social consequences of the production (if any) on the large estates like those of lower Iraq in the ninth century?

The distribution of plants that can be smoked may repay investigation, in the first place because the discovery of ancient pipes by archaeologists raises the problem of what was smoked before the introduction of tobacco and, secondly, because these plants were linked with social and religious phenomena.

Research into rice is badly needed. Various working documents acknowledge the valuable work carried out in Madagascar on this subject. Other studies in the Indian archipelago indicate that probably the method of rice cultivation by burn-beating was not—contrary to what was believed up to now—the most primitive but, rather, was the most advanced method. Rice 'follows its consumers' in their migrations, and these assumed massive dimensions in the Indian Ocean after the fourteenth century and, more especially, during the eighteenth and nineteenth centuries. Was this an important factor in the spread of rice cultivation and of production techniques? The rice trade in the nineteenth century (no doubt the trade was also carried on in earlier centuries) is dealt with in a number of the studies cited in the bibliography.

The generalized introduction of the eucalyptus tree may have produced consequences that are well worth investigating, particularly the health and social aspects.

The oral tradition or inquiries made among old persons should be used to study methods of working and cultivating agricultural land, and in this way to try to determine the antiquity of these agricultural methods and to discover the elements of a real agronomy which, although not in written form, was undoubtedly employed efficiently and consciously.

Parallel research is required concerning irrigation and water-use techniques (Engaruka) and their origins: so far it has been noted that the techniques became more and more sophisticated as one approached the coast of East Africa.

Exchanges concerning animals, even the smallest (insects or rats) should also be studied.

Trade relations

On this topic the meeting did not receive any really new information. Besides, in many cases it was difficult to separate the study of trade relations from that of population movements.

The meeting accepted the idea, however, that future research into trade relations should, within the limitations of the available documentation, employ modern methods of economic history, the object of which is to organize, quantify and identify the chronological sequences and not just (as was the practice in the past) to compile a purely descriptive catalogue of the commodities traded.

Similarly, research workers should investigate commercial usages, the organization of trading companies (e.g. the Karimi merchants, about whom some information has come to light in recent years), the monetary mechanisms used to regulate and effect payments for transactions, etc. Two periods are important:

The Pre-Muslim period: The sources of material for this period are as yet very few in number and not very informative, in spite of a good many publications. For some years now, however, archaeological findings in Ethiopia and Somalia have been yielding important evidence. As regards the Axumite period, there is evidence of actual trade with India.

The period of Arab-Muslim expansion: Exchanges developed greatly, from the eighth century onwards at least. Besides the Arab sources, which have long been known, there is archaeological evidence of the establishment of trading posts on the East African coast, first at Pemba and then at several points along the coast. Although a good deal is known about this period, many problems still await investigation.

In the first place, these problems concern the products. Although it is relatively simple to form an idea of the trade from the African coast towards the north and the east (ivory, gold, wood), it is less easy to estimate other important trade flows. Was iron ore exported to India? What was the importance of trade in chlorite schists from the Persian Gulf with the East African coast, and then between Africa and Madagascar? What kind of trade was there with Africa and the islands in semi-precious stones such as cornelian, cut or uncut (cornelian beads in the cutting stage have been found in Antongil bay)? By which routes were cowries imported into East Africa and re-exported to West Africa? Did these trade routes change from one century to another? What import trade was carried on in semi-precious articles such as glass beads, cosmetics (kohl), in East Africa and Madagascar?

Pottery, an essential import item, deserves to form the subject of a special and very critical study. In this case, archaeology is the only source of data, since traditional sources are virtually silent concerning this trade. With the possible exception of the short period of fifteenth-century Chinese voyages to the western basin of the Indian Ocean, the appearance of pottery raises a problem: Did it reach the African coasts through Chinese or Arab traders? Another phenomenon to be investigated is the sudden mass arrival on the east coast of Kenya of yellow glazed pottery of Hadrami origin and of decorated sgraffito ware from the Persian Gulf in the thirteenth and fourteenth centuries. Variations in this trade as regards period and volume and the origin of the pottery are likely to throw a great deal of fresh light on relations between East Africa, Madagascar, the islands and the other countries of the Indian Ocean.

In the second place, these problems concern the routes, main or secondary, by which Asian products arrived in Africa and African products in Asia. According to what still seems to have been the most likely pattern, the African coastal route was, in the main, used by coastal traffic from South Arabia and Aden. From there the goods were transported to Asia, the Persian Gulf, the Red Sea or Africa. But there were probably voyages from India to Kilwa as well, making use of the annual monsoon. It would be very desirable to study, in this field, the points at which cargoes were transshipped, either for general reasons (limits of the supervised shipping zone), or for technical reasons (change in tonnage of boats) or for commercial reasons (redistribution of freight according to origin and destination). In this connection, the island of Socotra and the south Arabian coast were mentioned as worthwhile subjects of study.

Yet other problems are connected directly with the spread of religion through personal contacts when exchanges were made. In the opinion of some experts, the spread of Islam was intimately related to the widening network of Muslim traders; others consider that the two are distinct phenomena. Some experts consider that specific regions of the Muslim world, identifiable by the names indicating the origin of persons from such regions (e.g. southern Arabia, which has not yet been studied sufficiently) have played a vital role, at certain times at least; others take the view that too much should not be read into names of origin, such as 'Shirazi', which meant very different things, politically and socially, in different periods.

Lastly, the commercial organization of the urban societies of East Africa still remains to be studied. The example of Kilwa was mentioned, where the local sovereign apparently tried to monopolize the large-scale export trade for his own profit, at least from the fourteenth century onwards. Unfortunately, only a short discussion took place on the recent period from the sixteenth century onwards. The experts stressed, however, that the quantitative survey methods commonly used nowadays by specialists in economic history should be applied to the abundant sources of that period. Likewise, it was suggested that a study should be made of the 'commercial diplomacy' of the countries that had no regular contact with the outside world.

It was already known from recent research that European trade in the sixteenth century had not taken the place, either in tonnage or in value terms, of the former Arab trade in the Indian Ocean.

An observer provided some new information about the nineteenth century. At that time, trade among ports on the Indian Ocean equalled in volume trade between those ancient ports and ports in Europe. The main items traded among ports on the Indian Ocean were consumer products; for example, coffee and cotton were regularly sold there as well as in Europe. A flourishing trade was carried on in rice, wood and textiles. There were, for example, substantial sales of cloth from Java to neighbouring countries until about 1840.

Population movements

The peopling of Madagascar

Given the theories advanced by the authors of the three working documents, the meeting could do no more than note the latest stage then reached by the discussion and form a view as to the importance of the arguments advanced by the different specialists: It noted the theory concerning the essential part played by the 'Swahili transition stage' in the peopling of the island. It was said that over 60 per cent of all the peopling of the island could be attributed to this 'Swahili transition stage'.

Beyond that, the stage currently reached by research being what it is, the theories remain vaguer.

Nobody questions that a large proportion of Madagascar's population and elements that decisively shaped its culture and language came from Asia. It is beyond this point that the difficulties begin to crop up.

Why did the people who leave Asia set out? Possible reasons mentioned by the meeting were political, economic and social structures, climatic and population factors, and wars. The answer can be found only through a close study of the conditions of life in South-East Asia at the time of the migrations.

Where did these migrants come from? India? Indonesia? There is a tradition in Indonesia that some ancestors set out westwards, but when does this tradition date from? At what periods did they leave? Were their migrations chance movements or organized ones? Mass migrations or scattered? Did people leave in large numbers?

What route did these voluntary migrants take? Did they land on the islands near Madagascar? The opinions of the experts diverged on this point, but no conclusive argument was put forward. Did the migrants sometimes land directly on Madagascar, or did they all arrive by way of the East African coast, as the 'Swahili hypothesis' would lead one to suppose? Did the Comoro Islands serve as a staging post during these migrations towards the African coast or from the African coast towards Madagascar?

The extent of the purely black peopling of the island has also to be reconsidered. The latest archaeological research has already provided considerable information. Several questions nevertheless continue to arise:

Were the very first inhabitants of the island Africans or not?

Did the 'Afro-Indonesians' who arrived from the sixth century onwards bring blacks with them? What was their status?

As regards recent periods, the Malagasy language distinguishes the 'Makwa', totally different from the Malagasy, and the 'Mozambiques', who came from the other side of the straits. What do these terms signify, and what was the chronological and geographical extent of this immigration?

What, for example, were the links with Madagascar of the copper-using peoples who were discovered in the Limpopo region by the Portuguese when they arrived and who may have been settled there since the eleventh century?

In the 'Malagasy melting pot', the various immigrant streams were amalgamated. It would be interesting to discover—outside the successful assimilations—what original cultural features were retained by the various groups of newcomers.

The peopling of Mauritius, Rodriguez, the Seychelles and Réunion

The meeting did not accept as proven the hypothesis that these islands were not peopled at all until the Europeans settled there in the seventeenth and eighteenth centuries. The majority of the experts expressed the hope that a survey would be carried out by all possible means, which would make it possible to give a clear and scientifically based reply to this question. Were there no travellers from anywhere who landed or lived on these islands before the seventeenth century?

The archaeological information (Réunion) on this point is still very sparse and inconclusive. Research is hampered by the abundant vegetation, which very rapidly covers all remains except those of buildings, and by possible changes of sea level, even small ones, in historical times.

The stages in the peopling of the islands have been quite clearly described:

Mauritius: the Portuguese and Dutch left very few traces of their brief stay on the island. The French, and subsequently the British, settled there. With the development of cotton, sugar-cane and coffee growing, a considerable amount of slave labour was imported. Before the abolition of slavery, Indians were brought in, together with black Africans and

Malagasy. After 1830, the influx from the East declined, but Indians and Chinese still came voluntarily as traders.

Rodriguez: This island was peopled essentially by Africans, mostly slaves from Mauritius or blacks freed in the nineteenth century by British warships, which intercepted clandestine slavers after the abolition of slavery.

The Seychelles: The peopling followed much the same lines as that of Rodriguez.

Réunion: An initial foundation for its peopling was provided by European peasants and Malagasy women in about equal numbers. Subsequently, as in Mauritius, imported slaves arrived who were needed on the plantations. (See Professor Gerbeau's paper.)

The methods used to transfer people varied. The slave trade proper was carried on (probably as from the ninth century) for nine or ten centuries; after the sixteenth century, other practices came into use (e.g. in Kilwa and Zanzibar), which were grafted on to the slave trade and which were based on 'free engagement' or on the 'redemption' by the slave of his liberty, as in the Humblot estates in the Comoro Islands. On Réunion, after the prohibition of slavery in 1817, slaves taken from slave ships were not set free but had to work as the 'King's Blacks' in public workshops.

On Mauritius, Réunion, Rodriguez and the Seychelles, an original Creole civilization developed, which the meeting suggested should be studied in detail. In their turn, the Creoles settled in large numbers in neighbouring countries, particularly on the east coast of Madagascar, at Tamatave, for example. To begin with, the word 'Creole' everywhere had the meaning of 'those born on the island'. Since the end of the nineteenth century the meaning of the word has changed in Mauritius, and it is now used almost exclusively to designate Mauritians of African origin.

East coast of Africa

If any peopling took place before the Muslim period, only very small numbers were involved, and the newcomers were absorbed in the general population.

In this region, studies should concentrate on the intermingling of peoples of varied origin in the 'Swahili melting pot'. Was this amalgamation successful at every level, ethnic, social and cultural, within the common mould of Islam? The situation is obviously not the same in the northern (Somalia) and southern (Mozambique) parts of the East African coast.

Asians forcibly transported by Europeans arrived on this coast from the sixteenth century onwards. Scarcely any study has been made of these movements so far.

The African diaspora

In general, the relative importance of Africans and islanders in the life of the Indian Ocean should be studied.

The African diaspora, whether voluntary or not, is a reality, the traces of which were mentioned by several experts, in India (Gujarat) and in the Hadhramaut.

Except in the case of forced emigration, these seem to have been less organized migrations than the movements from Asia to the western Indian Ocean. There appears to be no trace in the African memory of such migrations eastwards. Population movements could nevertheless still have taken place from Africa to Asia in a much more piecemeal way over a long period of time.

In the Malaysian archipelago and the Pacific Ocean, population groups can be found who may well be of African origin.

The meeting was unanimous in recommending that great attention should be paid to all forms of the black dispersion in the Indian Ocean.

Important staging posts for voluntary migrants existed in southern Arabia, where their ethnic and cultural influence is visible.

The transfer of persons against their will began very early, as witness is not clear from their Arabic name (Zanğ)—in the long social revolt that the position held in the ninth century by Africans—whose regional origin developed in Mesopotamia and the Basra region.

The transportations of the seventeenth, eighteenth and nineteenth centuries, until the abolition of slavery and sometimes even afterwards, led to considerable movements westwards (Indians, Malays) and from the west towards the east (Malagasy, Africans), which contributed greatly, although in unequal proportions, to the peopling of the islands.

All these transportations involved a majority of men. The number of women among the migrants was very small in the eighteenth and nineteenth centuries and probably during the preceding centuries as well. This disproportion, noted by a number of experts with reference to several regions, was obviously fraught with social and moral consequences. One cannot even rule out certain hypotheses, like that of the limitation of the slaves' reproduction rate to 'reasonable' levels, either by order of the owners, or through a decision on their own part to limit the number of births. This 'shortage of women' in slave societies is a major phenomenon whose importance was stressed by the meeting. Striking examples were mentioned: as late as the nineteenth century among the Indian or Kaffir hired labourers there was sometimes only one woman for every ten men.

Not all the migrants were slaves, and not all of them had a similar fate. Several of the experts referred to the numbers of blacks serving in ships' crews in the eighteenth century; and in the Seychelles blacks from Africa became very skilled in seamanship.

Slavery

The participants held a long debate on the definition of slavery, the forms of which varied as greatly in the early societies of Africa and the Indian Ocean as they did in many other parts of the world. While they were aware that a symposium[1] specially devoted to this problem would be held in connection with the drafting of the *General History of Africa,* they were anxious to show how much importance they attached to several aspects of the question.

The attempt to devise a satisfactory general definition of the term and its historical content is beset by difficulties, including the possibility that the terminology may well disguise the reality; for example, the 'free employees' (*engagés libres*) seem in fact to have suffered the economic and social fate of the slaves of the preceding period.

How did the slaves live and what did they think of their condition? To answer these questions, one should consult, besides the traditional sources, particularly abundant in the Mascarene Islands, the oral tradition as well as clandestine literature (examples of which have been discovered in Réunion and which include a 'Hare cycle'). The documentary material in this field, though sparse, is not totally lacking: fourteen letters exchanged by two Ethiopian slaves around 1840 have been discovered by Professor Pankhurst.

In what respects did the treatment of slaves vary from one type of society to another and at different stages of development?

The abolition of slavery seems to have produced very varied consequences in different places. In Réunion it led to a very high mortality rate among the emancipated slaves. The lot of the freed slaves deserves to be studied. Perhaps, as in the Seychelles, they remained tied to their former master by a client dependency.

An important and positive factor was the attention paid to the slaves by the churches (e.g. on Réunion). Was this also the case elsewhere? The example of the 'Bombay Africans', who returned to Africa after their liberation and after receiving a religious education, is perhaps the first in a series of similar cases. Freed by Scottish ministers, former slaves constituted veritable colonies with large numbers of children.

African intervention in the political and military life of the Indian

---

1. Meeting of Experts on the African Slave Trade, Port-au-Prince, Haiti, 31 January-4 February 1978. The working papers and report of this meeting have been published in *The African Slave Trade....* (The General History of Africa: Studies and Documents, 2.)

Ocean deserves study. One expert thought that the pirate attack on Aden in the twelfth century was probably carried out by Africans.

Linguistic exchanges

Swahili

The origins of Swahili are still obscure. The geographical area over which it spread has varied in time. It is interesting to trace the internal variants of this language, which are probably of great historical and social value. Swahili is spoken in the Comoro Islands, in the Hadhramaut, Zaire, Madagascar, Kuwait, etc., but not in quite the same way. Swahili deserves to be studied by research workers because it certainly played a part in the formation of the morphology of the Malagasy language.

Creole

The origins of Creole are uncertain. The meeting considered tentatively the theory that the Creole of the Antilles and the Creole of the Indian Ocean had a common origin, traceable to a mingling of African languages with Portuguese, on the coast of West Africa.

Even though French played an important part in the formation of the Creole now spoken, the modern vernacular has been heavily modified by borrowings from Bantu, the Indian languages, Malagasy and English. These modifications reflect, of course, the political and cultural vicissitudes experienced by the islands in the last two centuries or so.

Special reference was made to the contribution of sailors to the Creole spoken on the Mascarene Islands; sailors make up their language as they go along and they speak a spicy mixture of words borrowed from very varied sources.

The study of Creole or its local forms, which are so varied in Réunion, for example, should be expanded. It is essential for an understanding of Creole culture from the inside.

Reciprocal linguistic influences

These have not been studied. The influence of India on Africa frequently seems weak, but it is stronger on the languages of the islands. Nothing seems to be known as yet about the influence of African languages in Asia. Little is known about the position of Arabic in African and island cultures, except as regards the origins of Swahili.

Research into linguistic phenomena should be conducted by means of an interdisciplinary approach employing modern methods of linguistic analysis. At the same time, however, one should study the extent to which social and linguistic stratifications coincide and whether languages have acted as a link between regions or, on the contrary, have constituted an obstacle to communication.

Oral traditions

The meeting stressed that these traditions should be recorded in those regions which it was asked to study. The abundance of written sources should not lead historians to neglect this essential source of information—on the contrary. If oral traditions are subject to careful criticism, using techniques that are today well defined, they make it possible to deal with aspects and levels of historical inquiry that are not accessible through written sources, for the latter always originate in other social strata.

In the case of Réunion and Mauritius, for example, oral traditions might provide a clue to the culture of whole population groups on the islands, which for a variety of reasons have not been able in the past or are now unable to express their cultural identity through the traditional media of literature.

Religions

This subject has been discussed at many meetings in recent years. The participants tried to discuss it from other angles. The explicit premise was that African religions, in the full sense of the term, used to exist that were comparable to those imported into Africa at various periods in its history. Various communications, in particular those dealing with the religion of the Malagasy people, convinced the meeting that the only sound method of analysis would be one based on that premise.

The analysis of religious rites showed that important likenesses as to form can be discerned between Africans, Malagasy and islanders, and sometimes Asian religions represented in the islands. The two monotheistic religions reacted to these rites in various, more or less positive, ways. The power of social cohesion that is exerted by religion and its ethic in African societies can be observed in Madagscar as well. The solidarity of human beings created by the vital force and the even closer solidarity of the living and the dead in one and the same family seem to be cultural traits common to East Africa and Madagascar. These features ought to be compared with those of Asian origin in the islands and with those found in Asia itself. The value of the role of the islands as places where these features have been preserved was referred to repeatedly. This social and moral cohesion probably played an important part in the way in which African societies reacted to external religions; in some cases they rejected these religions; in others they superimposed on these religions, which were new to them, an African character, and in yet others, these social and moral foundations were destroyed by the imported religions. This subject deserves very careful study, each case being considered individually, in the light of the chronological evolution of situations, as regards Islam and Christianity.

From the metaphysical point of view there is an obvious theoretical incompatibility between the revealed religions and the African religions. It remains to be seen whether a confrontation in fact took place.

At a more mundane level, the role of religions in the life of the societies concerned requires closer study. The religious situation in Africa is by now fairly well known. So far as the religious situation in Madagascar is concerned, which was less well known until the present, the meeting heard some important contributions from several experts. Religion in Madagascar has still to be studied closely, and its study may cast as much light as other methods of approach on the share accounted for by Africa and Asia, respectively, in the origins of Malagasy culture. Similarly, religion in the Mascarenes, a combination of tolerance and loyalty to tradition, deserves study.

The evolution of Christianity amidst the societies and religions of Africa, Madagascar and the islands should be studied. The Christian attitude, which was relatively positive in regard to slavery, relatively negative in regard to the social and religious rites and traditions of Africa and the islands, has changed since the nineteenth century. The existence of African Christian communities has changed the attitude of the churches at the local level and their universalist approach.

Similarly, the spread of Islam, at various times from the earliest appearance until the present day, and the various forms it took, should be studied. Has Islam established a limited community of converts or has it penetrated deeply into the masses of the African population? Have its legal and religious leaders (ulama and qadi) constituted an aristocracy oriented towards the Arab world or have they been completely integrated in the African societies? What has been the role of the pilgrimage in the cohesion of the multireligious African societies? What was the influence of the propagation of Sufism on the societies in question? It was also suggested that the place of the African and island Muslim communities in the modern Islamic renascence should be studied.

In any case, it is important to observe the extent to which African religions and societies admit imported religions and the extent to which the monotheistic religions can be permeated by the network of institutions, social traditions and rites of the African societies and religions. Did the monotheistic religions, where they predominated, tend to produce uniformity in the religious affiliations of the African and island populations? And what active or passive resistance, if any, did these attempts arouse on the part of the minorities? (The example of the Indians in Réunion was mentioned.)

Forms of genuine religious syncretism seem rare but should not be overlooked. Indeed, instances of two or more religions existing side by side in the same ethnic or family group, and sometimes even in the same individual, seem to be common.

The meeting expressed interest in the evidence of the religious life of the slaves (possible means of resistance or refuge). The information is very hard to come by, though some material has been gathered in Réunion.

Lastly, the meeting drew attention to the modern problems of coexistence between the secular State and religious communities of all kinds in East Africa and the islands.

Arts

The dance of the Mascarenes, the Sega, was discussed. As it has been little studied as yet, it can hardly be said to be either African or Asian. The meeting therefore asked for a study of this important cultural phenomenon. The instruments traditionally used for it are known, but not its musical repertoire or the texts. The Sega cannot yet be classed as a popular dance for amusement, or as a religious dance or a 'magic' dance, nor does it seem to have any clearly discernible social function. A wealth of documentation exists for elucidating this point.

In Madagascar the dances deserve the same attention.

Music, too, raises many problems that have yet to be solved. It was hoped that a thorough survey would lead eventually to elucidating the origins of the xylophone.

A comparative study of poetry is in the project stage. No doubt the Indonesian poetry competitions are reminiscent of the poetic tournaments so popular with the Malagasy people on the occasion of important festivals. However, the function of the poet as chronicler, found both in East Africa and in Madagascar—where in the nineteenth century some poets were in the service of the queen for this purpose—is also to be found in southern Arabia. In this connection, the love songs and the worship of womanhood characteristic of the Malagasy people of all regions, and not just those of the plateaux whose poetry is known today, are features of so many cultures that a superficial comparison would be insufficient. In the experts' opinion,

African and Malagasy poetry, and that of the Indian Ocean area in general, will constitute a very rewarding research topic.

In the field of architecture the meeting noted a very serious lack of studies, except in regard to the east coast of Africa—studies on the various types of building (religious, funerary, military, harbour buildings, etc.). The experts recommended comparative research in this field rather than the collection of relatively unreliable random impressions. They hoped that building materials, private dwellings, decoration and rites for the inauguration of buildings would all be studied in the context of such research.

On painting, too, the information contributed to the meeting was very meagre. The experts hoped that an international survey would be carried out to show the respective influences of Asia and Africa on painting. The study should investigate the arts of calligraphy and illuminated manuscripts in East Africa, and also monumental and ornamental painting.

The meeting called more particularly for a study of the place of the artist in society and of the forms of modern painting, as an original expression of island and African cultures.

Cookery, a supremely social form of self-expression, deserves the attention of research workers. Apparently nothing had been done as yet in this respect.

There are both rice-eaters and bread-eaters in the Indian Ocean region. Pilaf is a universal dish throughout the region. The use of bread-fruit—probably the food of the poorest in the first place—in island cookery deserves attention.

Documentation is available for investigating the social levels of diet, imports and quantities consumed.

The experts, beyond noting that ideas as to what is 'good', edible, or forbidden vary greatly in the different areas in question, were of the opinion that a thorough study of the reasons governing those choices and prohibitions was required.

Of course, at this level of scientific observation, the phenomena noted in connection with cookery and eating quite naturally come within the ambit of the study of dietary deficiencies and imbalances and consequently of medicine. The experts urged therefore that surveys of medical exchanges should be expanded.

Regional examples

Many of the questions which were to have been considered under this head were dealt with in the preceding discussions.

The region of the Horn of Africa, which is quite distinct from those further south, has been in contact with neighbouring Asia and with India.

The old connection with the Arabian peninsula is well known. The importance of this connection during the Axumite period and the pre-Axumite period is being increasingly corroborated by archaeology. Persian influence in Ethiopia has been limited, however. On this particular point the meeting regretted the absence of the Iranian and Iraqi experts who had been invited.

Exchanges with India were more important, especially in the earlier periods, fourth to sixth centuries, and from the sixteenth to the eighteenth. It is thought that India was the source of the ship-building techniques and of the techniques of building with clay mortar employed in Ethiopia. Indian builders probably built bridges, palaces and churches. Games and banking techniques were imported as well. Right up until the Italian invasion Indians played an important part in the economic life of Ethiopia.

Aden's contribution as a clearing-house for all the exchanges in this region of the Indian Ocean, at least during the Muslim period, should be reappraised.

The experts found no satisfactory study available concerning the arrival of the Chinese on the east coast of Africa. The actual arrival of Chinese is not attested by any evidence before the fifteenth century. Archaeology has disclosed the importance in earlier times of Chinese contributions (ceramics) in East Africa and the Nile Valley (Han-type bronzes in the Meroitic tombs). Orientalists should therefore be asked to investigate further the voyages of the Chinese, the exportation of their goods beyond the eastern basin of the Indian Ocean, especially from the fourth to the sixteenth century, and also non-Chinese contributions from the Far East.

Recommendations

The meeting submitted the following recommendations to the Director-General of Unesco for his consideration:

Study of maritime relations among countries bordering on the Indian Ocean: ports, routes, equipment of ships, art of navigation, movements of ships, quantitative analysis of the traffic, mode of life of seafarers.

The timber trade, in all the periods that can be studied, on the basis of the source material, is a very important topic in the history of the Indian Ocean. The research should cover not only the trade in timber intended for ship-building, but also the trade in the various kinds of wood used for carpentry or roofing, cooperage and carving.

Compilation of a very precise catalogue of local plant-names, preceded by clear agreement as to their scientific identity. This simple precaution will forestall certain errors and misunderstandings which tend to recur again and again in too many publications.

Priority study of a number of plants, their distribution and the consequences of that distribution: sugar-cane, rice, coffee, tea, cotton and plants used for smoking.

The study of the peopling of Madagascar may usefully be approached afresh from new angles: (a) archaeological excavations in the Comoro Islands and on the east coast of Madagascar; (b) study of the historical situations in India and the Indian archipelago that may have encouraged emigration; (c) comparative study of the Malagasy religion and African and Asian religions.

Archaeological investigation in the Seychelles, the Maldive Islands and the Mascarene Islands, to determine whether these islands played a part in the early population movements in the Indian Ocean.

Study of the African diaspora in the Indian Ocean in all its forms and during all periods.

Study of Creole culture: study of the word itself, the connotation of which varies; study of the civilization and social life of the Creole world.

Study of slavery and the slave trade in the Indian Ocean and neighbouring countries: definition of slavery and the slave trade; terminology indicative of the origins of slaves (Zanǧ or Habashi, for Africa); the true economic and social position of slaves; protests and opinions of slaves concerning their fate; cases of emancipation and their socio-economic consequences; clandestine forms of slavery; consequences of abolition.

Study of the Swahili language, of Creole and of seafarers' language in the Indian Ocean, by means of the scientific methods of linguistic analysis; analysis of the socio-cultural levels of usage of these languages; comparison with the evolution of Malay.

Oral traditions in the eastern regions of Africa and in the islands should be recorded. Although there are many written sources, these traditions constitute a unique key to the cultures.

Study of island dances (Sega and Malagasy dances). In Mauritius, historians can draw on an abundance of documentary material covering a whole century that can be used for this study.

Study of architecture and of the exchanges that are reflected in the architecture. Examples include places of worship, military architecture and harbour installations. Mapping of monuments to be studied in East Africa and in the islands. Study of tombs and burial rites. Study of painting.

As regards all the researches envisaged, the meeting recommended that, in every case, the two-way traffic of influences and exchanges should be studied. It recommended in addition that, whenever possible, modern graphic and cartographic methods of processing historical data should be used.

The experts expressed the wish, furthermore, that, in all the volumes of the *General History of Africa,* the titles of chapters which, in the Paris synopses, relate to the history of Madagascar should be so amended as to include references to the other Indian Ocean islands close to Africa. In addition, they recommended that in these chapters, the authors should provide the necessary information about these islands and not only information about Madagascar.

It was considered desirable that Iranian and Iraqi research workers should associate themselves with the work undertaken by this meeting. Excavations like those carried out at Siraf would probably yield evidence answering some of the questions that have arisen in the course of this meeting of experts.

Liaison with the programmes on South-East Asia and on Arab culture has become indispensable in the light of many of the questions raised during this meeting. In the experts' opinion, and they so recommended, Unesco should henceforth act as the channel for this liaison, on a regular basis, so far as specific topics are concerned.

The meeting was of the opinion, to which it drew the Director-General's special attention, that it would be desirable to establish at some future time a new programme concerned with the study of the cultures and civilizations of the Indian Ocean and neighbouring countries. An institute should contribute to the realization of this new programme. The institute would co-ordinate and facilitate the research work, organize meetings of research workers and arrange for the circulation of the results of the research.

List of participants

Professor S. N. Al Attas, Head, Department of Malay Language and Literature University Kebangsaan, Jalam Pantai Baru, Kuala Lumpur, Malaysia.
Professor Neville Chittick, Director, British Institute in Eastern Africa, P.O. Box 47680, Nairobi, Kenya.
Professor J. Devisse, 14 Avenue de la Porte de Vincennes, 75012 Paris.
Professor Hubert Gerbeau, Institut d'Etudes Supérieures de Lettres et Sciences Humaines, Boîte Postale 847, Saint-Denis, Réunion.
Professor M. Mollat, Président de la Commission Internationale d'Histoire Maritime, 1 Rue Bausset, 75015 Paris.
Professor P. Mutibwa, Department of History, Makerere University, Kampala, Uganda.
Professor L. D. Ngcongco, Gaborone, Botswana.
Professor B. A. Ogot, Head, Department of History, University of Nairobi, P.O. Box 30197, Nairobi, Kenya.
Professor R. Pankhurst, Director, Institute of Ethiopian Studies, Haile Selassie I University, P.O. Box 1176, Addis Ababa, Ethiopia.
Mr Jacques Rabemananjara, 2 Rue Georges de Porto-Riche, 75014 Paris.
Professor G. Rantoandro, Institut d'Archéologie et de Civilisation, Boîte Postale 564, Tananarive, Madagascar.
Dr Yusef A. Talib, Department of Malay Studies, University of Singapore, Bukit Timah Road, Singapore 10.
Dr Auguste Toussaint, 3 Rue Pasteur, Forest Side, Mauritius.
Professor Pierre Vérin, Centre Universitaire Antilles-Guyane, U.E.R. de Lettres, Pointe-à-Pitre, Guadeloupe.

Observers

Dr K. Hazareesingh, Director, Mahatma Gandhi Institute, Port-Louis, Mauritius.
Professor A. C. Staples, Murdoch University, Perth, Australia.

Unesco Secretariat

Mr Maurice Glélé, Programme Specialist, Division of Cultural Studies.
Ms Monique Melcer, Division of Cultural Studies.
Mr B. Friedman, Unesco Regional Office for Education in Asia, Bangkok, Thailand.

Bibliography

Considerable bibliographical material, some of it recent, was supplied by participants in the meeting. In addition to titles listed in the select bibliographies at the end of the authors papers, the following references were submitted to the rapporteur.

Reference works

Encyclopédie de l'Islam. Articles on Indonesia.
JAL. *Nouveau Glossaire Nautique.* Fascicles already published: letters A and B, 1969–71; letter C, 1975. The Hague and Paris.
PEARSON, J. D. (ed.). *A Guide to Manuscripts and Documents in the British Isles relating to Africa,* compiled by Noel Matthews and M. Doreen Wainright. London, Oxford University Press, 1971.
Source material in the course of publication: in Portugal: log books, instructions to navigators, Albuquerque's letters. Gavetas. Iranian: collection Mare Luso-Indicum, 2 volumes issued. Studies of the École Pratique des Hautes Études. University of Paris, IVe Section. Professor J. Aubin. To be utilized: Istanbul Archives.

The Comoro Islands

MARTIN, J. Les Notions de Clans Nobles et Notables, leur Impact dans la Vie Comorienne d'Aujourd'hui. *L'Afrique et l'Asie,* a quarterly political, social and economic review, *Bulletin des Anciens du CHEAM,* 1968, Nos. 81–2, p. 39–63.
——. Les Débuts du Protectorat et la Révolte Servile de 1891 dans l'Ile d'Anjouan. *Revue Française d'Outre-Mer,* 1973, p. 45–85.

East coast of Africa

BERLICOUX, E. G. *The Slave Trade in Africa in 1872.* London, Frank Cass & Co., 1971.
SALEH, I. *A Short History of the Comorians in Zanzibar.* Dar es Salaam, Tanganyika Standard. 19 p.
SEEDAT, Z. *The Makoa Community of Durban.* (Describes a community that still uses the Makoa language.)

Ethiopia and the Horn of Africa

BECKINGHAM, C. F. Amba Geshen and Asirgath. *Journal of Semitic Studies,* 1957.
LESLAU, W. Arabic Loanwords in Amharic. *Bulletin of the School of Oriental Studies,* 1957.
——. Arabic Loanwords in Goez. *Journal of Semitic Studies,* 1958.
PANKHURST, R. The Ethiopian Slave Trade, 1800–1935: A New Assessment. *Journal of Ethiopian Studies,* 1964.

India and East Africa

GREGORY, R. *India and East Africa. A History of Race Relations within the British Empire 1890–1939.* Oxford University Press, 1972.

Madagascar

MILLE, A. *Les Villages Fortifiés des Hautes Terres Malgaches.* 2 vols, multicopied, postgraduate thesis. Clermont-Ferrand, 1970.

Miscellanies of the London Missionary Society (L.M.S. Miscellanies). 19 volumes. See in particular, in Vol. 19, the articles by James Sibree.

RAKOTOAMOU (?), Jean A. *Les Forts Merina Extérieurs.* Dissertation for master's degree. University of Madagascar, 1971.

Mauritius

LY TIO FANE, M. *The Career of Pierre Sonnerat (1748–1814), a Reassessment of his Contribution to the Arts and to the Natural Sciences.* Ph.D thesis, University of London, 1973.

TOUSSAINT, A.; ADOLPHE, H. *Bibliography of Mauritius, 1502–1954.* Mauritius Archives, 1956.

VAN STEENIS-KRUSEMAH, M. J. *Cyclopaedia of Collectors and Collections, Flora Malesiana.* Groningen, 1950.

VAUGHAN, R. E. Wenceslas Boyer, 1795–1856. In: *Proceedings of the Royal Society of Arts and Sciences of Mauritius*, Vol. II, Part I, 1958, p. 73–98.

Indian Ocean

BRUNNET-MILLON, C. *Les Boutriers de la Mer des Indes.* Paris, A. Pedone, 1910.

MAGALHAES-GODINHO, V. *L'Économie de l'Empire Portugais aux XVe et XVIe Siècles.* Paris, 1969.

MEILINK-ROELOFSZ, M. A. P. *Asian Trade and European Influence in the Indonesian Archipelago between 1500 and about 1630.* The Hague, 1962.

STAPLES, A. G. Asian traders and seamen in the Eastern Indian Ocean 1830–1840. Inter Programme Seminar, 28th Congress of Orientalists, Canberra. Maritime trade in Asia in the early modern period: 17th to 19th centuries.

———. Indian Maritime Transport in 1840. Reprinted from the *Indian Economic and Social History Review*, Vol. VII, No. 1, 1970, p. 62–90.

———. *The Trade of the Eastern Indian Ocean, 1830 to 1845, with special reference to the internal maritime trade of the region.* Ch. 2, The Indian Coastline. London, 1965 (Unpublished thesis.)

Research on scurvy (Dr. H. Carre, University of Nantes), on navigation and on medical problems (École Pratique des Hautes Etudes, Paris, IVe Section, Professor Huard.)

Theses on the history of health at sea, general editor: Professor Kerneis, University of Nantes.

Réunion

AZEMA, M. *De l'Ulcère du Mozambique.* Paris, Adrien Delahaye, 1863.

JOLLES, S. *Étude Hémoanthropologique des Habitants de l'Ile Cimandal* (La Nouvelle, Cirque de Mafate). Paris, MD thésis, 1970.

LOUGNON, P. *Essai sur l'Ethnologie et la Pathologie de l'Ile de la Réunion*(medical geography). Montpellier, Imprimerie de la Charité, 1944.

MORIZOT, J. *Considérations Historiques et Médicales sur l'État de l'Esclavage à l'Ile Bourbon.* Montpellier, Jean Martel, Imprimeur de la Faculté de Médecine, 1838.